Gender development

Gender Development is the first book to examine gender from a truly developmental perspective, filling a need for a textbook and source-book for college and graduate students, parents, teachers, researchers, and counselors. It examines the processes involved in the development of gender, addressing such sensitive and complex questions as what causes males and females to be different and why they behave in different ways.

The authors provide an up-to-date, integrative review of theory and research, tracing gender development from the moment of conception through adulthood and emphasizing the complex interaction of biology, socialization, and cognition. The topics covered include hormonal influences, moral development, play and friendships, experiences at school and work, and psychopathology.

GENDER DEVELOPMENT

Susan Golombok
City University, London

Robyn Fivush
Emory University

CAMBRIDGE
UNIVERSITY PRESS

Published by the Press Syndicate of the University of Cambridge
The Pitt Building, Trumpington Street, Cambridge CB2 1RP
40 West 20th Street, New York, NY 10011-4211, USA
10 Stamford Road, Oakleigh, Melbourne 3166, Australia

First published 1994

Printed in the United States of America

Library of Congress Cataloging-in-Publication Data
Golombok, Susan.
Gender development / Susan Golombok, Robyn Fivush.
p.   cm.
Includes bibliographical references and index.
ISBN 0-521-40304-9 (hc.) – ISBN 0-521-40862-8 (pb)
1. Sex role. 2. Gender identity. I. Fivush, Robyn. II. Title.
HQ1075.G645   1994
305.3 – dc20

                                                    93-14108
                                                        CIP

A catalog record for this book is available from the British Library.

ISBN 0-521-40304-9 hardback
ISBN 0-521-40862-8 paperback

To John, John, and Jamie

Contents

Acknowledgments

This book would not have been written if Dick and Arden Neisser had not introduced us. Warmest thanks to both of them for their encouragement and hospitality throughout. Thanks are also due to the people who read and commented on parts of the book at various stages of its development. We would particularly like to thank Aletha Huston, Melissa Hines, and Richard Green, and the many anonymous reviewers. A very special thank you to our editor, Julia Hough, for her support, enthusiasm, and friendship. Gregor (age 7), Celia (age 8), James (age 8), Thomas (age 8), Samuel (age 7), Hannah (age 6), Vanessa (age 8), Chantal (age 7), Natalie (age 5), Jamie (age 6), Katie (age 6), Laura (age 7), Daniel (age 8), and Lynsey (age 7) drew the pictures featured throughout the book. We thank them for their insights into children's understanding of gender.

Introduction

When Freud began to develop his ideas about gender development at the turn of the century, it was taken for granted that men and women were different. In all of Freud's theorizing on the subject it was assumed that psychological differences between the sexes stemmed from differences in reproductive function. The roles of women as homemakers and child rearers and of men as breadwinners were never questioned. Neither was the assumption that the presence of both a mother and a father was necessary for children's gender development to proceed in a "normal" fashion.

As large numbers of women began to enter the work force to help with the war effort in the 1940s, the notion of "biology as destiny" was challenged. It was now argued that reproductive function need not determine gender roles; just because women experience pregnancy and childbirth does not mean that their lives must be limited to housework and child care, and just because men cannot give birth does not mean that they are unable to perform a nurturing role. With the growth of the women's movement and the gay liberation movement in the 1960s and 1970s, new types of families emerged in which parents played less traditional roles. An increasing number of children were brought up in families where the mother worked outside the home, in one-parent families, in stepfamilies and in a wide variety of other living arrangements. More radical changes to family structure also took place with the emergence, albeit in relatively small numbers, of families in which fathers shared domestic work and child care and of families headed by two parents of the same sex.

As we approach the twenty-first century, a situation has arisen that was inconceivable just a few years ago: It is no longer necessary for a woman to experience pregnancy, or to have sex with a man, in order to have a child. The development of the reproductive technologies has enabled a woman's egg to be fertilized with a man's sperm in the laboratory, and the embryo to be implanted into the womb of another woman who will "host" the pregnancy. When the child is born, it is genetically related to the couple who provided the egg and the sperm, just as if they had produced their child in the usual way.

In spite of the loosening ties between reproductive and social roles, the worlds of men and women, and boys and girls, are clearly not the same. We have learned that there is much more to being female or male than our potential to mother or father a child. We have also learned that gender development does not simply depend on our relationship with our parents; it results from a complex interaction between the individual and the wider social environment, of which parents are just one part. In this book we examine the processes that determine gender development. We look at how gender differences come about, why they persist, and the consequences at different stages of our lives. Our aim is not to provide a comprehensive account of the ways in which males and females differ. Instead, it is to explore from the perspective of developmental psychology the mechanisms through which these differences arise. But, first, what do we mean by gender development?

Definitions

Many different terms are used to refer to various aspects of gender development. Anyone who has read even a very few articles on this topic is likely to have encountered "gender identity," "gender role," "sex role," "sex typed," "sexual orientation," "sex role orientation," and "sexual identity," to name but a few. To make matters even more confusing, different authors use identical terms to refer to different aspects of behavior, or sometimes the same behaviors are described by different terms.

The appropriate use of *sex* and *gender* has probably raised the greatest controversy. Some authors argue that sex should be restricted to a person's biological maleness or femaleness, and gender for the social traits and characteristics that are associated with each sex (Deaux, 1985; Unger, 1979). The term sex implies a biological basis for a behavior when none necessarily exists. Maccoby (1988), on the other hand, believes that sex and gender should be used interchangeably because biological and social aspects of sex may interact with each other and it is difficult to distinguish between the two. Following Maccoby, we use both terms here, without any assumption that sex implies biological causes or that gender results from socialization. For example, "gender role" and "gender difference" are used interchangeably with "sex role" and "sex difference," respectively.

A distinction is generally made among the terms gender identity, gender role, and sexual orientation. *Gender identity* is a person's concept of him- or herself as male or female, as reflected in the statements "I am a boy" or "I am a girl". *Gender role* includes the behaviors and attitudes considered appropriate for males or females in a particular culture. *Sexual orientation* refers to a person's sexual attraction toward a person of the other sex (heterosexual sexual orientation) or the same sex (lesbian or gay male sexual orientation). People sexually attracted toward both women and men are bisexual.

Biological sex, gender identity, gender role, and sexual orientation are separate aspects of maleness and femaleness that may relate to each other in different ways. Gender identity is almost always in line with biological sex, so that biological males develop a male gender identity and biological females develop a female gender identity. For a very small minority of individuals – transsexuals – the two do not match. When this happens, a person who is physically male feels that "he" is really a "she" or, in the less common case of a person with a female body and a male gender identity, that "she" is really a "he." Male-to-female transsexuals (who are physically male) often describe themselves as "a woman trapped in a man's body," and vice versa for female-to-male transsexuals (who are physically female). Sometimes transsexual men and women adopt the gender role and clothing of their desired sex. They may also wish to have sex-reassignment surgery to give them the physical characteristics of the sex they wish to be. The sexual orientation of transsexual men and women may be heterosexual, homosexual, or bisexual. Thus heterosexual female-to-male transsexuals are sexually attracted to women, and heterosexual male-to-female transsexuals are sexually attracted to men.

For the vast majority of people whose gender identity is consistent with their biological sex, gender identity is linked to gender role, although the extent of the association between the two varies from person to person. Some girls with a female gender identity may show feminine gender role behavior in terms of the way they dress and the activities they prefer, and others may have interests that are more commonly associated with boys. But girls who prefer Batman to Barbie are quite sure that they are girls. Just because boys and girls do not adhere to prescribed gender roles does not mean that they are uncertain about their gender identity.

Knowing a person's sexual orientation does not tell us about that person's gender role. Lesbian women may show traditionally feminine or traditionally masculine gender role behavior, just like heterosexual women, and the same is true of gay and heterosexual men. Whatever a person's sexual orientation, his or her gender identity and biological sex remain in line (unless the person is transsexual). Thus lesbian women, like heterosexual women, have no doubt that they are female, and gay men, like heterosexual men, have no doubt that they are male. The gender identity of most bisexual men and women also matches their biological sex.

Two other terms that you will come across in this book are sex typing and sex stereotypes. *Sex typing* refers to the extent to which a person conforms to prescribed male and female gender roles. Boys who love rough sports, fighting, and playing with cars, trucks, and guns are considered to be very sex typed, as are girls who love dolls and playing house. It is important to remember that there is a great deal of overlap between the preferred activities and interests of boys and girls, although girls are more likely to enjoy "boyish" activities than boys are to enjoy "girlish" ones. *Sex stereotypes* are the characteristics generally believed to be typical of men and women or boys and girls. As we shall see in Chapter 2, the sex stereotypes that abound may bear little resemblance to the behavior and attitudes of men and women in the real world.

It is perhaps surprising that the two gender-related terms psychologists seem to have the most difficulty in defining are those commonly used in everyday conversation – *masculinity* and *femininity*. In fact, the concepts of masculinity and femininity have been described as among the muddiest in the psychologist's vocabulary (Constantinople, 1973). Why are they so difficult to define and measure?

Measurement issues

Psychologists have been engaged in the measurement of masculinity and femininity since the 1930s. In the early measures, such as the Terman-Miles Test of M-F (Terman & Miles, 1936), it was assumed that masculinity and femininity lie along a single, bipolar dimension ranging from extreme masculinity at one end to extreme femininity at the other. According to this approach, masculinity and femininity are mutually exclusive, so that a person who is masculine is, by definition, not feminine. In constructing these measures it was also assumed that so long as a question was answered differently by men and women it could be included in the scale, regardless of whether or not it related to commonly held beliefs about appropriate male and female roles.

Many of the assumptions underlying the construction of these early measures were later challenged (Constantinople, 1973; Huston, 1983). It was questioned whether masculinity–femininity forms a single, bipolar dimension. Instead, the proposal was made that there may be two separate dimensions of masculinity and femininity that are independent of each other. This meant that the two need not be opposites, and that a person could be both masculine and feminine at the same time. Another criticism was that masculinity and femininity are broad, multidimensional concepts that cannot adequately be measured by a single score. It was also thought to be inappropriate to include a question in a masculinity–femininity scale simply on the ground that men and women respond to it differently. This issue has often been highlighted by pointing to an item in an early masculinity–femininity scale that asked whether the respondent prefers to take a bath or a shower. Because a sex difference exists in response to this question, with men preferring showers and women preferring baths, the response "shower" is scored in the masculine direction and "bath" as feminine.

Dissatisfaction with the traditional view of masculinity and femininity as opposite ends of a continuum gave rise in the 1970s to the development of measures of androgyny that treated masculinity and femininity as two independent dimensions. The most well-known instruments are the Bem Sex Role Inventory, or BSRI (Bem, 1974, 1977), and the Personal Attributes Questionnaire, or PAQ (Spence & Helmreich, 1978; Spence, Helmreich, & Stapp, 1974, 1975). The term *androgyny*, from the Greek *andro* (man) and *gyne* (woman), refers to people who show both masculine and feminine characteristics. The earlier scales could not measure androgyny because they were unable to differentiate a person who was high on both masculinity and femininity from a person who was low on these characteristics; both obtained a similar score at the midpoint of the scale.

The Bem Sex Role Inventory (see the sample in Table 1.1)

Table 1.1. *Selection of items from the Bem Sex Role Inventory*

Masculine items	Feminine items
Independent	Affectionate
Forceful	Compassionate
Ambitious	Warm
Aggressive	Gentle

Source: Bem (1974).

consists of 20 characteristics judged to be more desirable for a man than a woman (aggressive, competitive, dominant), 20 characteristics more desirable for a woman than a man (gentle, understanding, tender), and 20 characteristics equally desirable for men and women (loyal, friendly, theatrical). Respondents are asked to rate themselves on a 7-point scale ranging from *never or almost never true of me* to *always or almost always true of me*. The inventory produces a score on a masculinity scale as well as a score on a femininity scale, and respondents are classified as androgynous if they obtain a high score on both, as masculine if they have a high score on the masculinity scale and a low score on the femininity scale, as feminine if they have a high femininity and a low masculinity score, and as undifferentiated if both scores are low.

The Personal Attributes Questionnaire also contains a masculinity scale with items judged to be more characteristic of males than females and a femininity scale with items judged to be more characteristic of females than males (see the sample in Table 1.2). It differs from the Bem Sex Role Inventory in that the items in its masculinity and femininity scales are considered to be socially desirable in both sexes.

Although androgyny questionnaires were greeted enthusiastically as an alternative to the earlier unidimensional scales, it was not long before it became apparent that the new measures were also problematic. A fundamental difficulty is that the theory on which the new measures were based has not stood up to

Table 1.2. *Selection of items from the Personal Attributes Questionnaire*

Male valued	Female valued
Active	Emotional
Adventurous	Kind
Outspoken	Considerate
Intellectual	Creative

Source: Spence, Helmreich, and Stapp (1975).

empirical testing. Bem (1974) and Spence et al. (1975) have argued that androgynous people are better adjusted as a result of their ability to engage in both masculine and feminine behaviors and to switch easily between the two. This is in direct contrast to the earlier assumption that the outcome of successful socialization is the adoption of conventional sex role behavior. Though many studies have confirmed a positive relationship between androgyny and psychological adjustment, and also between androgyny and self-esteem, closer examination of the findings has shown that it is the high masculinity score, rather than the combination of high masculinity with high femininity, that is important for psychological well-being (Taylor & Hall, 1982; Whitely, 1983). Masculinity, it seems, benefits both women and men, whereas androgyny holds no additional advantage. Still, we should not place too much emphasis on this conclusion. Because of the similarity between masculinity items and items used to assess self-esteem, it is not surprising that a strong relationship has been found between the two.

In recent years attention has turned to an examination of what the masculinity–femininity scales are actually measuring. Although they were constructed to produce global measures of these concepts, it appears that the scales are really measuring rather narrower aspects of masculinity, such as instrumentality, self-assertiveness, or dominance, and of femininity, such as expressiveness, nurturance, or interpersonal orientation. Gender-related characteristics are multidimensional in nature (Spence,

1984, 1985, 1993). That is, the constructs of masculinity and femininity are made up of many different personality traits that may relate to each other in a variety of ways depending on the person and the situation. Few men and women show all or even most of the qualities and behaviors typical of their gender, and the particular combination of characteristics that people exhibit varies widely from one man or woman to the next. For this reason, Spence has argued that the constructs of masculinity and femininity are too simplistic to be useful, and rather than using scales that simply produce one or two scores to describe all of a person's gender-related attributes and behaviors, researchers should develop more complex measures that take account of the multidimensional nature of masculine and feminine characteristics. In the 1990s, psychologists have been less inclined to measure masculinity and femininity solely on the basis of personality traits, and have begun to develop a wider range of measures that focus on other domains of gender-related behavior, such as interests and abilities, and social relationships (Ashmore, 1990; Lippa, 1991; Lippa & Connelly, 1990).

In contrast to adult masculinity–femininity scales, which focus on personality traits, children's measures assess preferences for toys, games, and activities as indicators of sex typing. For example, in the Checklist of Games and Play Activities (Rosenberg & Sutton-Smith, 1964; Sutton-Smith & Rosenberg, 1971), children are presented with a list of games and play activities and are asked to indicate which ones they like and which they dislike, and in the Toy Preference Test (De Lucia, 1963; Newman & Carney, 1981), children are shown pictures of pairs of toys and are asked to select the one with which they would most like to play (see Table 1.3).

A distinction has been made between measures of sex role preference, where children are asked which toys, games, and activities they like best, and sex role adoption, which refers to children's actual toy and game choices in a natural situation (Brenes, Eisenberg, & Helmstadter, 1985; Eisenberg, 1983). Sex role adoption has been assessed by directly observing the toys children choose and the games and activities they engage in during play at home or at school, or by obtaining reports about

Table 1.3. *Selection of items from the Toy Preference Test*

Plane ———	Racing car
Doll buggy ———	Sewing machine
Tractor ———	Tool set
Cosmetics ———	Cleaning set
Doll wardrobe ———	Roller skates
Football ———	Dump truck
Teddy bear ———	Jump rope

Source: De Lucia (1963).

children's sex-typed behavior from parents or other adults who know the child well. For example, the Pre-School Activities Inventory (see Table 1.4) is a questionnaire measure of gender role behavior in young children that is completed by an adult who is in close contact with the child (Golombok & Rust, 1993a, 1993b).

Instruments composed of personality items that are similar to those in adult androgyny scales have been constructed for use with older children. These include the Children's Personal Attributes Questionnaire (Hall & Halberstadt, 1980), which is based on the adult Personal Attributes Questionnaire, and the Children's Sex Role Inventory (Boldizar, 1991), which derives from the adult Bem Sex Role Inventory.

Masculinity and femininity are just two aspects of gender that psychologists are interested in assessing. In her compendium of measures of gender roles, Beere (1990) describes 211 instruments ranging from measures of adults' and children's gender roles to gender stereotypes, marital roles, parental roles, employee roles, and multiple roles. There are also many other assessment methods developed for use in experimental and observational research on gender that Beere does not include. For example, investigations that derive from an information processing approach to gender development have measured children's memory for pictures of males and females engaging in sex stereotyped activities, and observational studies have produced measures of

Table 1.4. *Selection of items from the*
Pre-School Activities Inventory

Toys
Guns (or used objects as guns)
Dolls, doll's clothes, or doll's carriage
Trains, cars, or airplanes
Tea set

Activities
Playing house (e.g., cleaning or cooking)
Fighting
Dressing up in girlish clothes
Climbing (e.g., fences, trees, gym
equipment)

Characteristics
Enjoys rough and tumble play
Likes pretty things
Shows interest in snakes, spiders, or
insects
Avoids getting dirty

Source: Golombok and Rust (1993a, 1993b).

children's involvement in play with masculine and feminine toys.
Standardized interviews have also proved useful in a diverse
range of studies with both adults and children.

With this huge array of measures available, how do we decide
which ones are best? There is no straightforward answer to this
question. First we must ask what the measure is for. If, for
example, we are interested in attitudes toward women in the
workplace, then a questionnaire might be the most appropriate
choice, whereas observational methods might be more suited to
research on the selection of male and female playmates among
preschool children.

Whatever measure is used, two questions must always be asked:
Is it reliable? and Is it valid? *Reliability* is an estimate of the
consistency of an individual's response. A measure is reliable if a
person obtains a similar score on different occasions, providing
he or she has not changed during the intervening period in a way

that is likely to affect the response. *Validity* is the extent to which an instrument measures what it is intended to measure. This is usually assessed by the relationship between scores on the measure and scores on some other criterion measure. For example, a valid questionnaire measure of femininity should discriminate clearly between tomboys and feminine girls as categorized by independent assessors. Unless a measure shows good reliability and validity, it will not provide meaningful information however appropriate it seems to be. So, in thinking about what the studies discussed in this book tell us about gender development, it is always important to consider what aspects of gender are being measured, and whether the measures employed are reliable and valid for that purpose.

Bias in gender research

A more general problem facing researchers interested in gender is bias. As with all scientific investigation, it is not only the choice of measuring instruments that may bias research findings. The questions researchers decide to examine, the way in which they design and conduct their studies, and how they deal with their results – all can affect the types of findings that emerge (Wallston & Grady, 1985). For example, looking at the studies that have been carried out to investigate the influence of maternal employment on child development, we find that, until recently, most of this research focused on negative outcomes for children, assessed either by the presence of emotional and behavioral problems, by impaired cognitive performance, or by atypical gender roles. The question posed has been "What are the harmful effects for children of having a mother who goes out to work?" rather than "How do children of working mothers benefit from this experience?" Not surprisingly, the conclusions arrived at were, at best, that maternal employment does not have deleterious consequences for children. It was only when positive effects were explored, such as children's increased contact with fathers and more flexible gender stereotypes, that it became apparent that the outcome for children was often good.

Another source of bias comes from the behavior and expectations of both researchers and participants during the course of an investigation. Researchers may unwittingly treat male and female subjects differently, thus influencing their response, and participants may respond differently to a male and a female researcher. It seems likely, for example, that women would talk more freely about sexuality to a female than a male interviewer. Participants may also report what they think the researcher wants to hear. In describing her child's involvement in sex-typed play, a mother may be more inclined to report the toy preferences and activities that are considered to be appropriate for the child's sex than those she believes to be inappropriate.

The way in which research findings are interpreted and reported may also be biased. Sex differences are often presented in the literature as evidence for inherent differences between males and females without considering other possible explanations. For example, the higher rates of anxiety and depression among married women than married men have often been attributed to the biological makeup of women without taking women's social circumstances into account. Moreover, investigations that show differences rather than similarities between the sexes are more likely to be published in academic journals, which gives the impression that males and females are more different than they really are. We must remember that there is a great deal of similarity between males and females, as well as a wide range of individual differences within each sex.

As research progresses, so does psychologists' understanding of the processes involved in gender development. Whereas early theorists assumed that the behavior of males and females was intrinsically different, the lack of empirical support for this assumption gave way in the 1970s and 1980s to the view that few sex differences exist and those that do are small and unimportant. This was in striking contrast to popular beliefs about boys and girls and women and men. It is now generally accepted that some differences in behavior do exist between males and females. For example, boys, on average, are more aggressive and more interested in playing with cars and trucks than girls are (Maccoby & Jacklin, 1974). But this does not mean that males and females will necessarily behave in a sex-typed way. There is a great deal of overlap between the sexes; some boys are not at all aggressive, and some girls frequently play with cars and trucks. What is interesting is not so much whether there are sex differences in behavior, but why these differences exist.

More recently, psychologists have begun to ask different questions in different ways. Interest has shifted from the focus on male and female traits to the influence of sex role stereotyping and social roles. So how does the experience of growing up female differ from that of growing up male? It is this question that this book sets out to address.

Overview of the book

In Chapter 2 we set the scene by looking at the gender stereotypes we encounter in our daily lives. From the announcement of "It's a boy" or "It's a girl" – at the moment of birth – males and females are expected to differ from each other in all kinds of ways. Do these expectations reflect fundamental differences between the sexes? Or is it the expectations themselves that cause gender differences to exist? This is an issue to which we shall return at various points throughout the book.

Chapter 3 examines the role of biological factors in gender development. Most of our knowledge comes from studies of individuals whose prenatal development was in some way atypical. For example, studying genetic females who were exposed to unusually high levels of male sex hormones while still in the womb can help us understand whether it is only physical sexual characteristics that are influenced by genes and hormones, or whether psychological aspects of gender are, to some extent at least, also biologically determined.

We then move on to consider psychological theories. As we shall see in Chapter 4, Freud has been highly influential in shaping our thinking about the processes involved in gender development, although little empirical evidence exists to support his theory. More recent reformulations of psychoanalytic theory are examined in terms of their ability to explain gender differences in sexuality, and in moral reasoning as well. Explanations of gender development that derive from classic social learning theory are explored in Chapter 5. There we consider whether boys and girls are treated differently, whether boys and girls tend to imitate models of the same sex as themselves, and most importantly, whether gender development is influenced by either of these processes. Chapter 6 focuses on cognitive aspects of gender development. The way in which children come to understand the concepts of maleness and femaleness are examined from two related theoretical perspectives, gender concept theory and gender schema theory, both of which assume that children's understanding of gender is dependent on their level of cognitive development.

We then turn to an examination of gender differences in relationships. In exploring friendships in Chapter 7, we ask why it is that boys play with boys and girls play with girls, and consider the consequences for adult friendships. Chapter 8 examines whether it is hormones or aspects of the social environment that trigger interest in sexual relationships during adolescence, looks at the experience of sexuality from a male and female perspective, and asks why some people develop heterosexual and others lesbian and gay relationships. We also explore the roles of men and women as mothers and fathers. In Chapter 9 we consider the consequences for children growing up in a nontraditional family.

Chapters 10 and 11 examine the divergent experiences of males and females from the classroom to the workplace, and explore the various explanations of gender differences in academic and occupational achievement. Chapter 12 focuses on the various explanations of why psychiatric disorder is more common among women than men, a difference that is apparent from adolescence onward. Finally, in Chapter 13, we put all the pieces together and return to our original question: What processes determine gender development?

2

Gender stereotypes

Think about meeting people for the first time, at a party or in a classroom. What do you notice? Perhaps you take note of what they are wearing, or the color of their hair. Somewhat less likely, you might note the color of their eyes, or the rings on their fingers. Perhaps you notice the way they move their hands when they talk, or an unusual inflection in their speech. One thing, though, you are sure to notice – in fact, one thing that you cannot help but notice – is the person's gender. Is this person female or male?

Categorizing individuals by gender is such an essential and automatic aspect of our understanding of people that we are not even consciously aware of making this distinction. Indeed, in those instances where this distinction becomes problematic for some reason, for example, over the telephone, we are decidedly uncomfortable. Why should this be so? What is it about knowing someone's gender that allows us to interact more comfortably? In this chapter we examine research that suggests that simply knowing someone's gender allows one to predict, whether rightly or wrongly, a whole host of other characteristics about that person. These sets of beliefs about gender, or gender stereotypes, play an important role in how we perceive both other people and ourselves. Moreover, children learn culturally prescribed gender stereotypes very early in development.

In the first part of this chapter we define gender stereotypes and discuss the research examining the content and the structure of these stereotypes. We then turn to the developmental literature and explore how adults' stereotypes about gender influence their interactions with infants and young children, as well as children's knowledge about gender stereotypes. As we shall see in this chapter, and throughout the book, gender stereotypes are pervasive. In a very real sense gender stereotypes play a role in all aspects of gender development. In this chapter we focus on research aimed at explicating the stereotypes themselves; the ways in which gender stereotypes develop and operate in our everyday behavior and understanding of gender underlie all of the topics covered in this book. Thus, the issues discussed in this chapter provide much of the background for understanding and evaluating the material presented in the rest of the book.

What are gender stereotypes?

Stereotypes are organized sets of beliefs about characteristics of all members of a particular group. A *gender stereotype*, then, is defined as a set of beliefs about what it means to be female or male. Gender stereotypes include information about physical appearance, attitudes and interests, psychological traits, social relations, and occupations (Ashmore, DelBoca, & Wahlers, 1986; Deaux & Lewis, 1984; Huston, 1985, 1983). Most important, these various dimensions are interrelated; simply knowing that an individual is female implies that person will have certain physical characteristics (soft voice, dainty, graceful) and certain psychological traits (nurturant, dependent, weak, emotional) and will engage in particular kinds of activities (child care, cooking, gardening) (Deaux & Lewis, 1983).

Content of gender stereotypes

A great deal of research has examined what characteristics people believe to be stereotypically male and female. In the most widely used method, subjects are presented with a list of psychological traits or attributes and asked to indicate the extent to which each trait describes the "typical female" or the "typical male" on a scale ranging from *not at all* to *extremely well* (see Ashmore et al., 1986, for a review). Not surprisingly, there is extremely high agreement among members of the same culture in determining which traits are typically "feminine" and which are typically "masculine." Further, results are similar whether subjects are asked to rate the "typical" male or female or to rate themselves, indicating that the cultural stereotypes are important in forming one's own gender identity (Bem, 1974). Moreover, although there are some differences across different cultures, there is also a surprising degree of similarity in which traits are considered feminine and which are considered masculine across relatively diverse cultures (Williams & Best, 1990). In the introduction, we discussed the traits that are most commonly associated with females and males, across various studies asking a wide variety of people for their ratings. What this research indicates is that we share culturally defined beliefs about what it means to be female or male.

When we consider the combination of traits describing males and females, these clusters of traits can be conceptualized as describing two distinct orientations toward the world. Males are stereotypically considered to be agentive or instrumental; they act on the world and they make things happen. Females are stereotypically relational; they are concerned with social interaction and emotions (Bakan, 1966; Block, 1973). As we shall see throughout this book, these two styles or orientations toward the world have implications for virtually all aspects of psychological functioning, including emotional development, play and friendships, intimate relationships, moral reasoning, and attitudes toward work and family.

This is certainly not to claim that stereotypes necessarily reflect reality; rather, stereotypes represent culturally shared beliefs about what particular individuals will be like. Whether or not it is true that females are soft, dainty, nurturing creatures who spend their days caring for children and flowers, we all know that this is the cultural version of what it means to be feminine. In fact, as we shall see again and again throughout this book, stereotypes would suggest many differences between males and females, but often these stereotypes have no basis in real behavior. So it is important to keep in mind that what we believe about gender differences may or may not be true. Still, culturally prescribed stereotypes do express those characteristics that are considered socially desirable for women and men to possess. Individuals who deviate too much from the stereotyped views of masculinity and femininity are seen somewhat negatively (Basow, 1992). Think about the connotations of someone who does not conform to gender stereotypes – the aggressive woman who is seen as a bitch or the nurturant, compliant man who is seen as a wimp. Gender stereotypes define our culturally agreed-upon notions of gender-appropriate (and gender-inappropriate) behaviors and traits.

Of course, not everyone believes in these stereotypes to the same extent. There is a great deal of individual variability in what people believe and how strongly they believe it. Overall, males tend to hold more stereotyped views about gender than females, and individuals with more years of formal education tend to be less stereotyped in their views about gender than those with less formal schooling. Further, gender stereotypes are only one dimension of our understanding of others. Racial, ethnic, and economic stereotypes also play important roles, and in combination with gender stereotypes often produce complex patterns of beliefs about behaviors and traits. For example, black women are seen as less passive than white women in our culture, and working-class women are seen as more hostile and irresponsible than middle-class women (see Basow, 1992, for a review).

One final point about gender-stereotyped traits: Traits associated with males tend to be more highly regarded than traits associated with females (Ashmore et al., 1986). Being strong, independent, and willing to take risks is seen more positively than being weak, gullible, and easily influenced. This difference in the values associated with male- and female-typed traits may have a great deal to do with the way certain characteristics are labeled. For example, use of the label "trusting" instead of "gullible" for females has a more positive connotation, and "stubborn" rather than "defends own beliefs" for males has more negative connotations. The way in which we assign psychological meaning to specific behaviors can partly determine how positively or negatively these behaviors are seen. Because males are perceived more positively in our culture than are females, traits associated with being male are described in more positive ways as well. As women achieve more power and credibility in our culture, the values associated with stereotypically female attributes are becoming somewhat more positive. Such traits as being empathic, tactful, and gentle are now viewed more positively than they have been in the past (Basow, 1992).

Structure of gender stereotypes

Clearly, we know which traits and behaviors are stereotypically female and male. But how do we use this knowledge in making judgments about other people and ourselves? As discussed in Chapter 1, some controversy exists over the meaning and measurement of "femininity" and "masculinity." Research evidence suggests, not surprisingly, that people are very complex. Just because an individual subscribes to some traditionally feminine traits does not necessarily mean that she subscribes to all traditionally feminine traits, nor even that she does not subscribe to some traditionally male traits (Bem, 1981, 1974). Yet, as naïve observers of behavior, we seem to take a somewhat more simplistic view of human behavior. In our everyday interactions with people, we tend to assume that individuals who are stereotypically female in some ways are stereotypically female in other ways as well.

Deaux and Lewis (1984) presented college students with descriptions of target individuals who varied on several dimensions. The target individual was first labeled as male or female and then described in terms of physical attributes, psychological traits, and/or role behaviors. These dimensions were either sex typed (e.g., sex-typed males were described as strong, sturdy, financial providers, taking the initiative with the opposite sex, etc., and sex-typed females were described as dainty, gentle, taking care of children, cooking the meals, etc.) or mixed (a male or female described with both stereotypically male and female characteristics). Given information about two of these dimensions (e.g., physical traits and psychological attributes) subjects were asked to rate each of the target individuals on the probability that they exhibited sex-typed behaviors on the third dimension (e.g., role behaviors).

Information about one dimension definitely influences subjects' judgments about other dimensions. Target individuals who are described as sex typed in physical appearance and role behaviors are assumed to be sex typed in psychological traits as well. Similarly, target individuals who are described as more androgynous (mixed sex-typed information) on one dimension are assumed to be more androgynous on the other dimensions too. In this way, gender stereotypes are tightly organized. Knowing that an individual conforms to one aspect of the cultural stereotype implies that the person will also conform to other aspects of the stereotype. A woman who is described as physically dainty and fragile will be assumed to be nurturant and sympathetic and pursuing a career in teaching or nursing. But counterstereotypic information is very important as well. Individuals who do not conform to one aspect of the cultural stereotype are also assumed to be non–sex typed on other dimensions. A woman described as physically strong will be assumed to be aggressive and independent and pursuing a career in law or engineering. Thus, given very little information about an individual, we infer a great deal about the person's appearance, personality, and behavior – all based on the structure of our gender stereotypes.

Also, the male stereotype seems to be more rigid than the female stereotype. Hort, Fagot, and Leinbach (1990) asked male and female college students to rate adjectives for the extent to which they described either (1) the *social* construal of males and females (What do most people believe about males and females?); (2) the subject's *own* construal of males and females (What do you believe about males and females?); or (3) the subject's construal of the *ideal* male and female (What should males and females be like?). In all three conditions males were rated in highly stereotyped ways, especially by females; in contrast, ratings for females were more variable and less extreme. The female stereotype, being more flexible than the male stereotype, may change more as a function of the raters and whether they are judging others or themselves. Moreover, male subjects rated their ideal male as extremely gender stereotyped, suggesting that males view the culturally prescribed male stereotype as particularly desirable. Males especially want to possess those traits and attributes that are considered stereotypically masculine (see Chapter 1). Thus females in our culture may have more freedom to deviate from the female stereotype, whereas males may be more locked in a particular configuration of behaviors and attributes.

Developmental issues

Adults agree on the traits and behaviors associated with males and females. But how early in development do these stereotypes play a role? What are adults' stereotypes about gender-related characteristics of infants and young children? And what are young children's beliefs about gender-related behaviors and traits?

Adults' stereotypes about infants

When a baby is born, one of the first questions is Is it a girl or a boy? Female infants are dressed in pink and their rooms are decorated in pastels. Male infants are dressed in blue and their rooms have bright, bold colors (Rheingold & Cook, 1975). From the first day of life, human infants are living in a highly gendered world. Moreover, parents seem to have very different expectations about what a female or a male baby is like. Female infants are perceived as softer and more vulnerable than male infants (Rubin, Provenzano, & Luria, 1974), and this is true despite the biological evidence that females are physically hardier than males from conception through old age. Boys are played with more roughly than girls, beginning in infancy and throughout the childhood years. Further, parents assume their infant girls will be more vocal and more interested in social interaction than their infant boys, and parents work harder to engage girls in mutual social interaction, such as eye-gazing and reciprocal emotional expressions (Goldberg & Lewis, 1969).

One obvious difficulty in interpreting these kinds of findings is the direction of influence. Are parents treating infants differently because of their stereotypes about what female and male babies are like, or are they responding to actual differences between female and male infants? It is possible that parents may socially interact more with female infants than male infants because female infants are, in fact, better able to engage in these kinds of interactions. Chances are that the type of interactions observed between parents and their children are not completely caused by either parental beliefs or infants' behavior; rather, as we argue throughout this book, gender-related behavior is complexly influenced by many factors, including biologically based differences between females and males, children's developing conceptualizations about gender, and adults' gender-related beliefs and expectations. Still, it is important to try to determine the extent of each of these influences on gender-related behavior. How much of adults' differential treatment of infants is due to parental stereotypes and how much may be due to differences between female and male infants?

One way to address this question is to ask adults to interact with an infant when that infant is labeled as either female or male. Seavey, Katz, and Zalk (1975) conducted the first such "Baby X" study. Adults interacted with a 3-month-old infant dressed in a yellow jumpsuit. One third of the subjects were told the infant was a female, one third were told the infant was male, and one third were given no gender information. (The infant was, in reality, a female.) Subjects were free to interact alone with the infant for 3 minutes. Several toys were also available: a small rubber football (male gender–typed toy), a Raggedy Ann doll (female gender–typed toy), and a plastic ring (gender-neutral toy).

The gender label provided by the experimenter had a clear

effect on the subjects' behaviors. When the baby was labeled female, subjects were more likely to engage in play interactions with the doll. However, when the baby was labeled male, subjects tended to use the gender-neutral toy more than either the football or the doll. In the no-label condition, female subjects engaged in a great deal of social interaction with the infant, but male subjects engaged in little social interaction, perhaps because they felt uncomfortable interacting with an infant whose gender was unknown. Yet virtually all subjects in the no-label condition spontaneously decided whether the infant was female or male, often based on particular physical characteristics. For example, subjects thought the infant was a boy because of "his" strong grip and lack of hair, or they thought the infant was a girl because of "her" softness and fragility. It was the same infant in all three conditions, yet subjects engaged the infant in different ways depending on the given gender label.

So, when parents and other adults "see" sex differences in infants, it might very well be because they expect to see these differences and will interpret the very same behavior differently, depending on the baby's gender. And it is not just in choosing gender-typed toys. In a similar study, by Condry and Condry (1976), subjects watched a videotape of a 9-month-old infant reacting to several emotionally arousing toys: a teddy bear, a doll, a jack-in-the-box, and a buzzer. Condry and Condry wanted to find out whether adult males and females would interpret the infant's emotional reactions differently, depending on the gender label. They also thought that amount of experience an individual had with infants might make a difference, so half their subjects had little such experience and half had a great deal. After viewing the videotape, subjects were asked to rate the overall emotional responsiveness of the infant, and they were also asked to indicate what emotion the infant was experiencing upon presentation of each of the toys. Half the subjects were told the infant was female and half were told the infant was male. Again, it is important to emphasize that it is exactly the same videotape of exactly the same infant being viewed in these different labeling conditions.

When the infant was labeled male, subjects, especially males, rated the infant as showing more pleasure than when the infant was labeled female. Males with a great deal of experience with infants rated female and male infants as most different. In contrast, females with a great deal of experience with infants showed the least difference in ratings as a function of the given gender label. Thus experience with infants seems to lead to different patterns of interactions for males and females. With more experience with young infants, males tend to see more gender differences between males and females and females tend to see fewer gender differences.

Even more interesting, subjects rated the infant's emotional reactions to specific toys differently. This was particularly true of the jack-in-the-box, to which the infant reacted relatively negatively by startling and crying. When the infant was labeled male, this behavior was perceived by subjects as anger, but when the infant was labeled female, this very same behavior was perceived as fear. As Condry and Condry (1976) argue, gender differences in infancy may very much be in the "eye of the beholder." The very same infant behaving in the very same way was perceived quite differently by both male and female subjects, depending on the given gender label.

We can speculate that these differences in the way adults label and react to infants' emotional expressions will have important consequences for how children come to understand their own emotional experiences. Over time, as adults label children's emotional expressions in particular ways, males may come to see themselves and other males as experiencing more anger than females, whereas females may come to see themselves and other females as experiencing more fear than males.

These early Baby X studies demonstrate that adults perceive and react to infants in gender stereotyped ways. Adults hold certain stereotypes about male and female behavior, and they interpret infants' behavior in ways consistent with those stereotypes. As one might imagine, these findings generated a great deal of excitement, and many studies have been carried out to explore this phenomenon further.

Stern and Karraker (1989) reviewed 23 gender labeling studies to determine the effects of a given gender label on (1) ratings of an infant's traits and characteristics; (2) the way in which subjects interacted with the infant; and (3) the toys that subjects chose for the infant. Across these studies, a given gender label does not seem to have much of an effect on personality trait ratings of the infant. When subjects were asked to judge infants on a series of characteristics, such as loud, affectionate, friendly, or cooperative, infants labeled as male or female were seen as similar. However, when subjects were asked to interact with the infant, many differences based on the gender label emerged. Labeled females received more vocalizations, more interpersonal stimulation, and more nurturant play than labeled males did. In contrast, labeled males received more encouragement of activity and more whole body stimulation than labeled females did. And when choosing toys for infants, subjects were more likely to give dolls to labeled females and balls, tools, or other male-typed toys to labeled males.

These results suggest an important distinction between self-report measures and behavioral measures. On those measures for which subjects were asked to report on their beliefs about the characteristics of an infant, few differences due to the gender label emerged. But when subjects were observed actually interacting with infants, many differences based on the label became apparent. Even if adults do not consciously believe they are making a distinction in the way they perceive a female versus a male infant, they nevertheless behave in very different ways depending on the given gender label. Again, this is evidence of the pervasiveness of gender stereotypes. Even when we don't think we are behaving in gender stereotyped ways, or are encouraging gender-typed behavior in our children, examination of our actual behavior indicates that we are.

Of course, this does not mean that the actual gender of an infant has no effect on the way in which an adult interacts with that infant. In a clever extension of the standard Baby X studies, Lewis, Scully, and Condor (1992) asked adults to interact with a male or female infant about 10 months old, either labeled correctly (a male infant labeled male) or incorrectly (a male infant labeled female). As in previous studies, adults showed the expected patterns of different interaction depending on the gender label given the baby. But when asked to rate themselves after the interaction, adults who had interacted with a male baby rated themselves as more feminine and those who had interacted with a female baby rated themselves as more masculine, regardless of the gender label given the infant. It is not clear how interacting with a baby of a particular gender might change one's ratings of one's own gender-related behavior, but obviously, adults are reacting to both the labeled gender and the actual gender of the baby. In real-life situations, where the actual and labeled gender are the same, differential interactions with male and female babies most likely result from an interaction between adults' gender stereotypes and real differences between female and male babies.

Children's gender stereotypes

It is quite clear that adults have gender stereotypes and use these stereotypes in interpreting the behavior of other adults and even of young infants. But when and how do children learn these stereotypes? When do children begin to believe that females are soft and nurturing and males are strong and aggressive? Perhaps not too surprisingly, children learn about gender very early in development. Children begin to consistently label themselves and others as male or female sometime around the age of 2 years, and very soon after this, they begin to associate particular behaviors and traits with one gender or the other. Even more interesting, young children, between about 3 and 6 years of age, are even more strongly sex stereotyped than adults (Signorella, Bigler, & Liben, 1993); Stern & Karraker, 1989). Preschool children not only know what the culturally defined gender stereotypes are; they believe very strongly that these stereotypes are true. (We discuss various reasons why young children may be so rigid in their gender stereotyping in Chapter 6.)

Are young children's stereotypes about gender the same as adult's stereotypes? Urberg (1982) examined the content of 3-, 5-, and 7-year-old children's gender stereotypes. She told children a series of stories designed to illustrate specific gender stereotyped traits, such as independence, bravery, and nurturance. The story for bravery was: "Some people are brave. If a house was on fire they would go inside to rescue people." Children were then shown a picture of a male and a picture of a female and asked, "Who are the brave people? Are they women, men, both women and men, or nobody?" Thus children could choose the stereotyped response (in this case, the picture of the man), a counterstereotyped response (the picture of the woman), or a nonstereotyped response (both pictures or neither picture). For half the stories, the pictures were of adults, and for the other half, the pictures were of children. Children at all three ages used cultural stereotypes in assigning traits to females or males, but the stereotypes seemed to be most rigid at age 5, and by age 7 became more flexible. That is, at age 5, children claimed that only females engage in feminine-typed behavior and only males engage in masculine-typed behavior, but by age 7, children claimed that both males and females engage in various behaviors. Interestingly, children stereotyped other children more than adults; when pictures of adults were used, children at all ages were more likely to say that both males and females could engage in that behavior than when pictures of children were used.

Children's early knowledge of gender stereotypes is further elaborated in a Baby X study (Haugh, Hoffman, & Cowan, 1980). Three- and 5-year-old children viewed a videotape of two 12-month-old infants. The infants were shown side by side for 5 minutes engaging in play with gender-neutral toys. Half the subjects were told that the baby on the right was female and the baby on the left was male, and half were told the reverse. After viewing the tape, the subjects were asked to rate each of the infants on various dimensions. Both 3- and 5-year-old children rated infants labeled male as big, mad, fast, strong, loud, smart, and hard. Infants labeled female were rated as small, scared, slow, weak, quiet, dumb, and soft. Keep in mind that ratings of the same infant changed as a function of the gender label, so children were not simply responding to differences in the infants.

Even quite young children, then, have a great deal of knowledge about culturally prescribed gender stereotypes. But is this knowledge organized the same way for young children as for older children and adults? What kinds of inferences or predictions do young children make based on knowing someone's gender? Recall that adults will infer that an individual displaying one gender-typed behavior or attribute will display other gender-typed attributes as well. But if counterstereotyped information is given, adults assume the individual will display other cross-sex-typed behaviors. Do children make these same kinds of predictions?

Interestingly, they do but there are developmental differences. Martin (1989a) told 4 to 10 year olds stories about hypothetical children. In some of the stories the character was a male, and in some a female. In each story the character liked to play with a gender-consistent toy (a boy who likes to play with airplanes) or a gender-inconsistent toy (a boy who likes to play with dolls). Children were asked to decide what other kinds of toys the character would like to play with from a set of choices.

All children used the gender of the character to predict that character's interest in other toys, but younger children used only this information. Even when told about a girl who liked playing with airplanes, younger children predicted she would prefer dolls and tea sets over trucks and toolboxes. Older children modified their predictions somewhat, given counterstereotypic information. Similar to adults, they predicted a girl who liked to play with airplanes might also like to play with toolboxes. For younger children, then, an individual's gender overrides any other information; girls and boys will display certain behaviors and preferences simply because they are female or male. As children get older, they begin to understand that not all girls are alike, nor are all boys alike. But they still use their knowledge of gender stereotypes to make predictions, such that individuals displaying one gender-typed behavior will be predicted to display other gender-typed behavior, and individuals displaying one cross-typed behavior will be assumed to display other cross-typed behavior as well.

So it seems that the content and structure of children's stereotypes are similar to adults'. However, very young children's gender stereotypes are more rigid than adults', and information about someone's gender overrides any other information about that person. Further, children seem to believe that gender stereotypes apply more to their age-mates than to adults. Because young children are rigid in their beliefs about gender, and because they apply those beliefs most strongly to other children, friends may play a critical role in children's developing ideas about gender. As we discuss the ways in which children come to understand gender, keep in mind that it is not only adults that socialize young children – children may be socializing themselves and each other as well.

Gender stereotypes in the media

The research on adult's and children's gender stereotypes confirms that gender is an important and powerful way of understanding the world. Ours is a highly gendered society, and children quickly learn gender-related knowledge. The mass media – television, movies, newspapers, magazines, and books – both reflect and form the cultural stereotypes. Young children gain access to the larger culture through these media sources, and particularly for very young children, through storybooks and television.

Gender depictions in children's stories

Most preschoolers growing up in a literate culture spend time reading storybooks with adults. Reading stories is an important part of preparing young children for school and learning to read and write. The stories adults and children read together also provide the child with a great deal of information about the world, including information about what it means to be female or male. What kind of information about gender is being portrayed in children's books?

Not surprisingly, given the political climate of the times, research in the 1960s found that females were greatly underrepresented in the titles, central roles, and illustrations of popular children's stories (Weitzman, Eifler, Hokada, & Ross, 1972). Has this gender-typed portrayal of males and females changed with the political changes of the 1970s and 1980s? Collins, Ingoldsby, and Dellman (1984) examined the portrayal of gender roles in children's books that won the prestigious Caldecott Medal given by the American Library Association for the most distinguished picture book of the year. Although they found that females were better represented in the more recent books, male characters still outnumbered female characters by 2 to 1. Females in the leading character role were depicted as active and adventurous, just as males who were leading characters. However, few books had females as leading characters. When females were secondary characters, or when males and females shared the leading roles, females were depicted in fairly traditional terms, as passive and dependent. Although there has been some change toward more equal representation of females and males in children's storybooks, gender is still portrayed in relatively stereotyped ways.

Because preschool children cannot read storybooks for themselves, adults read the stories to them. Thus it is important to examine how adults present gender during book reading. It turns out that the "three bears are all male" (DeLoache, Cassidy, & Carpenter, 1987). Essentially, when reading books with their 2- to 3-year-old children, mothers label about 90% of characters for whom gender is unknown as male. In order to explore this finding in more detail, DeLoache et al. constructed a picture book in which all of the characters were bears of indeterminate gender. Some bears were big (i.e., adult bears) and some bears were small (i.e., child bears) but no other identifying information was depicted. Bears were shown expressing various emotions, engaging in various kinds of activities or as passive onlookers, and as hugging or disciplining each other. When asked to "read" these picture books with their young children, mothers labeled 62% of the bears as male and only 16% as female (the rest were never given a gender label). The only bears that were labeled female were big bears in close proximity to but not interacting with little bears. In other words, bears were female if they were watching over other bears.

In sum males are depicted more often than females, and even when the gender of the character is indeterminate, mothers overwhelmingly label the character male, thus inflating even more the overrepresentation of males in stories. Moreover, males are more likely to engage in active adventures. Only females not in the company of males are active and adventurous. More often, females are represented as passive in relation to the male or as caregivers. Children listening to these stories are most likely acquiring a very stereotyped representation of the roles of females and males in our society.

Gender depictions on television

Television has become the single most important source of information about our world. Current statistics estimate that a television is on 7.5 hours per day in the average household (Davis, 1990), and the average preschool child spends about 3 hours a day watching television (Greenfield, 1984), more time than for any other single activity except sleeping. Given the prevalence of television, it becomes important to examine what kind of a world television displays. Unfortunately, the picture is not an egalitarian one.

Research conducted from the 1950s through the 1970s indicated that men outnumbered women on television 2 to 1 despite the fact that women represent just over 50% of the actual population. More disturbing, women were portrayed as overly emotional, dependent, less able to deal with difficult situations, and less intelligent than men (see Davis, 1990, for a review). Has this image changed in more recent years? Examination of current television programming indicates it has not. Male major characters still outnumber females 2 to 1. Moreover, female characters are younger on the average than male characters, the marital status of female characters is known significantly more often than the marital status of male characters, and females are four times as likely to be provocatively dressed (wearing swimsuits, nightgowns, undergarments, etc.) as male characters (Davis, 1990). Almost 40% of the female characters on television have no clear occupation outside the home, whereas 68% of male characters can be categorized by occupation. Related to this, 20% of female characters are shown engaging in housework, but only 3% of the male characters are shown doing household tasks. Moreover, male characters are equally likely to commit a violent crime as to be the victim, but females are overwhelmingly more likely to be victimized than to commit violence (Signorielli, 1989). Thus the portrayal of females on prime-time television continues to be quite stereotyped; females are portrayed as young, sexy, and vulnerable, not that important to the plot, and interested in family and home.

It is not just television programs that portray gender in stereotyped ways; these stereotypes are also portrayed on television commercials. The average viewer sees 714 commercials per week; by the age of 17, he or she will have seen 350,000 commercials (Bretl & Cantor, 1988). There are dramatic differences in the ways in which males and females are depicted. First, although males and females are represented about equally as characters in commercials, females are more likely to be depicted without an occupation than are males. Whereas females are more likely to be in commercials advertising home and household products, males are more likely to advertise recreational and leisure products. Not surprisingly, females tend to be depicted in the home, but males are just as likely to be away from the home as in the home. Perhaps most telling, 90% of the narrators who talk about the product (i.e., the voice-overs) are male, and this figure is the same even for products aimed explicitly at women, such as cosmetics and feminine hygiene products (Bretl & Cantor, 1988; Lovdal, 1989).

Similar findings emerge in programming aimed at children (Calvert & Huston, 1987; Greenfield, 1984). The vast majority of cartoon characters are male; in fact, many cartoon programs have no female characters at all. On educational television only 15% of the lead characters are female; and on advertisements aimed at children 80% of the characters are male. Even when female characters are present, they are often depicted as helpless and dependent on males.

Does it matter how gender is portrayed in the media? What exactly are adults and children learning from watching these gender stereotyped depictions? If television plays a role in forming and sustaining stereotyped notions of gender, then we would expect that people who watch more television, and therefore are exposed to more stereotyped messages, would be more stereotyped in their views about gender than people who watch less television. Data collected during the 1970s suggested that heavier viewers were more sex typed, but this relationship lessens in data collected during the 1980s (Signorielli, 1989). Perhaps there is more conflict now between the way gender is portrayed on television and accepted gender roles in society. For example, although the majority of married females on television are shown working only in the home, the majority of married women in our society are working outside the home as well. These obvious discrepancies may lead adult viewers to question the portrayal of gender in the media.

But the research with children suggests a different pattern. Here there is clear evidence that heavier television viewing leads to more stereotyped views about gender (Calvert & Huston, 1987; Greenfield, 1984; Signorielli & Lears, 1992). Children who watch a great deal of television aspire to more sex-typed occupations and apply sex-typed personality attributes more rigidly than do children who watch less television. In one of the few longitudinal studies examining this question, Morgan (1982) followed sixth- to eighth-grade children over a 2-year period. Girls who watched more television became more sex typed in their beliefs over this period of time, but there were no effects for boys. However, it should be noted that all of the boys in the study were extremely sex typed in their views, even at the beginning of the study, and therefore it may not have been possible to measure increases in sex-typed beliefs.

Children thus seem to be learning gender stereotypes from television. They may be more influenced by television's portrayal of gender than are adults because they have less ability to evaluate television as an information source. Children may think television presents social reality to a greater extent than do adults, and therefore accept the gender stereotyped information presented as true.

Are gender stereotypes changing?

Because it is assumed that gender stereotypes reflect culturally prescribed beliefs about gender, one might also assume that as society's views of females and males change, the content of the stereotypes will change as well. Somewhat surprisingly, however, research indicates that gender stereotypes may not be changing as quickly as we might think given the cultural upheavals that have taken place since the 1960s and the beginning of the second women's movement.

McBroom (1987) examined changes in gender stereotypes over a 5-year period in three groups of subjects. One group had graduated college in 1974 and were 22 years of age at the beginning of the study. A second group had graduated college in 1964 and were 32 years of age at the beginning of the study, and a third group had graduated college in 1954 and were 42 years old when the study began. All subjects filled out questionnaires assessing the extent to which they subscribed to the cultural gender stereotypes in 1975 and filled out these same questionnaires again in 1980.

Overall, males subscribed to the stereotypes more than females, and males showed no decrease in their stereotyping over the 5-year period. One exception to this general pattern was that males who remained married over the 5 years did show a decline in stereotyping. In contrast, all three age groups of females showed significant declines in stereotyping over the 5-year period, and this decrease was especially pronounced for females who married and/or entered the work force during this period of time.

Thus females are more likely to question the culturally prescribed stereotypes than males are. Further, life experiences may call stereotyped beliefs into question. When females marry and/or enter the work force, they may be confronted with the more negative expectations associated with being female, and this may lead them to reexamine cultural beliefs. Similarly, men who remain married may be more likely to question more traditional beliefs in the process of negotiating a long-term intimate relationship.

One of the problems with interpreting results on changing stereotypes is the difficulty of determining whether changes are due to developmental differences or to cohort differences. Developmental differences are assumed to reflect changes in an individual's way of viewing the world. Cohort differences refer to the fact that individuals growing up in a particular time period (e.g., the 1940s versus the 1980s) will share certain ways of looking at the world that are a function of events occurring during critical historical periods during their lives.

To try to tease out these possibilities, Halohan (1984) examined data on gender stereotypes in a group of married couples in 1941, when the subjects were 30 years of age. She then collected data on these same couples 40 years later, in 1981, when they were about 70 years old. Finally, she collected data on the gender stereotypes of a group of married couples who were 30 years old in 1981. Thus she was able to examine changes in gender stereotypes as a function of aging from 30 to 70 years of age and also as a function of cohort group by comparing couples who were 30 years old in 1941 to couples who were 30 years old in 1981. Basically, Halohan found that subjects became much more egalitarian in their gender role beliefs from age 30 to age 70, but there was little difference between the two groups of 30 year olds. Gender stereotypes did not seem to change much from 1941 to 1981, especially for males. So, as people age, they may become less stereotyped in their attitudes about gender, but there has been little change in gender stereotypes over a 30-year period in which we might have expected great change.

The same pattern emerged when possible changes in adolescents' beliefs about what it means to be female or male were examined from 1956 to 1982 (Lewin & Tragos, 1987). Similar to the findings with adults, there was little evidence of changing stereotypes across this time period. In fact, if anything, adolescents were more sex typed in 1982 than they were in 1956. Again, these findings were especially true for males.

Across all these studies, then, it is apparent that gender stereotypes have remained relatively stable over the past 30 to 40 years. Although there have been many changes in the roles that females and males play in our society, beliefs about gender-related traits and characteristics have not undergone much change.

Summary

There is no doubt that children and adults share a common, culturally defined view of what it means to be female and male.

These gender stereotypes are pervasive both in the culture at large and in our everyday social interactions. From the beginning of life children are bombarded by gender stereotypes. This information is pervasive in books and on television and is communicated by the gender-typed expectations of parents, other adults, and other children. As early as 2 to 3 years of age, children already know a great deal about the cultural stereotypes of gender, and this knowledge will influence their understanding of gender throughout their lives.

3

Prenatal influences

One question that has vexed researchers is the extent to which social and behavioral aspects of gender development are biologically determined. Clearly, our physical appearance as male or female has a profound effect on our experience of the world and on how we are viewed by others. It is genes and hormones in the developing fetus that are responsible for the formation of a male or female body. But is the function of genes and hormones simply to establish physical sexual characteristics, or does our biological makeup have a more direct effect on gender by influencing the development of gender identity, sex role behavior, and sexual orientation as well?

This issue has been addressed by studying people with an

unusual biological makeup to discover whether an atypical genetic pattern or an excess or deficiency of sex hormones has an effect on gender development. If so, the variation in sex-typed behavior can, at least in part, be attributed to the biological anomaly under investigation, and can help us to understand the role of specific biological factors on normal gender development. For example, if children exposed prenatally to unusually high levels of male sex hormones are found to be extremely masculine and those exposed to unusually low levels of male hormones are much less so, then male hormones would appear to be influential in the development of male sex role behavior. This approach is not as straightforward as it seems. But before going on to examine the research on individuals with biological anomalies, we must first look at the processes involved in normal sexual differentiation.

Sexual differentiation

At conception a female egg containing 23 chromosomes unites with a male sperm, also containing 23 chromosomes, to form a single cell with 23 chromosome pairs. One of these, the sex chromosome pair, determines the genetic sex of the child. The sex chromosome provided by the egg is always an X chromosome; the sperm can donate either an X or a Y chromosome. If the sperm contributes an X chromosome, the child will be a genetic female with an XX sex chromosome pair. A Y chromosome from the sperm will result in a genetic male with an XY pattern.

The single cell formed at conception immediately begins to divide to produce an embryo. For the first few weeks, XX and XY embryos appear to be identical, each developing neutral gonads (sex glands). Sexual differentiation begins at about 6 weeks. At this time, messages encoded in the XY chromosome pairs cause the gonads of genetically male embryos to develop as testes. The gonads of genetically female embryos remain neutral until about 12 weeks at which time they develop as ovaries. The direct influence of sex chromosomes on sexual differentiation appears to end at this stage.

By 7 weeks, the embryo possesses two sets of rudimentary internal reproductive structures: (1) Müllerian ducts, which have the potential to become female internal reproductive organs, and (2) Wolffian ducts, which eventually can become male internal reproductive organs. Which system develops depends on the presence or absence of testes. When testes are present, a predominance of male sex hormones (androgens) are secreted that cause the Wolffian ducts to develop as male internal reproductive organs (seminal vesicles, prostate, vas deferens, and urethra) and Müllerian inhibiting factor causes the Müllerian ducts to diminish. When testes are absent, as in the female fetus, the Müllerian ducts develop as female internal reproductive organs (uterus, fallopian tubes, and upper vagina) and the Wolffian ducts diminish. Female sex hormones are not thought to be necessary for development to proceed in a female direction, as the female reproductive system develops even in the absence of ovaries.

As shown in Figure 3.1, the external genitals of males and females originate from the same basic structures: a genital tubercule and a single opening surrounded by a fold of skin and a small swelling on either side (labioscrotal swellings). Development is identical until about 3 months of pregnancy, when the genital tubercule becomes a penis in males and a clitoris in females, and the labioscrotal swellings become the male scrotum or female labia (vaginal lips). As with the internal reproductive organs, a male pattern of hormones is necessary for the development of male genitals, whereas the absence of male hormones rather than the presence of a female hormonal pattern produces female genitals.

During sexual differentiation some individuals are exposed to biological influences that are female at some stages and male at others, so that the major indicators of sex – chromosomes, gonads, hormones, internal reproductive organs, and external genitals – do not match. For example, an infant with male genitals may in fact have female chromosomes, gonads, hormones, and internal reproductive organs. Studies of the development of people with such anomalies can help increase our knowledge of the influence of biological factors on gender development (for reviews, see Ehrhardt & Meyer-Bahlburg, 1981; Hines, 1982; Hines & Green, 1990; Money & Ehrhardt, 1972).

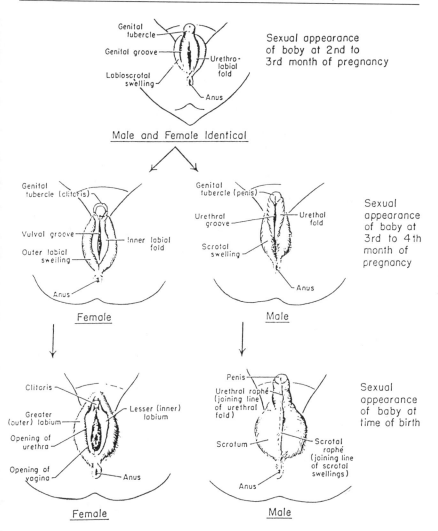

Figure 3.1. External genital differentiation in the human fetus. (From Money & Ehrhardt, 1972; reprinted by permission of Dr. John Money.)

Sex chromosome influences

Four major sex chromosome disorders have been examined in terms of their effects on gender development: XO (Turner) syndrome, XXX syndrome, XXY (Klinefelter's) syndrome, and XYY

. Individuals with Turner syndrome have only one X
me. Although their genitals look like those of other
gonads do not properly differentiate and, as a con-
_, they do not menstruate or develop breasts at puberty.
They can be given hormone replacement therapy, however, so
that breasts and other female secondary sex characteristics will
develop. Girls with Turner syndrome have a female gender identity
and female sex role behavior. If anything, they are more feminine
in their behavior than chromosomally normal girls (Downey,
Ehrhardt, Morishima, Bell, & Gruen, 1987). Girls with XXX
syndrome have a normal female body. Again, gender identity is
female and they do not differ in sex role behavior from XX girls.

Males with Klinefelter's syndrome have a male body but have
small genitals and underdeveloped secondary sex characteristics
and are infertile. Gender identity is usually male, but they may
show some diminished masculine behavior in comparison to XY
men. Although those with XYY syndrome have been described as
"supermales" and were once thought to be more masculine than
other men because of their extra Y chromosome, this seems to
be because they are particularly tall and because the early studies
were carried out on prisoners who tended to be aggressive. XYY
men are, in fact, no more masculine than XY men in their
interests and behavior.

Thus it seems from investigations of people with atypical
chromosomal patterns that sex chromosomes have little direct
influence on gender development. Further evidence for this
conclusion comes from studies of genetically female pseudo-
hermaphrodites raised as males and genetically male pseudo-
hermaphrodites raised as females, both discussed in the following
section.

Hormonal influences

Before we examine hormonal influences on behavior, it is important to point out that the categorization of hormones as either
male or female can be misleading. Androgens are commonly
referred to as male hormones because of their role in male sexual

differentiation, whereas progesterone and estrogens are often described as female hormones because they control the female reproductive cycle. In fact, both sexes produce all three hormones, but in different relative amounts. Moreover, the so-called female hormones can act like androgens. Both estrogen and some synthetic forms of progesterone can have a masculinizing effect on behavior (Hines & Green, 1990).

To gain an understanding of the influence of hormones on gender development, investigators have studied people who have been exposed prenatally to abnormally high or low levels of male or female sex hormones. Such exposure has come about in two ways. First, certain genetic conditions cause an overdose or a deficit of specific sex hormones in the developing fetus. These infants are born with genital malformation, either masculinization of the genitals of genetic females or feminization of the genitals of genetic males, depending on the effect of the condition on sex hormone production. The extent of the masculinization or feminization varies from one child to another, so that in some cases the genitals are ambiguous in appearance and in others a genetic female appears to be male, and vice versa. These individuals are called pseudo-hermaphrodites, meaning that they possess both male and female sexual structures.

Second, synthetic hormones have been prescribed to women experiencing a difficult pregnancy. This practice began in the 1940s and continued until the 1970s, when it became clear not only that this treatment was largely ineffective but also that women who had been prescribed the hormone diethylstilbestrol (DES) were at risk for vaginal and cervical cancer. There was also a small increase in the rate of female infants born with masculinized genitals and of male infants born with feminized genitals.

Gender identity

Congenital adrenal hyperplasia is a genetically transmitted disorder in which malfunctioning adrenal glands produce high levels of androgens from the prenatal period onward. Girls with this syndrome are genetically female and have female internal reproductive organs but are born with masculinized external genitals. When assigned and raised as boys, these genetic girls adopt a male gender identity and role, showing that a Y chromosome is not necessary for gender development to proceed in a male direction. The condition is usually treated by surgically feminizing the genitals during infancy and by administering corticosteroids thereafter, which reduces the level of androgen production. Genetic boys with congenital adrenal hyperplasia are also treated with corticosteroids to prevent an early puberty, but they do not need surgery, as their genitals are normal in appearance.

Studies of the effects of prenatal androgenization on gender identity have examined children who were treated early in life to avoid the confounding effects of increased levels of male sex hormones postnatally. If genetic females with congenital adrenal hyperplasia are raised as girls from birth, they develop a female gender identity in spite of their prenatal androgenization. They are quite sure that they are girls and have no desire to change sex (Money & Ehrhardt, 1972). Thus prenatal androgenization does not affect the formation of gender identity. Boys with congenital adrenal hyperplasia are always raised as boys and develop a male gender identity.

Studies of genetic males with *complete androgen insensitivity syndrome* tell us what happens when the body cannot respond to male sex hormones. This is a condition in which the tissues of a genetic male are insensitive to androgen, causing the genitals to be female in appearance. These infants are raised as girls. When they reach puberty they develop breasts and look just like other adult women. They do not menstruate, however, and are infertile. The syndrome is often not detected until puberty, when menstruation fails to occur. Individuals with complete androgen insensitivity syndrome develop a female gender identity in spite of the presence of a Y chromosome (Masica, Money, & Ehrhardt, 1971; Money & Ogurno, 1974).

These studies of pseudohermaphrodites provide strong evidence that gender identity is determined by psychological rather than biological factors (Money & Ehrhardt, 1972; Money & Tucker,

1976). Biological males who look female at birth and who are raised as girls can develop a female gender identity, and biological females who look like boys and who are treated as boys can develop a male gender identity – in spite of incongruent sex chromosomes, gonads, hormones, and internal reproductive organs. The most important factor in determining gender identity seems to be the sex to which the infant is assigned and reared.

But not everyone believes that biology plays no role in the development of gender identity. Studies of pseudo-hermaphrodites may not provide adequate evidence, as their biological ambiguities may well result in greater susceptibility to the influence of assignment and rearing (Diamond, 1965). A particularly interesting example involved a pair of identical twin brothers who had no genital malformation. The penis of one of the twins was accidentally ablated during circumcision when he was 7 months old. After plastic surgery at 17 months, this boy was reassigned as a girl and given hormone replacement therapy. When followed up into childhood she was found to have a female gender identity, although she tended to be masculine in appearance and tomboyish in behavior, which may be explained by her prenatal exposure to male sex hormones. As a teenager, she experienced identity problems, including concern about her masculine appearance and preference for a masculine occupation. She was also reported to be unhappy and to feel that being male would be easier (Diamond, 1982). It is impossible to say whether these feelings and behaviors were a response to her masculine appearance or a direct consequence of her exposure to male hormones. The effect of the parents' knowledge of her unusual history is also unclear. All of these factors show just how difficult it is to determine the role of biological factors in the development of gender identity.

Once gender identity is established, at about 3 years of age, it tends to remain fixed throughout life. After this age, gender reassignment becomes progressively more difficult. Later gender identity changes do occur, however. Thirty-one genetic females with congenital adrenal hyperplasia who were born with masculine genitals and who did not receive surgery or hormone treatment were examined by Hampson and Hampson (1961). The parents had been told that their children were female and raised them as girls. Although the large majority retained their female gender identity, five adopted a male identity at puberty following the development of male secondary sex characteristics.

Findings reported by Imperato-McGinley, Peterson, Gautier, and Sturla (1979) also challenge the view that once gender identity is formed it is fixed for life. They investigated a group of boys in the Dominican Republic who, due to a rare genetic disorder, were born with underdeveloped male genitals, which made them look like girls. The children were reared as girls until the increased levels of male hormones produced at puberty caused them to develop a penis and male secondary characteristics. These genetic males then turned into men, adopting a male gender identity and male sex role behavior.

This research suggests that male hormones may be important in gender identity formation. But social factors cannot be ruled out as an explanation. The parents may have been aware of the condition because the children's genitals were not identical to those of normal females. In fact, the children were nicknamed "*guevodoces*," meaning "testicles at 12." And because fertile men hold a much higher status in the Dominican Republic than infertile women (the alternative had they remained female), both the children and their families would have benefited from the change. Just imagine what might have happened if, as a teenager, your body had transformed from one sex to the other. Do you think it would have been easier to adapt to or resist this change?

So what can we learn from research on pseudohermaphrodites? It seems that gender identity is largely determined by psychological rather than biological factors, and that the sex to which an infant is assigned at birth is the first crucial step in this process. We cannot, however, definitively conclude that biological factors play no part in the development of gender identity.

Sex role behavior

Although prenatal sex hormones are not a major influence on gender identity, they do appear to play a part in the development of gender roles. It seems that prenatal androgens predispose us toward masculinity. Comparisons between girls with congenital adrenal hyperplasia who were treated early in life and control groups of girls unaffected by this disorder found the androgenized girls to be more interested in active outdoor play, to prefer boys as playmates, to spend more time playing with masculine toys, and to see themselves and be seen by others as tomboys. They were less interested in traditionally female activities such as doll play, baby care, and fantasy games involving role play as a wife or mother (Berenbaum & Hines, 1992; Dittman, Kappes, Kappes, Borger, Meyer-Bahlburg, Stegner, Willig, & Wallis, 1990; Dittman, Kappes, Kappes, Borger, Stegner, Willig, & Wallis, 1990; Ehrhardt & Baker, 1974; Ehrhardt, Epstein, & Money, 1968). Boys with congenital adrenal hyperplasia also showed higher levels of energy expenditure in play and sports than did a control group of their unaffected brothers (Ehrhardt, 1975).

Progesterones can have either a masculinizing or feminizing influence on sex role behavior. Natural progesterone and some synthetic progesterones are feminizing because they interfere with the action of androgens. Other synthetic progesterones mimic androgens and thus have a masculinizing effect (Goy & McEwen, 1980; Hines, 1982). Both natural and synthetic progesterones have been used to treat problem pregnancies (Reinisch, Ziemba-Davis, & Sanders, 1991). Girls prenatally exposed to synthetic progesterones with androgenic properties show a similar pattern of tomboyish behavior to that of girls with congenital adrenal hyperplasia (Ehrhardt & Money, 1967; Money & Ehrhardt, 1972). Also, higher scores on a projective test of aggression have been obtained by both females and males exposed to androgenic progesterones (Reinisch, 1981). These studies provide further evidence that prenatal androgenization causes a predisposition toward male sex role behavior.

In contrast, the outcome of prenatal exposure to nonandrogenic progesterones is a tendency toward female sex role behavior, particularly for girls. Prenatally exposed girls show more interest in doll play, child care, feminine clothing, and less physically active play and less interest in tomboyish behavior than do unexposed controls (Ehrhardt, Meyer-Bahlburg, Feldman, & Ince, 1984; Zussman, Zussman, & Dalton, 1975). The consequence for boys is less conclusive. There are some reports of less energetic, assertive, aggressive and athletic behavior (Yalom, Green, & Fisk, 1973; Zussman et al., 1975). Other studies have failed to demonstrate a clear effect for boys (Ehrhardt et al., 1984; Kester, 1984; Kester, Green, Finch, & Williams, 1980). One explanation is that sufficient androgens are present in the male fetus to override the effect of the natural or synthetic progesterone. And because boys are under pressure to conform to stereotypically masculine behavior, any tendency toward less typically male behavior that may arise from an elevated level of natural or nonandrogenic synthetic progesterone may be counteracted by cultural influences.

Although it seems that the development of sex role behavior may be influenced to some extent by sex hormones, with androgens masculinizing behavior and nonandrogenic progesterones having a feminizing effect, a number of methodological problems are associated with this research (Bleier, 1984). The samples studied were small and often included children across a wide age range; furthermore, the interviewers were sometimes aware of the nature of the child's condition, which may have biased the results. It is also conceivable that knowledge about the unusual hormonal condition may affect the behavior of parents or the children themselves, so that tomboyish behavior in girls prenatally exposed to an excess of male hormones may be noticed more by parents, and their daughters may be under less pressure to conform to the female role. In the past, many girls with congenital adrenal hyperplasia did not receive surgery until after they had become aware of their masculinized genitals, which may well have affected their behavior. Nowadays, however, the majority of these girls are feminized in infancy, and yet they continue to be less feminine than their peers. Interestingly, the findings of more recent studies of prenatal androgenization that have corrected for the methodological problems summarized by Bleier are similar to those of the original investigations.

Differences in the children's behavior may also stem from the mother's illness or from pregnancy complications. Many mothers who were administered progesterones during pregnancy were diabetic and may have been less encouraging of their children's active and energetic play. However, an examination of pregnancy complications in girls exposed to prenatal progesterones established that the more feminine behavior shown by these girls cannot be fully explained in this way (Meyer-Bahlburg, Feldman, Ehrhardt, & Cohen, 1984).

So what can we conclude about the influence of prenatal hormones on sex role development? Although the methodological difficulties prevent us from drawing any firm conclusions, the research findings are relatively consistent in suggesting that there might be a link between sex hormones and sex role behavior, with androgens predisposing toward masculinity and nonandrogenic progesterones toward femininity.

How might prenatal sex hormones influence sex role behavior? It is thought that sex differences in prenatal hormone levels produce sex differences in the organization of neural substrates of the brain, causing the threshold for some behaviors to be lower for girls and for other behaviors to be lower for boys. According to this theory, a high level of prenatal androgens masculinizes the brain so that it takes a weaker stimulus to evoke male sex-typed behavior such as play with cars and trucks and a stronger stimulus to evoke female sex-typed behavior such as doll play, whereas a low level of androgens has the opposite effect. These prenatally determined differences in sensitivity to stimuli are thought to help explain why boys and girls differ in patterns of play, in levels of activity, and in aggressive behavior (Ehrhardt, 1987; Hines & Green, 1990; Money & Ehrhardt, 1972; Money & Tucker, 1976).

There is also growing evidence that prenatal sex hormones may play some part in the development of sex differences in specific cognitive abilities. Although there is much overlap between the sexes, males tend to perform better than females on visuospatial tasks, whereas females do better than males on tests of verbal fluency (Halpern, 1992). Males also show greater language lateralization – that is, greater reliance on the dominant hemisphere of the brain for processing verbal material (McGlone, 1980). As we shall see in Chapter 10, these sex differences are very small and are influenced by social factors. Still, studies of individuals exposed to unusual hormonal environments during fetal development suggest that low levels of androgens are associated with the female profile of cognitive abilities and high levels predispose toward the male pattern (Hines, 1990).

The theory that prenatal sex hormones produce sex differences in brain structure and behavior has aroused a great deal of controversy, particularly because it derives from animal research, which is often criticized as irrelevant to human behavior, and because the mechanisms involved in the link between sex hormones, sex differences in brain structure, and sex differences in behavior in humans have not been clearly determined. Nevertheless, anatomical differences between the human male and female brain have been identified in areas of the hypothalamus associated with sex differences in reproductive function (Allen, Hines, Shryne, & Gorski, 1989; LeVay, 1991) and in cortical regions that are implicated in sex differences in cognition (de Lacoste & Holloway, 1982; Witelson, 1989).

The theory has also been criticized for failing to take account of psychological and social influences on sex typing . Once an infant is born, environmental influences are thought to play a major part in increasing or decreasing sensitivity to different stimuli, so that the original slight difference in thresholds between the sexes may be maximized or overridden depending on the culture in which the child is reared. Boys and girls may be more likely to behave in a sex-typed way if they are encouraged to do so because of the initial threshold differences, but they are also quite capable of behaving in ways that are typical of the other sex in an environment that is supportive of less traditional roles. Thus any effect of sex hormones on sex role behavior is mediated by the social environment of the child. It may even be the case that the social environment can directly influence sex differences in the brain. Recent animal research shows that social environments that differ in complexity produce different patterns of sex differences in brain structure (Juraska, 1991). Whether the same processes operate in humans remains to be seen.

Sexual orientation

If fetal sex hormones influence childhood gender roles, might not adult sexual orientation also be rooted in the prenatal hormonal environment? Let us take a look at research that addresses this question. The role of androgens in sexual orientation has been examined by studying genetic females with congenital adrenal hyperplasia who had been assigned and reared as girls. Many of these women consider themselves bisexual or lesbian, either on the basis of actual sexual relationships with a woman or because their sexual thoughts involve a female partner (Dittman, Kappes, & Kappes, 1992; Money, Schwartz, & Lewis, 1984). This suggests that prenatal exposure to raised levels of androgens predisposes females toward sexual attraction to women.

Genetic females with congenital adrenal hyperplasia who are assigned and raised as boys become attracted to female partners and have sexual relationships with women just like other heterosexual men (Money & Lewis, 1982). Although this may be explained by the high levels of prenatal androgens promoting sexual attraction to women, these men have a male body, gender identity, and sex role that may have contributed to their heterosexual orientation. Female sex chromosomes do not prevent these genetic females from becoming heterosexual males, showing that a male chromosomal pattern is not necessary for a male heterosexual identity. Even in the case of physical feminization, genetic females with this disorder who are raised as boys continue to identify as heterosexual men (Money, 1987, 1988). A genetic girl who was born with a fully formed penis and diagnosed as a boy with undescended testes was discovered to have congenital adrenal hyperplasia at the age of 10 years. The boy's doctor prescribed female sex hormones in the misguided belief that, in addition to feminizing his body, the hormones would feminize his mind. The physical effect of hormone treatment on this heterosexual boy was breast development and the onset of menstruation through his penis. The emotional effect was devastating. Rather than identifying as a heterosexual girl, he became extremely distressed about the changes to his body. Hormone therapy was stopped (Money, 1987, 1988).

Individuals with complete androgen insensitivity syndrome who have been assigned and raised as women develop a sexual orientation toward men. This may be due to their lack of prenatal androgens or to their female appearance and identity (Money et al., 1984). These genetically and gonadally male women have been compared with a control group of genetically and gonadally female women with Rokitansky syndrome, a disorder involving the absence of a uterus and fallopian tubes (Lewis & Money, 1983; Money & Lewis, 1983). Both groups are physically similar in that they have a shallow vagina and no internal reproductive organs and do not menstruate, but they differ in chromosomal sex. All of the women were found to be heterosexual in fantasy and in practice. This tells us that female sex chromosomes are not essential for the development of a female heterosexual orientation.

If high levels of androgens promote sexual attraction to women and low levels to men, do estrogens, because they are derived from androgens, do the same? Women prenatally exposed to the synthetic estrogen diethylstilbestrol (DES) have been compared with unexposed women from the same clinic and with their unexposed sisters (Ehrhardt et al., 1985). In comparison with both control groups, the women who had been exposed to DES reported increased bisexuality and lesbianism in terms of sexual fantasy or sexual behavior. Thus estrogen seems similar to androgen in its effect on sexual orientation. But, as the researchers themselves point out, 75% of the DES-exposed women were heterosexual and only one identified as lesbian from the start of her sexual life. For men, no differences in sexual orientation have been found between those exposed prenatally to raised levels of DES and a nonexposed control group (Kester et al., 1980).

So what can we conclude from this research? Money (1987, 1988) believes that prenatal sex hormones, but not sex chromosomes, play some part in the development of later sexual orientation, although he emphasizes that whether an individual will identify as heterosexual, bisexual, or homosexual is also strongly dependent on postnatal experience. Prenatal hormones may act on the brain to facilitate development as heterosexual or homosexual, providing the individual's socialization experiences are compatible. According to Money, androgenic hormones predispose both sexes toward a preference for female sexual partners, and men and women who lack a critical amount of these hormones are more likely to prefer men. Thus men who are prenatally exposed to high levels of androgens and women who are prenatally exposed to low levels of androgens or estrogens are more likely to be heterosexual, whereas men who are prenatally exposed to low levels of androgens and women who are prenatally exposed to high levels of androgens or estrogens are more likely to be homosexual. This does not mean that nature is more important than nurture in the development of sexual orientation. The fact that male pseudohermaphrodites with ambiguous genitals can become either heterosexual males or heterosexual females according to their sex of rearing demonstrates the overriding influence of postnatal factors on sexual orientation.

An alternative explanation for the higher incidence of bisexuality or lesbianism among women with congenital adrenal hyperplasia is that the genital abnormality is responsible, or possibly the increased attention paid by parents and doctors to the child's condition. It is also important to remember that most women with congenital adrenal hyperplasia, and most women prenatally exposed to DES, are heterosexual in spite of their unusual endocrine history. A further difficulty with the existing studies is that some women who were classified as lesbian or bisexual had simply reported feelings of sexual attraction toward women rather than involvement in sexual relationships, and many were young at the time of interview so that their sexual orientation as heterosexual, bisexual, or lesbian may have changed as they grew older.

The studies of the effects on sexual orientation of prenatal hormones have been few, the samples small, and biases in sampling procedures have not been ruled out. Although we cannot conclude that prenatal hormones have no effect on later sexual orientation, clear evidence for their involvement does not exist. As research progresses we shall no doubt learn more about the role of biological factors in gender development. However, from the work done so far, it seems unlikely that sex hormones will be found to determine directly gender identity, sex role behavior, or sexual orientation independently of the child's social environment. It is to these social and psychological processes that we now turn.

Summary

Studying people with an unusual prenatal history has helped us to understand the role of biology in gender development. Though gender identity is primarily socially influenced, prenatal sex hormones set the foundations for later sex role behavior, and possibly sexual orientation as well. Prenatal hormones do not determine gender development. Instead, their effect is augmented or diminished according to the social environment in which the child grows up.

4
Psychoanalytic approaches and moral development

Probably more than any other single psychologist, Freud has fundamentally changed the way in which human beings think of themselves. Following Freud, we have accepted the idea of an unconscious and that much of our behavior is motivated by impulses of which we are only dimly aware at best (Freud, 1916/1963; see also Lee & Hertzberg, 1978, and Lerman, 1986, for discussions). Moreover, Freud stressed the importance of early experiences and thoughts in influencing later personality. But because these early thoughts are often unacceptable due to their sexual and aggressive content, they are repressed. Thus, even though as adults we no longer remember these early experiences, they are assumed to play a critical role in behavior.

In this chapter we examine Freud's theory of psychosexual development and discuss his ideas on the development of the male and the female personality. As we shall see, the different developmental paths that females and males follow lead to gender differences in sexuality and, interestingly, in moral reasoning as well. According to Freud's theory, females are both sexually and morally inferior to males. After explicating Freud's views, we consider some reformulations and reinterpretations of Freud's theory of sexuality, and then turn to a more detailed discussion of gender differences in moral reasoning.

The traditional psychoanalytic account

Freud's theory of personality is inherently developmental. Freud (1931/1967; see also Stockard & Johnson, 1992) argued that infants are born as pure biological creatures, motivated by intense erotic and aggressive desires. The psychological locus of these desires is the *id*. The major task of development is to modify these desires and to harness psychological energy, known as *libido*, into more culturally appropriate avenues. He postulated several psychosexual stages in children's development, each of which involves a conflict between the child's erotic and aggressive desires and the demands of the socializing culture. In resolving each of these conflicts, children come to invest their libidinal energy in more and more culturally appropriate activities.

During the first two stages of psychosexual development, females and males are quite similar. In the first stage, called the *oral stage*, the infant's erotic energy and desires center on sucking. The erogenous zone is the mouth and the love object is the mother's breast. In fact, Freud argued that infants are not really aware that they are separate from the mother at this point; infants may believe that the much desired breast is really a part of themselves. Conflict arises between the infant, who wants the breast all of the time, and the mother, who controls feeding and access to the breast.

The conflict is resolved through the establishment of the *ego*, which is a mechanism for reality testing and rationalization. Essentially, the formation of the ego allows the infant to cope with the all-encompassing desires of the id through rational thought. The ego allows the infant to reason that although the breast is not available now, it will be available again at some point in the future. This is the early beginning of the ability to delay gratification, that is, to learn how to wait for something that we want very much. It is also, for Freud, the beginning of children's understanding that they are separate from the mother. This idea will become important later when we discuss some reinterpretations of Freud's theory.

The second stage of psychosexual development is the *anal stage*. At this time, young children become critically concerned with the retention and elimination of feces. The erogenous zone is the anus, and the conflict is between the child, who wants to control retention and elimination, and the parent, who is trying to toilet-train the child, and thus wants the child's anal control to conform to socially accepted standards. The conflict is resolved as children begin to derive pleasure and feelings of mastery from anal control.

It is during Freud's third stage of psychosexual development, the *phallic stage*, that sexual identity is formed. It is during this stage, occurring at about 5 years of age, that children shift their libido to their genitals. Both boys and girls masturbate and begin to have fantasies, however unrealistic, about engaging in sexual activities. However, the love object for both boys and girls is still the mother. Because Freud saw the male pattern of development as the norm, and the female pattern as somehow deviant, we discuss male development first.

On entering the phallic stage, boys discover that not only do they have a penis but that their penis is a source of great pleasure. Moreover, they develop some vague idea that they can do something with their penis that will give them even more pleasure, and that this activity has something to do with what their parents do together. Boys thus become sexually interested in their mother. Although this is very exciting, it also causes a great deal of anxiety in boys. Specifically, boys fear the father's retaliation. But what kind of retaliation could the father engage in? Boys look around and realize that not everybody has a penis. This means that they could possibly lose their penis as well, a thought that creates an extreme amount of fear, known as *castration anxiety*. Boys see that their father is much more powerful physically and sexually, and begin to fear that if they act on their sexual urges toward their mother, their father will castrate them.

The conflict between wanting the mother sexually and fearing the father's retaliation is known as the *Oedipal conflict*, after the Greek tragedy. Freud argued that the fear of castration is so great that, in order to retain their penis, boys give up their sexual love for their mother. Although they are giving up their mother now, boys come to understand that when they grow older, they will be able to have sexual access to their own female, just as their father does, by virtue of having a penis. In this way they identify with their father, and this identification forms the basis of boys' identity as a male sexual being. Further, in identifying with the father, boys also identify with and internalize the father's moral standards and values. Thus the resolution of the Oedipal conflict results in the formation of the *superego*, which Freud posited was the source of all moral judgment and reasoning. Boys resolve the phallic stage with a secure sense of their sexual identity and power and with the basis for a strong moral stance.

Freud believed that girls, too, were sexually in love with their mother. However, because the impetus for giving up the mother as a love object is castration anxiety, girls face a peculiar problem. What girls discover during the phallic stage is that they do not have a penis. They have already been castrated, and because they see that their mother also lacks a penis, girls blame her for this basic psychic wound. Girls turn toward their father as a love object because he has the coveted prize, a penis. Girls' sexual identity is ruled by *penis envy*. Notice, however, two things. First, girls do not have to give up their father as a love object, because they do not fear their mother's retaliation; they are already castrated. Second, and following from this first problem, girls never fully identify with their mother. Rather, they see their mother as weak and ineffectual because she has no penis.

Because they do not fully identify with the mother, girls have problems both with their sexual identity and with their moral understanding. Girls continue to want a penis of their own; but in order to achieve a healthy sexuality, they must convert this desire into the wish for sexual penetration by a penis, and this transition is accomplished with great difficulty. Further, because there is no compelling need to identify with the mother, the superego is not as fully formed in females as in males. Thus,

Freud argued, females are both sexually inferior and morally inferior to males.

Freud's theory of sexual development created quite a controversy, and it continues to be controversial to this day. It must be stated at the outset that there is virtually no empirical support for his theory. No research findings suggest that young children have these serious sexual conflicts with their parents. But Freud and his followers would argue that much of sexual development goes on at the unconscious level, and all of these feelings are strongly repressed as children grow older because they are so unacceptable. So it is not clear exactly what evidence might exist to confirm the theory. On the other hand, a theory that is not open to scientific test and confirmation is not really a scientific theory at all. Most researchers concerned with gender do not consider Freud's ideas about gender development to have serious scientific merit.

Still, Freud's contribution to our understanding of human psychology is immeasurable. First and foremost, Freud was the first psychologist to focus on developmental issues and particularly on very early development as an important psychological period. Second, Freud was the first psychologist to bring sexuality into discussions of human development and to argue that sexuality was an important aspect of human life that needed to be studied and understood. Finally, Freud's notion of the unconscious has changed the way we conceptualize behavior; we do not always know why we do the things we do, but following Freud, we always assume there is some reason for our behavior. Thus, although psychoanalytic theory fails as a scientific theory, it has continued to influence the way we think about development and sexuality. Over the years many of Freud's followers and critics have refined, reformulated, and reinterpreted aspects of Freud's theory.

Neo-Freudian approaches to gender

One of Freud's basic assumptions was that, by biological definition, being male and having a penis was better than being female and having a vagina. For Freud, masculinity was identified with activity and femininity with passivity, and this distinction was based on biological aspects of sexual union, with the male being the aggressor. Moreover, it is this basic biological fact that leads to the concept of penis envy. Many of Freud's critics have questioned this assumption. More specifically, they have argued that although penis envy may indeed be a real phenomenon, it is based more on culture than on biology. Freud developed his theory during the early twentieth century in Vienna. At that time Vienna was the cultural center of a sexually repressive society. Females in that society had few, if any, opportunities outside of marriage. Thus, even psychoanalysts who trained under Freud, such as Helene Deutsch (1933/1967), Karen Horney (1933/1967), and Clara Thompson (1943/1967), argue that females come to envy the penis because the penis represents power and control in society. In other words, what little girls come to realize early in development is not that a penis, per se, is important but that having a penis means having power and control over one's life, and not having a penis means being denied opportunities and autonomy.

Although this reformulation of Freudian theory may make a great deal of sense, it does not change any of the basic ideas about sexual development. These theorists still assume that penis envy is a major factor in female sexual development. Further, being male is still seen as better than being female, although for cultural rather than biological reasons. Most important, the resolution of the Oedipal conflict is still in question for little girls, and girls are still assumed to have less developed superegos than boys. In a very real sense males are still seen as the norm and females as other or deviant from this norm.

More radical reinterpretations of traditional psychoanalytic theory have questioned the assumption of male superiority. From this approach females are examined in their own right rather than in comparison to males. Erik Erikson (1968/1974), who was a student of Freud's and later went on to formulate his own theory of development, argued that the female experience of body was fundamentally different than the male experience of body. Whereas the male sense of bodily self involves protrusion and projection into external space, the female sense is directed toward inner space, a feeling of containment and surround. Females do not have penis envy; rather they have a different but very positive sense of their own body. In fact, Erikson argues that males may envy females because females have the ability to create life. To overcome this "womb envy," males feel the need to accomplish things in the world, leading to their being more outer-directed. Males become concerned with creating objects that will empower them. Females are more secure because of their creative powers. Females remain inner-directed, in the sense of creating secure and calm spaces, and develop caring and nurturing relationships.

As discussed in Chapter 2, the notion that females are more caring and nurturant than males is pervasive in Western conceptions of gender, and quite possibly in most other cultures as well. It is certainly the case that it is females who provide the vast majority of child care in all cultures. Why is it that women mother? In order to answer this question, Nancy Chodorow (1978) reinterpreted some of Freud's basic ideas about early development. Instead of focusing exclusively on the phallic stage of psychosexual development as critical in forming a gender identity, Chodorow argues that gender identity begins in infancy. At this early point in development, Chodorow agrees with Freud that the breast, and by extension the mother, is the most important object in the infant's world. Both boys and girls see the mother as the source of all comfort, as all-caring and all-sacrificing. This view sets the stage for later notions of femaleness. More important, this early period is characterized by merging and identification with the mother. Both boys and girls are assumed to begin with a female gender identity.

Because the mother is female, Chodorow further argues, the mother identifies more closely with a daughter than a son. Because mother and daughter mutually identify with each other, daughters maintain a sense of interpersonal merging. With sons, the mother does not identify as strongly but, rather, reacts in terms of separateness and individuation. Although males have an early identification with the mother, they quickly begin to separate from her and to define themselves in terms of difference from females.

As they grow older, females continue to identify with the mother, and their self-concept develops from this interpersonal relationship. Females remain merged with others in the sense that their self-concept is dependent on mutuality and relatedness. Females are relationally oriented. Because their self-concept depends on mutuality and interpersonal relatedness, women are psychologically prepared to mother when they reach adulthood. This, in turn, perpetuates the cycle of development, and explains why women mother. Males, in contrast, begin to differentiate more and more from the mother, and in the process of forming a male gender identity, turn away from all that is female. Males define themselves as separate and individuated; moreover, they repress all feminine tendencies in themselves and begin to denigrate femininity in others. Males' self-concept depends on being a separate, independent individual. But because of their very early experiences, both males and females continue to think of females as self-sacrificing and nurturant. Thus both males and females assume that women are better caregivers than men.

There have been many criticisms of Chodorow's theory (see especially Sayers, 1983). Similar to Freud, Chodorow seems to assume that gender roles are biologically given. Although she discusses how males and females come to different gender identities because of early experiences, she also claims that these experiences could not be other than what they are. Females must be the ones to conceive, carry, and birth the baby; and in most cultures females must also be available to breast-feed if the infant is to survive. Because women must mother from a biological viewpoint, Chodorow argues that there is no other way that cultures could exist other than females becoming relationally oriented and motivated to mother.

Although it is true that biology plays an important role in how cultures come to define gender, it is not clear that biology provides one, and only one, solution. Chodorow pays little attention to the different ways that various cultures define the role of mothering. For example, cultures vary in how much time the mother is expected to spend with her infant, in the kinds of mother–child interactions that are deemed appropriate, and even whether to breast-feed and, if so, for how long. Also, as with traditional Freudian theory, there is little empirical evidence for Chodorow's claims. Although it does seem to be the case that mothers and infants have an intense emotional bond with each other (e.g., Ainsworth, 1979; Sroufe, 1985), there is no evidence that this bond is different between mothers and daughters than between mothers and sons – a difference that is a cornerstone of Chodorow's theory.

Still, Chodorow's ideas are provocative. Moreover, they fit with much of what we know about gender differences in adults, at least in this culture. As discussed throughout this book, it does seem to be the case that females are more oriented toward others and relationships than males are (what has come to be called a relational orientation) and males are more oriented toward independence and autonomy than females are (an autonomous orientation). Of course, as also discussed, there are many other possible explanations of this gender difference.

Interestingly, Chodorow's reformulation of traditional psy-choanalytic theory also leads to a different interpretation of gender differences in moral reasoning. From a strict Freudian perspective, females are morally inferior to males. However, arguing from Chodorow's ideas, Carol Gilligan (1982) has proposed that females have a different, but not inferior, moral orientation than males. Before considering these arguments in more detail, we need to discuss the way in which moral reasoning has been studied within developmental psychology over the past several decades.

The development of moral reasoning

Although morality and moral development are integral to Freud's psychoanalytic theory, most of the research on moral reasoning in the developmental literature has stemmed from a cognitive developmental approach (see Chapter 6 for an extended dis-cussion of this theoretical approach). Yet even from this approach, many theorists have argued that females are morally inferior to males.

As with many other topics in developmental psychology, Piaget (1966) was the first theorist to discuss the cognitive basis of moral development. After observing and interviewing children ranging in age from 6 to 12 years, Piaget postulated a developmental shift in children's understanding of morality. At first, children are concerned only with the consequences of behavior and pay little attention to the underlying intentions of the actor. For example, when told about a child who broke one dish while trying to steal a cookie from the cookie jar, and another child who broke several dishes while helping to set the table, young children claim that the second child should be punished more, because she broke more dishes. Older children begin to take into account the actor's intentions, and so would argue that the first child should be punished more because her intentions were morally wrong.

The shift of focus from consequences to intentions is a critical turning point in moral understanding. According to Piaget, a major impetus for this shift comes from interacting with the peer group and especially from negotiating and resolving conflict, a process that involves understanding and coordinating others' points of view. Because males are more likely than females to play in large groups and negotiate rules (see Chapter 7 for a discussion of childhood play patterns), Piaget argues that males begin to understand the consensual nature of rules earlier than females do and are better able to coordinate multiple points of view, leading to higher levels of moral reasoning.

Kohlberg and his colleagues (Colby, Kohlberg, Gibbs, & Lieberman, 1983; Kohlberg, 1969) extended Piaget's notions of moral reasoning and developed a formal model of moral development. Kohlberg assessed individuals' level of moral reasoning by presenting them with a series of stories, each of which contained a moral dilemma. For example, one story, called "the Heinz dilemma," involves a husband, Heinz, whose wife is dying of a rare disease. There is a drug that will save her, but only one druggist sells this drug, and he is asking an exorbitant amount of money for it. After exhausting various avenues for getting the drug (e.g., trying to get a loan, arranging payments with the druggist) Heinz is still unable to buy the drug. The moral question posed by this dilemma is whether or not Heinz should steal the drug to save his wife.

Based on the way subjects respond to these kinds of moral dilemmas, and especially based on the reasons they give for their decisions, Kohlberg concluded that there are three major stages of moral reasoning. During the first, *preconventional*, stage, individuals base their moral reasoning on the physical conse- quences of actions. For example, children at this stage might respond that Heinz should not steal the drug because he will be punished for it.

The second stage of moral reasoning is called *conventional*, because individuals base their decisions on the conventionalized rules and laws of society. In the first substage of conventional moral reasoning, the focus is on conformity to society's rules and interpersonal expectations. Essentially, morality is based on being good toward others so that others will be good toward you. An individual at this substage might argue that Heinz should not steal the drug because Heinz would not want anyone to steal anything from him. In the second substage of conventional reasoning, the focus is on maintaining law and order. An in- dividual at this stage might argue that Heinz should not steal because stealing is against the law.

The last stage is called *postconventional*. Now individuals base their moral judgments on a concern for individual rights and justice. According to Kohlberg, this is the highest form of moral reasoning because it is based on universal concerns for the rights of all people and on principles of equal justice. Individuals at this level might argue that Heinz should steal the drug because the preservation of life is a high moral principle based on the universal rights of individuals.

In Kohlberg's original research, only males were studied. When females began to be examined using Kohlberg's model of moral development, they tended to score lower than males. In particular, females most often responded at the first substage of conventional reasoning, the level of concern for interpersonal expectations. Males, in contrast, even when using conventional reasoning, focused on maintaining law and order, which is seen as a higher level in Kohlberg's scheme. Further, few females progressed to the third level of reasoning based on rights and justice.

In 1982, Gilligan published *In a Different Voice*, which challenged Kohlberg's theory and argued that females were not morally inferior. She presented data from interviews with women facing a real-life moral dilemma, whether to continue an unwanted pregnancy or to have an abortion. In analyzing these interviews, Gilligan presented evidence that females had a different moral orientation than did males. Whereas males were mainly concerned with issues of rights and justice, females seemed more concerned with issues of caring for others and preserving interpersonal relationships.

According to Gilligan, female morality also develops through three stages. In the first stage the focus is on caring for self; this stage is similar to Kohlberg's preconventional level. The second stage centers on caring for others, and often involves issues of sacrificing one's own needs or desires in order to help other people. In an example of this kind of reasoning, a woman talks about her decision whether to continue an unwanted pregnancy:

> I don't know what choices are open to me. It is either to have it or the abortion; these are the choices open to me. I think what confuses me is it is a choice of either hurting myself or hurting other people around me. Which is more important? If there could be a happy medium, it would be fine, but there isn't. (Gilligan, 1982, p. 80)

This women views her moral dilemma as a conflict between hurting herself and hurting others. She is unable to decide which decision is right because she sees these moral imperatives as incompatible.

The final stage in Gilligan's theory involves an integration of concern for self and concern for others. Individuals achieving this level are able to coordinate and balance their own needs with those of others. Again, an example from a woman thinking about terminating an unwanted pregnancy:

I have this responsibility to myself, and you know, for once I am beginning to realize that that really matters to me. Instead of doing what I want for myself and feeling guilty over how selfish I am, you realize that that is a very usual way for people to live – doing what you want to do because you feel that your wants and your needs are important, if to no one else, than to you, and that's reason enough to do something you want to do. (Gilligan, 1982, p. 94)

The woman's moral dilemma is finding the right balance between meeting her own needs and meeting the needs of others. She no longer sees these goals as incompatible, but is struggling with their integration.

Gilligan's stages of female morality are based on Chodorow's theoretical formulation of female development. Because females never fully separate from the mother in order to form their gender identity, females define themselves in terms of their relationships to others, and their moral reasoning reflects this concern. When assessed according to Kohlberg's model, Gilligan argues, females score lower because the model is biased toward males. Specifically, because of their concern with others' needs and desires, even females reasoning at a high moral level would be classified at the first substage of conventional reasoning in Kohlberg's scheme. Only males, who have an individuated self-concept, are able to ignore the needs and desires of others and base their moral judgments on abstract principles of equal justice. This is why it is usually males who evidence moral reasoning at Kohlberg's postconventional level. Gilligan's ideas began a major controversy about gender differences in moral development. Is it the case that males and females are morally different, and if so, why?

Gender differences in moral reasoning

Recall that in a traditional moral reasoning study, subjects are read a series of hypothetical moral dilemmas and asked to discuss appropriate courses of action. Do females and males differ in their responses? Although early research in the 1960s indicated females scored lower than males when measured by Kohlberg's scale, more recent research has found little if any difference. Walker (1984) reviewed 79 research studies that explicitly analyzed for gender differences in children, adolescents, and adults. Of the 31 studies of children, only 6 found significant differences between females and males, and in most of these females scored higher in moral reasoning than did males. Of the 35 studies of adolescents, 10 found significant gender differences, and most of these showed males scoring higher on moral reasoning than did females. Few studies examined moral reasoning in adults; of 13 studies of adults, 4 found gender differences favoring males, but this is difficult to interpret because the males also tended to have higher levels of education than the females (we return to this issue later). Overall, then, there are few consistent gender differences in moral reasoning (see Thoma, 1986, for similar conclusions). Only during adolescence were consistent differences found, and even here the differences were small and only found in about a third of the studies conducted.

Does this mean that there are no gender differences in moral reasoning? The answer is complicated. Clearly, when faced with hypothetical moral dilemmas, both males and females are capable of abstract reasoning based on universal principles of justice. Still, as Gilligan and others (Gibbs, Arnold, & Burkhart, 1984; Thoma, 1986; Walker, deVries, & Trevethan, 1987) have argued, there may be gender differences in preferred *style* of moral reasoning. It is not a question of moral competence, but a question of the different kinds of reasoning that people bring to bear on moral problems. In standard studies of moral reasoning, individuals are assigned to a stage of moral reasoning based on the "highest" or most frequent kind of reasoning shown in their response. But a few studies have delved more deeply into subjects' responses. In these studies, rather than assigning each subject to one particular moral level, all of the subject's reasons and arguments are evaluated. While it is true that both females and males are capable of justice-based reasoning, it is also the case that females ground more of their arguments on empathy and care than do males (Donenberg & Hoffman, 1988; Gibbs et al., 1984). Females, more than males, temper their abstract moral principles with concern for others and relationships.

A deeper criticism of moral development research concerns the use of hypothetical dilemmas. Rather than examining moral reasoning about unknown people in personally uninvolving situations, perhaps we should examine real people making real moral decisions in their day-to-day life (see especially Gilligan, 1982, for a full discussion of this argument). A few studies have asked people to generate and discuss real-life moral dilemmas, and in these studies, there are consistent gender differences. First, when asked to generate a personal moral dilemma, females mention family issues and interpersonal relations more frequently than do males (Walker et al., 1987). And when discussing a real-life dilemma, females use more care-based reasoning than do males (Ford & Lowery, 1986; Gilligan & Attanucci, 1988; Walker et al., 1987). This is not to say that females do not use justice-based arguments in personal dilemmas; they do. But they do not rely on justice-based arguments to the same extent as do males. So females are showing a relational, care-based orientation in thinking about their own life problems. Females also rate their personal moral dilemmas as more important and more difficult than do males (Ford & Lowery, 1986), suggesting that females may be more concerned with resolving personal dilemmas than are males.

An intriguing finding is that when males generate a more interpersonally oriented moral dilemma, for example, a family dispute, they are just as likely as females to use more care-based reasoning (Walker et al., 1987). Perhaps it is the type of moral dilemma that calls for a particular kind of reasoning. Some moral dilemmas revolve around interpersonal relationships, such as dilemmas about lying to friends or family (should you tell your mother where you really were last Saturday night?), or interpersonal and family commitments (should a surrogate mother have the right to keep the baby once it is born?). Other dilemmas do not involve close personal relationships; for example, dilemmas about personal standards of behavior (should you cheat on the chemistry test or face certain failure?), or equality of justice (should a black person be tried by an all white jury?). Obviously, care-based reasoning and justice-based reasoning are relevant for both kinds of dilemmas, but perhaps more interpersonally situated dilemmas lead to a greater amount of care-based reasoning than less interpersonally situated dilemmas. Because females are more likely than males to focus on interpersonally oriented moral dilemmas, they may use more care-based reasoning as a consequence.

If this interpretation is correct, then given a more interpersonally situated moral dilemma, both males and females should show care-based reasoning, and given a less interpersonally situated dilemma, both should show justice-based reasoning. Rothbart, Hanley, and Albert (1986) examined this possibility by asking subjects to discuss two hypothetical dilemmas. The first was the Heinz dilemma presented earlier, which pits two abstract justice concerns against each other, stealing and saving a life, so subjects should use abstract principles of justice. The second hypothetical dilemma concerned a moral question about physical intimacy; this topic should lead to more concern with care and interpersonal relations. In fact, this is exactly what was found. Both males and females showed more justice-based reasoning when discussing the Heinz dilemma and more care-based reasoning when discussing the physical intimacy dilemma. Most telling, subjects were also asked to generate a personal moral dilemma. In this context, females generated more interpersonally situated dilemmas than did males. And, not surprisingly, females relied heavily on care-oriented reasoning and males relied heavily on justice-oriented reasoning.

Overall, both males and females use both care and justice in thinking about moral problems, although females seem to use more care-based moral reasoning than do males. More important, it appears that the dilemma itself partly determines what kind of moral reasoning individuals use. Both males and females use more care-based moral reasoning when discussing interpersonally situated moral dilemmas, whereas they use more justice-based reasoning when discussing more abstract, impersonal moral dilemmas. The real locus of a gender difference in moral reasoning seems to lie in the way in which females and males conceptualize moral issues. When discussing their own moral lives, females focus on interpersonal dilemmas and care-based reasoning, whereas males focus on impersonal dilemmas and justice-based reasoning. It is not that females and males differ in their ability to reason morally but rather that females and males differ in the kinds of issues that they consider morally important (see Brabeck, 1987, for a fuller discussion).

Explaining gender differences in moral reasoning

Gender differences in moral reasoning are small but consistent. ← When asked to select and discuss real-life moral dilemmas, females tend to choose problems that focus on relationships and use care-oriented reasoning. Males tend to select problems that focus on more impersonal issues and argue about individual rights and equal justice. Why? Two possibilities have been examined: gender differences in level of education and gender differences in early socialization experiences.

In general, level of education is related to level of moral reasoning as assessed by the standard Kohlberg scale (see, e.g., Baumrind, 1986; Boldizar, Wilson, & Deemer, 1989; Lifton, 1985). Because formal education focuses on abstract principles, people with higher levels of education may use more abstract principles of rights and justice. Further, the argument goes, because males tend to achieve higher levels of formal education than do females (see Chapter 10 for a discussion of why this might be so), they would be expected to use higher levels of moral reasoning than females. Can differences in education explain gender differences in moral reasoning?

In a study addressing this question, Baumrind (1986) found, surprisingly, that higher levels of education predicted higher levels of moral reasoning for males but not for females. Males with more years of formal education reasoned at a higher moral level than did males with fewer years of formal education; but for females, there were no consistent relationships between level of education and level of moral reasoning. Moreover, males who had completed some postgraduate education reasoned at the highest moral level, outperforming females. But for those subjects who had completed no more than 2 years of college, females reasoned at higher moral levels than did males.

Why would we see these different patterns in males and females? Perhaps there is a better fit between males' preferred style of moral reasoning and the skills learned in formal schooling. Because males prefer a more abstract mode of reasoning, those males who learn abstract reasoning skills through formal education use these skills in thinking about moral dilemmas. For females, on the other hand, the abstract reasoning skills learned in school are not used in thinking about moral issues. The care-based reasoning females prefer is not taught in school, and so there is no relationship between education and moral reasoning. It is simply not the case that females use more care-based reasoning than males because they have not achieved the same level of education and thus have not learned more abstract moral principles.

Another possible explanation for gender differences in moral reasoning focuses on differences in socialization. This is essentially the argument that Gilligan advances. Because females are socialized to be relationally oriented, they will be oriented toward care and interpersonal concerns in their moral reasoning. In contrast, males are socialized to be autonomously oriented, and will therefore use principles of individual rights and justice in their moral reasoning. If this is accurate, then we might expect differences in moral reasoning depending on an individual's gender role identity. Those individuals who define themselves in terms of gender-typed traits and behaviors should also be more likely to show the gender-related moral orientation.

Indeed, this seems to be the case. Pratt, Golding, and Hunter (1984) examined the relationship between moral reasoning and gender role, as measured by the Bem Sex Role Inventory. Recall from Chapter 1 that, according to this scale, individuals who describe themselves in terms of the stereotyped gender traits are considered sex typed or traditional, and those who do not define themselves exclusively in terms of the gender-typed traits are considered androgynous or nontraditional. In general, males at the highest level of moral reasoning tended to base their arguments on fairness and justice, whereas females at the highest moral levels used arguments based on maintaining and preserving relationships. More interesting, nontraditional males used more arguments focusing on relationships than did traditional males, but there were no differences between traditional and nontraditional females.

In related research, higher levels of moral reasoning are associated with a sense of self as individuated for college males, but for college females, higher levels of moral reasoning are associated with sense of self as social. For middle-aged adults, higher levels of moral reasoning are associated with a balanced social and individual sense of self for both genders (Lifton, 1985). In early adulthood, when definition of self and gender becomes critically important, people who define themselves in gender-typed ways also show gender-typed patterns of moral reasoning. With age, both males and females may come to incorporate more cross-gender aspects into their sense of self, leading to a more balanced sense of self and a more balanced moral orientation.

Gender differences in moral orientation, then, seem to stem from gender differences in socialization. We need to take a closer look at how girls and boys are treated by parents, peers, and teachers, and to examine how these early interactions influence the development of gender differences, not just in moral reasoning but in many other domains as well. In the next few chapters these questions are explored in depth.

Summary

Freud's psychoanalytic theory of gender development posits that females are sexually and morally inferior to males. Although Freud has had a major impact on our thinking about human behavior, there is no evidence that boys and girls progress through the psychosexual stages outlined by his theory. Nor is there any evidence that little girls experience penis envy, which is supposedly the basis of female sexual identity.

The question of moral reasoning is more complicated. Stemming from Chodorow's reinterpretation of psychoanalytic theory,

Gilligan proposed that females have a different moral orientation than males. Yet there is little evidence of gender differences in the ability to reason about moral dilemmas. Both males and females use care- and justice-oriented reasoning in discussing moral problems, although females seem to use more care-based reasoning than do males. However, females and males seem to conceptualize their own moral life in different ways. When asked to discuss personal moral dilemmas, females focus on interpersonal dilemmas and use care-based moral reasoning, whereas males focus on abstract, impersonal problems and use justice-based moral reasoning. Gender differences in moral reasoning, then, are not based on underlying ability but rather on different moral styles or orientations.

5

Social learning theory

Why is it that girls use ropes for skipping and boys use ropes for climbing, women cook the turkey and men do the carving, and women become air stewardesses and men become airline pilots? These sex differences in social roles cannot be explained by physical differences alone. After all, housework, a traditionally female activity, is often much more strenuous than many male occupations. And it is extremely unlikely that prenatal hormones would predispose males and females to such specific social roles. In this chapter we consider the influence of social factors on gender development and, in particular, examine the contribution of classic social learning theory to our understanding of the mechanisms by which social factors shape gender roles.

According to social learning theory, behavior is acquired in two ways; through reinforcement and modeling. The process of reinforcement is based on the principle that behavior is modified by its consequences; behavior that has favorable consequences (reinforcement) is more likely to be repeated, whereas behavior that is not rewarded or is punished is less likely to be performed again. Though reinforcement has a powerful influence on shaping behavior, social learning also occurs through the observation and imitation of others in the absence of reinforcement. This process is known as modeling or observational learning.

Social learning theory has been applied to gender development by Mischel (1966, 1970) and Bandura (1977), who believe that gender role behaviors are acquired through the same processes as all other behaviors. Sex-typed behavior is thought to result from the differential reinforcement of boys and girls. The consequences for children of various behaviors depend on their sex; girls, for example, will generally receive a much more favorable response than boys for playing with dolls, and boys are more likely than girls to be reinforced for playing with cars and trucks. And because these behaviors produce different outcomes according to the child's sex, they come to be performed with different frequency by boys and girls; girls more often than boys play with dolls, and boys more often than girls play with cars and trucks.

Modeling of same-sex individuals is also considered important for gender development. Children learn about both male and female sex role behavior through observational learning. But they are more likely to imitate models of the same sex as themselves, as this is expected to yield more favorable consequences, and because children come to value behavior that is considered appropriate for their sex. Although the focus of this chapter is on the role of parents in the socialization of their children, it is important to remember that it is not just parents who treat boys and girls differently and act as models of sex-typed behavior.

Teachers and friends also play a part in this process, and images presented by the media are important as well. These influences are discussed in detail in other chapters.

Differential reinforcement

A great deal of research has been done on whether or not parents really do socialize boys and girls differently. Maccoby and Jacklin (1974) have reviewed early studies and have found little evidence for the differential reinforcement of boys and girls. Both sexes were equally allowed and encouraged to be independent, equally discouraged from dependent behavior, treated with equal affection in the first 5 years of life, and experienced a similar response to aggressive behavior. There were some differences in how parents treated boys and girls. Boys were handled and played with more roughly and received more discipline, both physical and nonphysical, than girls. There was also evidence for differential reinforcement of specifically sex-typed behaviors. As well as dressing their children differently, parents encouraged them to develop sex-typed interests and play with sex-typed toys and discouraged activities considered to be more appropriate for the other sex, particularly for boys. However, Maccoby and Jacklin played down the importance of differential reinforcement of children's activities and interests, describing these aspects of sex typing as "superficial," and concluded that differential reinforcement cannot account on its own for the wide range of sex-typed behavior shown by boys and girls.

Block (1976, 1978) challenged Maccoby and Jacklin's conclusions on the ground that most of the studies in the review focused on preschool children and few examined fathers, which, she argued, is likely to have resulted in an underestimate of the differential treatment of boys and girls by their parents. Both of these shortcomings reflect biases in the research. The review was further criticized for failing to take account of the quality of the studies under consideration, and for lumping together diverse behaviors under single, broad categories.

More recently, a meta-analysis of 172 studies of parental differences in the treatment of boys and girls has been carried out (Lytton & Romney, 1991). Meta-analysis is a statistical technique by which the results of a large number of studies can be combined and common effects evaluated. As this quantitative method of reviewing is less open to bias than the traditional narrative approach, it is thought to provide a more objective summary of large bodies of research. The researchers included a wide range of studies that they categorized according to distinct areas of socialization, such as the encouragement of dependency, warmth and nurturance, encouragement of achievement, discouragement of aggression, physical punishment, and the encouragement of sex-typed activities. Like Maccoby and Jacklin, Lytton and Romney found few consistent differences between the treatment of boys and girls except for the encouragement of sex-typed activities. This was in spite of the inclusion of many investigations that had been conducted since Maccoby and Jacklin's earlier review. Taking the quality of each study into account in the meta-analysis did not change these results.

Thus it seems that parents do not differentially reinforce their sons and daughters for social and personal aspects of sex-typed behavior, such as aggression and dependency, but they do promote specific sex-typed activities and interests. Contrary to the view of Maccoby and Jacklin, it is now generally accepted that toy, game, and activity choices are important aspects of gender development (Block, 1983; Fagot & Leinbach, 1987; Huston, 1983; Lytton & Romney, 1991).

So how exactly do parents treat their boys and girls differently? We have already seen from the Baby X studies discussed in Chapter 2 that adults respond differently to infants according to whether they are thought to be boys or girls. For example, they are more likely to give a doll to an infant they believe to be female than to one they believe to be male. In these studies the adults did not know the infants, and unfamiliarity might have caused them to behave in a stereotyped way.

But what about parents? Do they treat their own girl babies differently from their boy babies? It seems that they do. In Chapter 2 we saw that right from birth, parents have different perceptions of their sons and daughters. When Rubin et al. (1974) asked parents of newborns to describe their babies they found that daughters were described as softer, finer-featured, and more delicate, whereas sons were thought to be firmer, more alert, and stronger. Mothers and fathers also interact with their sons and daughters differently from early in infancy. Male infants are given more physical stimulation than female infants, whereas female infants are held, touched, and talked to more than male infants (Moss, 1967; Parke & Sawin, 1980; Power & Parke, 1982). Parents seem keen to ensure that no confusion arises about their child's gender. They dress their girls in pink, decorative clothes and their boys in blue, functional ones (Shakin, Shakin, & Sternglanz 1985), and surround them with sex-typed toys and furnishings (Rheingold & Cook, 1975). And from as early as 12 months, infants are encouraged to play with sex-typed toys and to avoid play activities considered more appropriate for children of the other sex (Snow, Jacklin, & Maccoby, 1983).

The differential encouragement of sex-typed activities in boys and girls becomes even more apparent as infants grow into toddlers. Fagot (1978) observed 24 children between 20 and 24 months of age at home with their parents and found clear differences in the way parents responded to the activities of their sons and daughters. The girls were given approval for dancing, dressing up in female clothes, playing with dolls, asking for help, and following their parents around, and were discouraged from running, jumping, climbing, and manipulating objects. The boys, on the other hand, were punished for feminine activities, such as playing with dolls and seeking help, and were encouraged to play with toys considered to be sex appropriate, such as blocks.

Broadly similar findings were obtained by Langlois and Downs (1980) in an observational study of 3 and 5 year olds and their parents in a nursery school setting. Both the boys and the girls were presented with masculine and feminine toys and were asked to play with them in a sex-appropriate way with either their mother or their father present. The results showed that girls were rewarded by their parents with praise, affection, or attention for playing with feminine toys and punished for playing with masculine toys. Boys were rewarded for playing with masculine toys, but it was only the fathers who punished them for playing with feminine toys.

A consistent finding is that boys are more likely to be discouraged from engaging in feminine behavior than girls are for engaging in masculine behavior (Fagot, 1978; Langlois & Downs, 1980; Maccoby & Jacklin, 1974). The age of the child also makes a difference. It used to be thought that the differential reinforcement of boys and girls becomes more marked as children grow older, but more recent research suggests that the opposite is true. In an observational study of parents' reactions toward boys and girls age 12 months, 18 months, and 5 years, parents were most likely to reinforce differentially their sons and daughters at 18 months, and few differences between parents' reactions to their children were apparent by age 5 (Fagot & Hagan, 1991). So differential socialization of the sexes was most marked in the second year of the child's life. In their meta-analysis of the differential reinforcement literature, Lytton and Romney (1991) also found that parental differences in treatment decrease as children grow up.

Many studies have shown that mothers and fathers respond differently to the sex-typed behaviors of their sons and daughters. For example, Fagot (1978) found that fathers more than mothers encouraged proximity in girls and discouraged doll play in boys, and mothers more than fathers encouraged girls to help. Fagot and Hagan (1991) found that with children age 18 months fathers gave fewer positive reactions to boys engaging in feminine play than did mothers, and mothers gave more instructions to girls when they attempted to communicate than did fathers. The diversity of behaviors investigated in the different studies makes it difficult to draw general conclusions about how mothers and fathers differ in their treatment of sons and daughters. Block's (1976, 1978) suggestion that boys and girls are treated *more* differently by fathers than by mothers was not supported by Seigal's examination (1987) of studies that compared mothers' and fathers' treatment of their sons and daughters. No evidence for greater sex differentiated socialization by fathers than mothers was found other than for discipline and physical involvement. Lytton and Romney's meta-analysis also failed to lend much

support to Block's suggestion that fathers make greater differences between sons and daughters than do mothers. Restrictiveness was the only area of socialization where this was found to
occur.

Taking all of the studies together, it seems that children
of preschool age, particularly boys, do receive differential encouragement of sex-typed play and activities. But what effect
does this have on the child? Block (1983) argues that differential
exposure to toys with dissimilar characteristics results in different
play and problem-solving experiences for girls and boys, and that
this has far-reaching implications for cognitive and personality
development. While boys' toys encourage invention, manipula-
tion, and understanding of the physical world, girls' toys encourage imitation, proximity to the caretaker, and understanding
of the interpersonal and social world. According to Block, the
greater opportunity that boys have to explore the physical world
gives them a greater sense of competence and mastery than girls,
who are reared in a more restrictive way and are not encouraged
to learn about their physical environment.

Caldera, Huston, and O'Brien (1989) support Block's theory
by showing that masculine and feminine toys do lead to different
patterns of parent–child interaction. They examined the interactions of toddlers and their parents during play with masculine,
feminine, and neutral toys. Equal numbers of boys and girls were
observed with mothers and fathers. Regardless of the sex of the
parent or the child, masculine toys were associated with relatively
low levels of questions and teaching and low proximity between
parents and children, whereas feminine toys elicited close physical
proximity and more verbal interactions in the form of questions
and comments. It is not just parents' selection of toys and activities but also the influence of this selection on parent–child
interaction that results in sex-typed behavior in their children.

Although there seems to be no doubt that parents do treat their
sons and daughters differently, this does not necessarily mean
that they influence their children's gender development. An important question still remains: Does the differential socialization
of boys and girls by parents cause children to develop sex-typed
behavior? Or are parents simply responding to sex-typed be-

haviors that would occur even if they did not treat their sons and daughters differently? More simply, are parents reacting to differences or creating them?

One way of addressing this question is to determine whether parents show differences in their reactions to boys and girls before children show clear and consistent sex differences in behavior. In a study of parent–child interaction with 16 to 18 month olds, fathers responded more to sons than daughters and mothers responded more to daughters than sons, fathers responded primarily with emotional feedback and mothers gave more instructions (Fagot & Leinbach, 1987). So boys and girls do appear to receive different reactions from their parents from a very early age. But studies of toddlers do not allow us to rule out the possibility that sex typing results from biological influences rather than differential socialization. Sex-typed toy preferences are shown by children as young as 1 year old; by this age, boys show a weaker preference than do girls for dolls regardless of parental encouragement (Snow et al., 1983). Sex differences in temperament have also been demonstrated in 1-year-old children; boys, on average, show higher activity levels than do girls, as well as more negative reactions to frustration (Kohnstamm, 1989; Prior, 1992). So we cannot be sure that parents are not simply reinforcing and amplifying preexisting, biologically based behaviors, rather than producing sex-typed behavior in their children (Lytton & Romney, 1991). The research discussed in Chapter 3 on hormonal influences on behavior supports the view that boys and girls are to some extent biologically predisposed to behave in a sex-typed way.

The interaction between parents and their children is a dynamic, two-way process. Whether or not children bring to this relationship a biologically based predisposition toward sex typing, there is much evidence to suggest that parents do shape the behavior of their sons and daughters through the process of differential reinforcement so as to maximize sex-typed activities, interests, and possibly other aspects of gender-related behavior as well. One way of examining how much influence parents have on their children's sex-typed behavior would be to investigate families in which parents were making a deliberate effort to encourage their children to engage in non-sex-typed activities and interests. However, a study of this type is difficult to carry out. Even parents with nontraditional sex role attitudes relate differently to their sons and daughters.

In a small study of communication style with 2- and 3-year-old children, mothers gave more verbal stimulation of the type thought to facilitate cognitive development to their sons than to their daughters, regardless of their attitudes toward women's rights and roles (Weitzman, Birns, & Friend, 1985). Similarly, parents who reported actively playing down sex typing in their socialization values and practices still admitted that, while discouraging children of either sex from playing with guns, they were more likely to discourage girls than boys, and while rarely discouraging children of either sex from playing with dolls, they were more likely to encourage doll play for girls but, at most, only permit it for boys (Weisner & Wilson-Mitchell, 1990). Not surprisingly, the 6-year-old children raised in families with sex egalitarian beliefs did not differ from children in more conventional families in their play activities, appearance, preference for friends, or in parents' ratings of their sex-typed attributes, although these children did hold less sex stereotyped beliefs. As the authors point out, no matter how fervently parents commit themselves to emphasizing sex egalitarian values and beliefs, they are constrained by the wider cultural context to which they belong. We take another look at the parental socialization of sex roles when we discuss nontraditional families in Chapter 9.

Modeling

In their daily lives, children are continually exposed to models of sex-typed behavior. At home, children are more likely to see their mother cooking, tidying up, and mending clothes; their father is more likely to be mowing the lawn, fixing a fuse, and emptying the garbage. If the mother goes out to work she will probably earn less and have a lower status job than the father. The type of work mothers and fathers do is also likely to be different. Most secretaries and nurses are women, whereas most managers and doctors are men. And it is usually women who hold primary responsibility for child care. More often than not, it is the mother who bathes and feeds the baby and who collects the children from school, even when both parents are employed. It is not just parents who are models of masculine and feminine behavior. Teachers, other adults, and peers are all potential models, and so are characters presented in books and on television. As discussed in Chapter 2, media characters tend to portray particularly traditional roles.

There is no doubt that children have plenty of sex stereotyped models to observe and imitate, but do they learn masculine and feminine behavior in this way? According to classic social learning theorists, boys and girls imitate same-sex models, particularly the same-sex parent. However, Maccoby and Jacklin (1974) concluded from their review of research on modeling that imitation of a same-sex parent does not play a major role in the development of sex-typed behavior. They found no evidence to show that boys had more contact with their father and girls with their mother, or that boys closely resembled their father and girls their mother, which would be expected if there were greater imitation of the same-sex than the other-sex parent. They also pointed out that in observational studies where children are given the opportunity to imitate either a male or a female, they do not characteristically select the same-sex model. Further, children's sex-typed behavior does not closely resemble that of adult models so that girls play sex-typed games such as skipping without seeing their mother do so and boys play with cars even when their mother and not their father drives a car.

The idea that children acquire sex-typed behavior by direct imitation of same-sex models is now considered simplistic, and a modified version of social learning theory has been proposed to explain the contribution of modeling to gender development (Perry & Bussey, 1979). In the real world, children do not simply imitate the behavior of individual models of the same sex as themselves. Instead, they learn which behaviors are considered appropriate for males and which for females by observing many men and women and boys and girls and by noticing which behaviors are performed frequently by females and rarely by males, and vice versa. Children then use these abstractions of sex-appropriate behavior as models for their own imitative performance. In other words, children imitate behaviors that they have observed to be typical of their own sex.

In a first experiment by Perry and Bussey, children observed four male and four female models choosing between pairs of items (e.g., a banana and an apple) and were then asked which items they themselves preferred. When all of the female models chose the same item and all of the male models chose the other item, the children were more likely to choose the item preferred by the models of the same sex as themselves when asked which they liked best. But when two of the men and two of the women chose one item and two men and two women chose the other, the children were much less likely to prefer the item chosen by the same-sex models. This shows that children learn which behaviors are appropriate for each sex by observing differences in the frequencies with which male and female models perform certain behaviors in given situations, and then use these abstractions of male- and female-appropriate behavior as models for their own imitative performance.

In Perry and Bussey's second experiment, it was shown that a child's imitation of a model is strongly influenced by the degree to which the child believes that the model usually displays behaviors that are appropriate to the child's sex. That is, children are most likely to imitate models whom they perceive to be good examples of their sex role. The children again observed four male and four female models choosing between two items. In this experiment three of the women and one of the men chose one item, and three of the men and one of the women chose the other. It was always the same man and women who chose the same item as the three models of the other sex, so that the children learned that one man and one woman were behaving sex inappropriately. When the children were asked to give their own preferences, they were more likely to imitate a same-sex model whose behavior was typical of others of the model's sex.

So children learn about sex-typed behaviors of both sexes through observation, not just their own. They form concepts of masculinity and femininity, not just concepts of "what is appropriate for me" (Huston, 1983). From her review of a large number of empirical investigations of observational learning, Huston confirmed that whether or not a model is imitated does depend on the child's perception of the sex appropriateness of the model's behavior. Children are much more likely to imitate same-sex models who behave in ways that are thought to be typical of their sex. Thus girls are more likely to imitate their mother changing the baby than changing a tire, and boys are more likely to imitate their father caring for the car rather than for the baby.

The relative importance of the sex of the model versus the sex appropriateness of the behavior being exhibited for children's imitative behavior has been examined by Masters, Ford, Arend, Grotevant, and Clark (1979). Non-sex-typed toys (a balloon or a xylophone) were presented to children as being appropriate for girls or for boys. The children then watched a video of a boy or a girl model playing with the toys. Following the video, they were observed playing with the toys themselves and were asked which they preferred. The children's imitative play and reported preferences were found to be more influenced by the sex-typed labels given to the toys than the sex of the model, but when there was correspondence between the two the effect was even stronger. Thus the perceived sex appropriateness of a behavior is a more important determinant of imitation than the sex of the model. Nevertheless, the situation in which imitation is most likely to occur is when sex-appropriate behavior is exhibited by a model of the same sex as the child.

Just as boys are less likely to engage in female sex-typed behavior than girls are to engage in male sex-typed behavior, boys are less likely to imitate female models than girls are to imitate male models. There is an exception to this rule, however. When female models are perceived to command power, boys are quite prepared to imitate them. So it appears to be the lack of power attached to the female role, rather than the female role per se, that discourages boys from emulating female models. As males generally hold greater power than females in our society, girls have much to gain, and boys much to lose, by emulating female models, which may explain the gender difference in imitation of models of the other sex (Bussey, 1986; Bussey & Bandura, 1984).

Although modeling is now generally viewed as an important aspect of gender development, the mechanisms through which this process operate appear to be more complex than previously thought. Contemporary social learning theorists, now called social cognitive theorists, believe that cognitive skills play a fundamental part in same-sex modeling. These include the ability to classify males and females into distinct groups, to recognize personal similarity to one of these groups, and to store that group's behavior patterns in memory as the ones to guide behavior (Bandura, 1986; Bussey & Bandura, 1984). Cognitive social learning theorists also emphasize the importance of social factors in influencing the behaviors and characteristics that are adopted through same-sex modeling. Children's social experiences interact with their developing concepts of gender to determine which particular gender-related characteristics will be exhibited (Spence, 1985). If, for example, it is socially acceptable within a particular subculture for boys to cook and sew, boys who like to cook and sew consider themselves to be just as masculine as boys who do not like these activities. Thus, children of the same sex can develop a variety of gender-related attributes while remaining certain of their gender identity. Evidence for the contribution of social influences comes from a study of sex typing in middle childhood. It was found that children whose mothers frequently performed nontraditional household and child-care tasks were themselves less sex typed in their preferences for activities, occupations, and playmates (Serbin, Powlishta, & Gulko, 1993).

Whereas social learning theorists have contributed greatly to our knowledge of the role of modeling in the acquisition of sex-typed behavior, cognitive theorists have extended our understanding of the cognitive mechanisms involved in this process. In Chapter 6 we look at the child's cognitive understanding of gender. The gap between social learning and cognitive theories of gender development has narrowed to such an extent that it is no longer meaningful to separate the two.

Summary

According to classic social learning theory, children acquire sex-typed behavior through differential reinforcement and by modeling individuals of the same sex as themselves. In this chapter we have focused on the role of parents in these processes. Other adults and peers and the images presented by the media are also influential. There is clear evidence that parents do treat their sons and daughters differently. But we cannot be sure whether parents are producing sex-typed behavior in their children, or whether they are responding to preexisting differences between boys and girls. The imitation of same-sex models as the child is also important for the acquisition of sex-typed behavior. Children are most likely to imitate models whom they consider to be typical of their sex. The processes of modeling and the development of gender concepts appear to be so closely intertwined that one cannot be discussed independently of the other.

6

Cognitive developmental theories

Developmental theorists agree that children are actively engaged in their own development. Children try to make sense of the world around them, and in doing so, construct ideas and hypotheses about how the world works. Theorists with a cognitive developmental perspective further assume that the way in which children are able to make sense of their world is qualitatively different at different points in development. That is, children's understanding of the world depends on their ability to understand information, to make logical inferences, and to draw conclusions, and these skills develop throughout childhood. In this chapter we discuss two major cognitive developmental theories of children's developing understanding of gender: the development of the gender concept and gender schema theory. Although these theories differ in substantial ways, they share two basic assumptions about development. First, children's understanding of gender may be quite different at different ages, and second, the development of gender understanding parallels the development of children's growing abilities to reason about other aspects of the world.

The gender concept

Piaget was one of the first psychologists to examine seriously the way in which children think and reason. His theory of development spawned a mass of research in the 1960s and 1970s, and much of his theory has had to be reevaluated in light of the empirical evidence (e.g., Donaldson, 1978; Gelman, 1979). Still, many of Piaget's basic assumptions have been proven correct. Of relevance for understanding gender is his finding that young children tend to focus on the surface appearance of things rather than on their underlying identity (DeVries, 1969; Piaget, 1968). For example, a child is shown a cat and identifies it as such. An adult then places a mask on the cat that makes the cat look like a dog, and again asks the child to identify the animal. Preschool children tend to say that the animal is now a dog because it looks like a dog; they rely on the perceptually available information. By age 5 or so, children understand that it is still a cat "pretending" to be a dog; children now understand that change in some of the superficial features is irrelevant to true identity.

Kohlberg (1966) extended Piaget's findings to explain children's developing concept of gender. Kohlberg argued that the major developmental task facing children is coming to understand that gender is constant and cannot be changed regardless of surface features. Based on extensive interviews with young children, he posited that children develop through three stages in coming to understand gender. At the very beginning, children do not use gender to categorize themselves or others at all. If asked if they are female or male, they may respond "female" when asked the first time and "male" when asked again. Essentially, they do not have any understanding that gender is an unchanging characteristic of an individual.

At about 2 years of age, children enter stage 1, called *gender identity*. Children are now able to label themselves and others consistently as female or male, but they base this categorization on physical characteristics. Thus, a person is female because she has long hair and wears skirts, and a person is male because he has short hair and wears a necktie. If these superficial physical characteristics change, then gender changes as well. At about 3 to 4 years, children move into stage 2, called *gender stability*. They now understand that if one is a female or male at the present time, then one was a female or male earlier in life and will remain a female or male later in life. Little girls will grow up to be mommys and not daddys and little boys will grow up to be daddys and not mommys. Thus, stage 2 children understand that gender is stable across time. However, they do not yet understand that gender is constant across situations. If a male engages in female-typed activities, such as doll play, stage 2 children believe the male might change into a female. It is only at about age 5, when children progress to stage 3, called *gender constancy*, that they understand that gender is constant across time *and* situations. Now children claim that gender will not change regardless of the clothes worn or the activities engaged in. They have come to understand that gender is an underlying, unchanging aspect of identity.

Research has confirmed that children do indeed progress through Kohlberg's three stages of understanding the concept of gender (see Stagnor & Ruble, 1987, for a review, and Martin & Halverson, 1983, and Siegal & Robinson, 1987, for methodological critiques), although the exact ages at which individual children understand different aspects of gender varies widely. But there is a great deal of controversy about the meaning and importance of these stages of the gender concept. Kohlberg believed that a complete understanding of gender relied on children's attainment of *gender constancy*. Before children understand gender in this relatively sophisticated way, they would not show much knowledge of gender-related information, nor would they pursue gender-related activities. In essence, gender constancy is the explanation of gender-typed behavior. Because children understand gender constancy, they identify with their own sex, prefer their own sex, and engage in activities to enhance their identification with and membership in their own gender group.

Is there any support for Kohlberg's predictions? Are there clear relationships between children's understanding of gender constancy and their more general knowledge about gender and preferences for own-gender activities? The answer is both yes and no. For example, Slaby and Frey (1975) examined the relationship between children's understanding of gender and their attention to same-sex models. If cognitive developmental theory is correct, then children should begin to pay more attention to same-sex models as they gain a more sophisticated understanding of gender.

In order to assess children's concept of gender, Slaby and Frey (1975) developed a Gender Concept Interview (see Table 6.1). Children's ability to answer these questions confirmed Kohlberg's model of the development of gender understanding. That is, children were able to answer stage 1 questions correctly before they could answer stage 2 or stage 3 questions correctly, and they were able to answer stage 2 questions correctly before they could answer stage 3 questions correctly. Children were then shown a videotape in which a male model and a female model were performing similar activities. All children paid more attention to the male model than to the female model, supporting the idea that males are generally seen as more powerful and reinforcing than are females. But children who achieved higher levels of understanding gender showed an increasing tendency to watch the same-sex model. Boys who had achieved an understanding of gender constancy looked almost exclusively at the male model, and girls who had achieved a similar understanding looked at the female model more than did girls who had not achieved gender constancy. As children come to understand more fully what their gender label means, they begin to seek out information relevant for their own gender.

An obvious question is how children develop the idea of gender constancy. It would seem that gender constancy is grounded in

Table 6.1. *Gender Concept Interview*

1 and 2.	(For a boy doll and for a girl doll): Is this a girl or a boy? Is this a [*opposite sex of subject's first response*]?
3–8.	(For a man doll, for a woman doll, for two men's photographs, and for two women's photographs): Is this a woman or a man? Is this a [*opposite sex of subject's first response*]?
9.	Are you a girl or a boy? Are you a [*opposite sex of subject's first response*]?
10.	When you were a little baby, were you a little girl or a little boy? Were you ever a little [*opposite sex of subject's first response*]?
11.	When you grow up, will you be a mommy or a daddy? Could you ever be a [*opposite sex of subject's first response*]?
12.	If you wore [*opposite sex of subject, i.e.,* "boys' "*or* "girls' "] clothes, would you be a girl or a boy? If you wore [*opposite sex of subject*] clothes, would you be a [*opposite sex of subject's first response*]?
13.	If you played [*opposite sex of subject*] games, would you be a girl or a boy? If you played [*opposite sex of subject*] games, would you be a [*opposite sex of subject's first response*]?
14.	Could you be a [*opposite sex of subject*] if you wanted to be?

Source: Slaby and Frey (1975). Reprinted by permission of the Society for Research in Child Development.

knowing that gender is a biological as well as a social category. Males remain males and females remain females because of some underlying biological difference, and one of the manifestations of this difference is genitalia.

Bem (1989) investigated what preschool children know about genitalia and how this knowledge relates to Kohlberg's sequence of gender understanding. She showed children photographs of two nude toddler-age children, a girl and a boy, and asked the children to identify the gender and to state how they knew whether the depicted child was male or female. In this way Bem determined young children's knowledge of, and reliance on, genitalia to make gender categorizations. She then presented photographs of these same children dressed in cross-sex-typed clothing from the waist up. For example, one picture showed the same male toddler the children had just seen nude, but dressed in a frilly blouse and a long-haired wig. Bem asked the children if the depicted child was male or female, and how they knew. Basically, the vast majority of children who based their gender categorization of the nude children on genital knowledge were able to ignore the surface appearance of the cross-dressed children and say that they were still female (or male) based on their genitals. In contrast, the majority of children who did not use genitals in making their initial gender categorizations (e.g., they used hair length or facial characteristics) relied on the type of clothing the child was wearing.

Thus children's understanding of gender constancy is related to knowledge of the biological basis of gender identity. Children who understand that males and females have different genitalia, and use genitalia to make gender distinctions, also understand that gender remains constant regardless of other aspects of physical appearance.

Still, our knowledge about gender includes more than information about genitalia. Is it the case that children must achieve gender constancy before they begin to learn the traits and behaviors associated with being female or male? Clearly not. In Chapter 2 we discussed that even very young children know a great deal about culturally defined gender stereotypes, and they seem to know this long before they understand gender constancy, at about age 5. Recent research has taken a much broader approach to examining children's understanding of gender. Two types of tasks have been developed to assess this understanding: gender knowledge tasks and gender preference tasks. In Chapter 1 we discussed general issues involved in measuring gender knowledge and gender roles, and the problems and limitations of these kinds of tasks should be borne in mind in evaluating the research presented here.

Gender knowledge tasks measure how much information children know about gender and gender stereotypes. Typical versions of these tasks include children's knowledge of gender-typed clothing and toys. Children are shown pictures of a boy and a girl and asked to match various clothes (skirts, baseball shirts) and toys (dollhouses, trucks) to the "appropriate" child. Examples of some of these picture choices are shown in Figure 6.1. In gender preference tasks, children are asked to rate how much they would like to play with toys that are either gender consistent (a dollhouse for a female subject) or gender inconsistent (a dollhouse for a male subject), and how much they would like to play with various children who are either of the same or the other sex. Note that a child may know a great deal about gender but still show little preference for gender-typed activities. Alternatively, a child may show very strong gender-typed preferences but have little knowledge about gender stereotypes (although preferences are, to some extent, based on knowledge of gender stereotypes). Thus gender knowledge and gender preferences may be separate. What kinds of developmental relationships do we see between gender knowledge and preferences? And how do gender preferences relate to gender constancy?

These questions were examined in a study of preschool children ranging in age from 35 to 65 months conducted by Martin and Little (1990). Overall, children showed a great deal of knowledge about gender-appropriate toys and clothes and had high preferences for gender-typed toys and same-sex playmates. Most important, even the youngest children, who were able to label gender accurately but had not yet achieved gender stability, still showed strong preferences for gender-typed toys. Children who had achieved gender stability but not yet gender constancy also showed strong preferences for gender-typed toys, as well as strong preferences for same-sex playmates. Clearly children are showing sex-typed behavior long before they understand gender in any sophisticated way. So we need to reconsider the relationships between children's concepts of gender and children's gender-related behaviors. Children may only need to know some very basic information about gender to begin to use gender as a way of thinking about the world.

Gender labeling

The ability to label gender consistently, which is only stage 1 thinking in Kohlberg's model, means children are beginning to

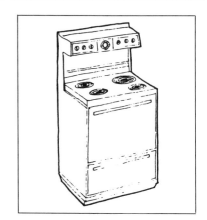

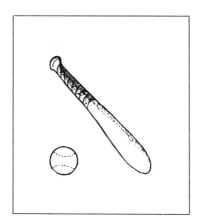

use gender as a category for dividing up the world, and that they have come to understand that gender is an important category to know. Perhaps children's ability and propensity to categorize and label by gender are more important in gender understanding than Kohlberg believed. Perhaps children's ability to label gender consistently is enough for them to begin to associate particular activities and traits with one gender or the other.

Children begin to label themselves and others as male or female sometime between 2 and 3 years of age (see Fagot & Leinbach,

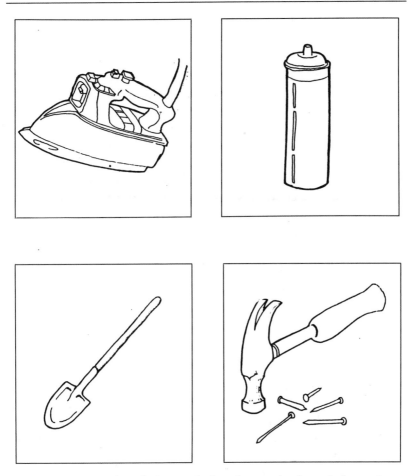

Figure 6.1. Examples of picture choices for gender knowledge tasks.

1993, for a review). In a simple but reliable test of ability to label gender, children are shown a series of photographs displaying various adults and children from the neck up, and are asked if the picture is of a male or a female (Leinbach & Fagot, 1986). Interestingly, there is wide variability in when individual children can respond to these questions correctly. Some children can make this discrimination as early as 24 months of age, and others still have some difficulty as late as 40 months of age. Children are also able to make this discrimination substantially earlier when shown pictures of adults than when shown pictures of children. Perhaps adults' gender characteristics are more distinctive than children's, or perhaps for young children gender is a more important dimension to notice about adults than about other children. But recall from Chapter 2 that children stereotype other children more than they stereotype adults, so once children do consistently label other children as male or female, this categorization carries a great deal of information and importance.

Most notable, children's ability to label gender consistently is related to some aspects of gender-related behavior but not others. Children who label gender consistently prefer same-sex playmates more than children who do not label gender consistently. And girls who label gender consistently show lower levels of aggression than girls who do not label gender consistently. But children prefer to play with gender-typed toys whether or not they can label gender consistently (Leinbach & Fagot, 1986). So gender labeling does seem to be an important step in children's understanding and adoption of some sex-typed behavior, but children show some aspects of gender-typed behavior even before they can consistently label gender. We return to questions of gender-typed toy choice and play behavior in Chapter 7, but here we note that children's understanding of gender begins very early in development, and may influence their behaviors even before they are explicitly aware of gender as an important social category.

It is also intriguing that there is such wide variability in the age at which individual children label gender consistently. Maybe children growing up in families that emphasize gender and gender roles learn about gender earlier. Certainly, as we discussed in Chapter 5, children learn a great deal about gender-"appropriate" behavior from their parents. Do parents who encourage sex-typed behavior also encourage learning about gender as a category? In order to answer this question, Fagot and Leinbach (1989) studied children from 18 months of age, before any of them could consistently label gender, to when they were 4 years old, when all the children consistently labeled gender. Those children who began to label gender consistently early in development (early labelers) also began to show more sex-typed play earlier than children who were not yet labeling gender consistently (late labelers). Early labeling girls also showed less aggression than later labeling girls. So early labelers may be more sex typed than later labelers.

Moreover, parents of early labelers, and especially fathers of early labelers, gave a great deal of feedback, both positive and negative, to their children's displays of gender-related behaviors when the children were very young. In addition to teaching their children that gender-typed behavior is more acceptable, these parents may also be teaching their children to pay attention to gender, thus leading to earlier labeling. At age 4, those children who had labeled gender earlier still knew more about gender than did later labelers. But there were no differences in sex-typed preferences. Both early and late labelers strongly preferred sex-typed toys and activities and same-sex friends. This emphasizes the need to keep distinct children's *knowledge* about gender from their *preferences* for gender-typed behaviors.

Simply being able to label gender consistently sets the stage for children's understanding of gender. This important developmental step leads children to engage in more sex-typed activities, although we must keep in mind that some sex-typed activities, such as toy choice, is in place even before children can consistently label gender. Further, gender labeling is only a first step. Children's knowledge of gender continues to develop throughout early childhood. Children learn more about gender, and their knowledge about gender becomes more organized.

Gender schema theory

As discussed in Chapter 2, there are stable, complex stereotypes of what it means to be male or female in our culture, and even quite young children know a good deal about these gender stereotypes. But there are developmental differences in gender-related knowledge as well. Gender schema theory describes and explains the developing content and organization of gender knowledge. Schemas have a long history in psychology (e.g., Bartlett, 1932); essentially a schema is an organized body of knowledge.

Thus a gender *schema* is conceptually quite similar to a gender *stereotype*.

The organization of gender schemas

One of the basic assumptions of gender schema theories is that gender knowledge is multidimensional. Distinct dimensions or components of gender-related knowledge include behaviors, roles, occupations, and traits (Deaux & Lewis, 1984; Huston, 1983; Martin, 1993). Being female is associated with specific behaviors (gardening), specific roles (homemaker), specific occupations (elementary school teacher), and specific traits (nurturance). Being male, on the other hand, is associated with a different set of behaviors (playing football), roles (father), occupations (engineer), and traits (aggressive). Our knowledge is organized such that simply knowing the gender label leads to clear links to these gender-related components. Note that knowledge about female-related components is conceptually distinct from knowledge about male-related components. One could have a great deal of information about the behaviors, roles, occupations, and traits associated with females but little knowledge about these components for males. And, of course, each component of knowledge is also independent, so that one might know a great deal about female-related behaviors but little about female-related occupations.

The development of gender schema

Children continue to learn more and more about gender throughout childhood (Best et al., 1977; Leahy & Shirk, 1984). Gender schema theory posits that as children learn more about each of these components, they also begin to organize their knowledge in more complex ways. Specifically, knowledge becomes organized such that there are associations both within and across components (Martin, 1993; Martin & Halverson, 1981). Within-component associations link information within each category of knowledge. For example, for gender-related behaviors, there are strong associations between "likes to cook" and "likes to sew" as female-related behaviors, and strong associations between "likes to play baseball" and "likes to drive fast cars" as male-related behaviors. Across-component associations link behaviors from different categories of knowledge. For example, "likes to cook," a female-related behavior, is associated with "being nurturant," a female-related trait, and with "mothering," a female-related role. These links within and across components allow us to make predictions. Knowing one thing about a person leads to inferring other things, both within the same category and across categories. In this way, the structure of gender schemas provides a great deal of predictability given very little information.

Most of the research on children's gender-related knowledge has examined only the simplest kind of gender associations, that is, links between the gender label and associated behaviors, traits, occupations, and the like (see Martin, 1993, for a review). As we have seen, preschool children already have much of this kind of knowledge. But what about more complex kinds of associations? When do children begin to make associations within and between knowledge components?

Preschool children rely almost exclusively on the gender label. Once they are told someone is male or female, they will predict that the individual will engage in gender-typed behaviors and activities regardless of any other information provided. So even if told about a boy who likes to play with dolls, preschool children will predict that the child will like to play with trains and toolboxes. Further, if told about someone who likes to play with toolboxes, preschool children will assume that that person is male (Martin, 1989b; Martin, Wood, & Little, 1990).

Older children begin to make more complex predictions. Told about a boy who likes to play with dolls, older children think he will also enjoy other female-related behaviors, such as dress-up play. Rather than relying solely on the gender label, older children consider counterstereotypic information; they make predictions based on relations within and among knowledge components regardless of the gender label. Interestingly, though, children have more complexly organized knowledge about their own gender before they have such knowledge about the other gender. At about age 6, children will draw complex inferences both within and between components when making predictions about same-gender characters, but it is not until about age 8 that they are able to draw these complex inferences about the other gender (Martin et al., 1990; Martin, 1993).

In addition to more complex knowledge, older children also have more *detailed* knowledge about their own gender. For example, children have more detailed information about same-sex gender-typed activities than other-sex activities. In order to understand this gender-related knowledge, we must first understand how children organize their knowledge of activities and events in general. Activities and events conform to a unique schematic organization called a script (Shank & Abelson, 1977).

Essentially, a *script* is a temporally organized sequence of actions that specifies what is most likely to occur during an activity and the order in which it will occur. When asked to report about familiar activities such as grocery shopping, having a birthday party, or going to school, young children give scriptlike reports. For example, a typical 5 year old's report about grocery shopping might be, "You go to the store, and you get a shopping cart and then you choose the food you want. And then you pay for it and go home." That young children report the various actions involved in grocery shopping in their correct temporal order indicates a great deal of detailed, schematically organized knowledge about this event (see Nelson, 1986, for a review of this research).

Recently, Levy has argued that children's knowledge of events may be different depending on whether these events are stereotypically associated with males or females (Boston & Levy, 1991; Levy & Fivush, 1993). Boys may know more about stereotypically male events, such as fixing a car or going fishing, whereas girls may know more about stereotypically female events, such as sewing a dress or changing a diaper. Indeed, when asked to sequence four pictures of each of two masculine-typed activities (building a birdhouse and barbecuing) and two feminine-typed activities (preparing dinner in the kitchen and doing laundry), 43- to 78-month-old children sequenced own-sex activities more accurately than other-sex activities, and this was especially evident for boys (Boston & Levy, 1991). Sequencing pictures in their correct temporal order relies on detailed knowledge of these activities; so preschool children have more detailed knowledge about same gender-typed events than other gender-typed events.

In fact, children may have differential knowledge of same- and other-sex activities as early as 2 years of age. Bauer (1993) modeled six event sequences for 25-month-old children. Two of the sequences were feminine typed (change teddy bear's diaper and make breakfast), two sequences were masculine typed (shave teddy bear and build a garage), and two were gender neutral (go on a treasure hunt and have a birthday party). After modeling four actions for each sequence with a set of small toys, she asked the children to reenact the sequences they had been shown. Girls reenacted all three sequence types equally well, but boys reenacted the masculine-typed activities and the neutral activities much better than the feminine-typed activities. (Notice that in all this research boys showed great differentiation between own-gender and other-gender information, whereas girls were more likely to know information about both genders. We return to this intriguing gender difference later in the chapter.)

Why might children know more about their own gender than the other gender? One obvious possibility is that children spend more time interacting with gender-typed objects and engaging in gender-typed activities, and this provides more opportunity to learn about one's own gender. In fact, in Bauer's (1993) study, boys played more with the toys from the masculine-typed activities than any other toys. Simply labeling an object "for boys" or "for girls" is enough to make a difference. Preschool children ask more questions about and spend more time playing with novel objects that are labeled appropriate for their gender than novel objects labeled appropriate for the other gender (Bradbard & Endsley, 1983). Children's preferences for engaging in gender-typed activities, then, would lead to differences in gender-related knowledge.

Overall, even young children have a good deal of gender-related knowledge, although this knowledge may be organized simply around the gender label. With development, children learn more about gender, and their gender knowledge becomes more complex, such that older children begin to make inferences about gender-related behaviors and attributes based on limited information. Of course, these inferences may be wrong. Just because someone likes to cook does not necessarily mean that that person is also nurturant or even female. Given that the world may not be organized the same way as our gender schemas, why do we continue to use this knowledge to make predictions?

Schema-driven memory bias

Gender schemas not only organize our knowledge about gender; they also guide the way in which we understand new information about gender. In general, we tend to pay more attention to information in the world that conforms to our schemas than information that violates our schemas. In fact, we may even misremember or distort information in ways that make it more consistent with our schemas (Taylor & Crocker, 1979). Even when we encounter information that is different from what we would have predicted on the basis of our gender schema, we will try to make sense of this information in terms of what we already know.

Let's take an example. Suppose a child goes to the doctor and a female nurse weighs and measures the child. The child knows that females are nurturant, that they take care of people, and that nursing is a stereotypical occupation for females. Therefore, this child should have no difficulty understanding the situation and remembering that the nurse was female. Now suppose the nurse is male. The child is faced with a seeming paradox. This does not fit with the child's gender schema. Therefore, it will be difficult for the child to understand the situation, and the child may even distort memory of the event such that the child remembers the nurse as female or recalls the male nurse as a doctor. Thus schema theory predicts that children will understand and recall schema-consistent information quite well but will have more difficulty understanding and recalling schema-inconsistent information, and may even distort schema-inconsistent information to make it consistent with the gender schema.

In fact, this is exactly what happens. When 5- and 6-year-old children are shown videotapes of male doctors and female nurses, they have no difficulty recalling what they saw. But when they see female doctors and male nurses, they misremember, and claim they saw female nurses and male doctors (Cordua, McGraw, & Drabman, 1979). And it is not just doctors and nurses. When asked to recall pictures of various gender-consistent occupations (a male fire fighter, a female teacher) and activities (a male mowing the lawn, a female cooking a meal), as well as gender-inconsistent occupations (a male secretary, a female chemist) and gender-inconsistent activities (a male doing laundry, a female building a house), school-age children show clear memory biases. Children recall many more gender-consistent than gender-inconsistent pictures (Martin & Halverson, 1983; Signorella & Liben, 1984). More interesting, children make recognition errors as well. After viewing all of the pictures, children are then shown two pictures at a time and asked which picture they saw before. One picture shows the gender-inconsistent information they had just seen and one picture is switched to make it gender consistent (a female chemist as just seen versus a male chemist, which was never seen). When faced with this choice, children often claim they had seen the gender-consistent pictures (Liben & Signorella, 1980), and they are extremely confident that they are remembering correctly (Martin & Halverson, 1983)!

Children's knowledge about gender clearly leads to biases in memory. By recalling more information that is gender consistent than gender inconsistent and by distorting gender-inconsistent information to conform to their gender schemas, children are paying attention to information that confirms their stereotyped beliefs about gender and they are not paying attention to information that might disconfirm these stereotypes. Overall, then, it may be very difficult to change children's stereotypes about gender, even by presenting counterstereotyped information. Yet, clearly, children's knowledge about gender changes over time. How can we explain this seeming contradiction?

Flexibility of gender knowledge

Although children believe the culturally defined definitions of masculinity and femininity, there may be differences in how strong these beliefs are. Children may know that females are more likely than males to cook and sew but still believe that it is perfectly appropriate for males to engage in these behaviors (Martin, 1989b; Signorella et al., 1993). Are some children more flexible in their gender stereotypes than others?

Serbin and Sprafkin (1986) propose that knowledge about gender should be most inflexible just as children are acquiring that knowledge and more and more flexible as they acquire more and more knowledge about gender. This is because in the early phases of acquiring knowledge, individuals have a limited amount of information and therefore are able to use the information only in a constrained, either/or way. So males are either aggressive or not and females are either emotional or not, but there are no real shades of gray. As more information is acquired, the individual's knowledge becomes more complex and more probabilistic. So now males are, on average, more aggressive than females, but not all males are aggressive, nor are all females nonaggressive, and so on. This suggests that early in development children should use gender more inflexibly as a way of categorizing the world, but with increasing age, they should come to rely on other ways of carving up the world as well.

Unfortunately, most research on gender knowledge does not assess flexibility. Recall that in the typical gender knowledge task, children are shown various toys and clothes, or various activities or traits are described, and children must say whether this attribute belongs with a female or a male. It is a forced-choice task; for each attribute, the child must choose between the genders. In general, studies using forced-choice measures find that older children assign more traits and behaviors to males or females than younger children. This might suggest that children become more gender stereotyped with age.

But a few studies have allowed children to choose both males and females as a response. That is, the child must say whether this attribute belongs with a male, a female, or both. Such studies find that the "both" response increases substantially with age (Serbin & Sprafkin, 1986; Urberg, 1982). Although older children know more about gender than do younger children, they also view gender in more flexible terms than do younger children (see Signorella et al., 1993, for a full discussion of this issue).

In summary, whereas children learn a great deal about gender during the preschool years, this knowledge seems to be quite rigid. At about age 5 or so, they not only believe that females are soft, dainty nurses and males are tough, athletic doctors; they believe that this is the way the world must and should be. During the elementary school years, children continue to learn more and more about gender, but this knowledge also becomes more flexible. Females may be likely to be nurturing and emotional and males may be likely to be independent and aggressive, but this may not necessarily be true all of the time for all of the people.

Individual differences in gender schematization

Of course not all children follow exactly the same developmental path. Some children may know more about gender than do other children, and some children may be more rigid in their beliefs about gender than are others. Some children may even have a great deal of well-organized knowledge about gender stereotypes but still not choose to play with gender-typed toys or engage in gender-typed behaviors. Although it is certainly important to describe general developmental changes in children's understanding of gender, we also need to consider individual differences in how children understand and use gender-related knowledge (Bem, 1981; Levy & Carter, 1989).

Levy and Carter (1989) developed the concept of *gender schematization* to explain these kinds of individual differences. They argue that for some children gender is an important way of thinking about the world; these children pay a great deal of attention to information relevant to gender and organize information in terms of gender-appropriate and gender-inappropriate categories. Knowing that females are empathetic and males are self-sufficient is an important and valuable way of understanding the world. These children are considered to be highly gender schematized. Other children, in contrast, do not see gender as such an important category for understanding the world; they may know that males take risks and females are emotional, but this doesn't seem to matter very much. These children are not highly gender schematized.

In order to measure gender schematization, Levy and Carter (1989) devised a special type of preference task. In this task children are shown pictures of two toys simultaneously and asked to select the one they would like to play with. For some pairs the toys are feminine typed, some pairs are masculine typed, and some pairs have both feminine-typed and masculine-typed toys. A highly gender-schematized child will always want a gender-typed toy. So, when given a choice between a same-sex-typed toy and an other-sex-typed toy, the choice will be made very quickly and easily: the gender-appropriate one. But when given a choice between two masculine or two feminine toys, the child cannot choose on the basis of gender typing. A highly gender-schematized boy, for instance, will want both masculine-typed toys and not either feminine-typed toy. So in these conditions, the choice will be difficult and slow. For children who are not that highly gender schematized, selection of a toy will be based more on personal preference than gender appropriateness, and therefore, there should be no significant difference in how long it takes them to choose between two toys regardless of the gender typing of those toys. Thus, by measuring the time it takes a child to choose between sets of two toys, we can determine how gender schematized that child is.

Using this method, Levy and Carter (1989) were able to classify individual children as highly gender schematized or not. Not surprisingly, more highly gender-schematized children know more about gender stereotypes than less gender-schematized children. More interesting, highly gender-schematized children show larger memory biases than less gender-schematized children when re-calling gender-consistent and gender-inconsistent pictures (Carter & Levy, 1988; Levy, 1989). Children who are highly gender-schematized recall very few stereotype-inconsistent pictures. And they distort their memory more than less schematized children, such that they are even more likely to claim they saw gender-consistent pictures that they did not see and believe they did not see gender-inconsistent pictures that they did see.

Gender is indeed a more important category for some children than others, and these children pay more attention to, and subsequently learn more about, gender-relevant information. Moreover, children who are highly gender schematized may have a much more rigid view of gender-appropriate and gender-inappropriate behaviors than do children who are not so highly schematized. What is left unanswered is why some children are more highly gender schematized than others.

Gender schema theory offers no clear explanation. As Bussey and Bandura (1992) argue, gender knowledge alone cannot predict gender-related behavior. Just because a child knows the cultural stereotypes about gender does not guarantee that she will want to conform to that stereotype. In integrating cognitive and social learning theory approaches, Bussey and Bandura theorize that it is the child's evaluation of gender-typed behaviors that is critical in her adoption of these behaviors. They asked children ranging in age from 2 to 4 years to rate how good or bad they would feel after playing with either a gender-typed toy or a cross-gender toy, as well as how other children would feel after playing with these toys. They also observed children's actual toy play. Overall, boys played with "boy" toys and girls played with "girl" toys at all ages. Further, children of all ages claimed that other children would feel good after playing with sex-typed toys and bad after playing with cross-sex toys. But only the older children showed this pattern when evaluating themselves. And self-evaluations based on gender stereotypes were strongly related to gender-typed behaviors. Children who claimed they would feel good after playing with a sex-typed toy and bad after playing with a cross-sex toy also spent more time actually playing with sex-typed toys than did children who did not evaluate themselves by the gender typing of their behaviors.

According to Bussey and Bandura, gender-typed behavior is initially guided by children's anticipations of others' response. In classic social learning theory terms, younger children engage in sex-typed behavior because they are reinforced for doing so. But as children get older, they construct their own personal standards based on their cognitive understanding of gender and on their history of reinforcements. Now children evaluate their own behavior, and gender appropriateness becomes an important dimension of children's own self-evaluations.

Gender differences in gender understanding

An intriguing finding that emerges in study after study is that girls know more about gender than do boys (see Signorella et al., 1993, for a discussion). Moreover, whereas both boys and girls know more about their own gender than the other gender, girls know more about males than boys know about females. Because stereotypically male behaviors and activities are more highly valued in our culture, girls may pay more attention to male-relevant information than boys pay to female-relevant information. Recall that both boys and girls pay more attention to a male model than to a female model (Slaby & Frey, 1975). Yet girls are also more flexible in their gender knowledge than are boys. Maybe this is because they have more information overall about gender, but it may also be that the female stereotype is not as constrained as the male stereotype. Females in our culture can engage in many cross-gender activities with little penalty, but males are not able to cross gender lines quite so easily.

Summary

In this chapter we have discussed the ways in which children come to understand gender. Children at different ages have very different ideas about the stability and constancy of gender, as demonstrated by Kohlberg (1966). Yet, somewhat surprisingly, children's concept of gender bears little relation to gender-related behaviors. It is not the case that children must achieve gender constancy before they begin preferring gender-typed activities or behaving in gender-typed ways. Rather, it seems that children engage in gender-typed activities and prefer same-sex playmates virtually as soon as they know the categories of male and female, which is as early as 2 years of age (Fagot & Leinbach, 1993).

From a cognitive developmental approach, the ability to label gender consistently begins a long developmental process of understanding what is associated with each gender label. Over the course of the preschool years and well into middle childhood, children learn more about gender and their knowledge becomes more complex. Although children are learning more and more about the culturally prescribed gender stereotypes with increasing age, they also seem to be using this knowledge more flexibly, suggesting that gender stereotyping may peak during the preschool years and diminish somewhat during middle childhood. Interestingly, children learn about their own gender before learning much about the other gender, and girls know more about gender than boys do.

We must also keep in mind that there are individual differences in how important gender seems to be as a way of understanding the world. Although individual differences in gender schematization have been amply demonstrated, gender schema theory does not have an explanation for these differences. We may need to turn to other theories about gender development, such as social learning theory (see Chapter 5), as well as to other aspects of gender-related development, such as play behavior and toy choice (see Chapter 7), to help explain some of these differences. One thing is abundantly clear, however: Gender is not simply something that is imposed on children; at all points of development, children are actively constructing for themselves what it means to be female or male.

7

Play and friendships

Observation of any playground will confirm the commonsense knowledge that girls play with girls and boys play with boys. In fact, during the elementary school years, children play in same-gender groups more than 10 times as often as in mixed-gender groups (Maccoby, 1988). Moreover, children are more likely to segregate by gender during unstructured free play than during adult structured play, suggesting that it is children, themselves, who are initiating and maintaining gender segregation.

How early in development does gender segregation in play begin? And why does it occur? Perhaps most important, what consequences does it have as we get older and begin to develop deeper and more intimate friendships with both same-gender and other-gender peers? In this chapter we examine various aspects of the development of play and friendship. We begin with early play patterns and discuss various explanations of how and why gender segregation occurs. We then move on to a discussion of friendship and connect early gender-related patterns of play with the emergence of gender differences in friendship and style of conversational interaction. We end the chapter with a discussion of friendship patterns among adults.

Early play patterns

Infants and children spend much of their time in play. Although there are no good definitions of exactly what constitutes play, most researchers agree that play can be best conceptualized as the active exploration of the physical and social worlds, usually accompanied by positive emotional involvement (e.g., Fagot & Leinbach, 1983; Fein, 1981). Moreover, play is believed to be an important part of the way in which children learn about the world (Fein, 1981; Garvey, 1977). Infants begin to engage in active exploration during the first months of life. However, at this early point in development, play is either solitary or structured by an adult. Although infants show a great deal of interest in other babies and young children, they are not yet capable of initiating and maintaining a social relationship with a peer (see especially Piaget, 1962, and Selman, Jaquette, & Lavin, 1977, for detailed discussions of the cognitive aspects of the development of play and friendships).

By about 1 year of age, infants begin to approach other children and may even begin rudimentary attempts to interact. However, although 1 and 2 year olds seem to enjoy greatly being with other children, they still have difficulty coordinating play together. At this age, children tend to engage in "parallel" play, sitting near each other but engaging in separate activities. Sometime around the second birthday, children begin to play together in more coordinated and structured ways, and by age 3, they are able to construct and coordinate complex play scenarios, including fantasy play, such as cowboys and Indians, and role play, such as playing house (see Garvey, 1977, for a review). Interestingly, it is also between the second and third birthdays that we begin to see gender segregation in children's play – that is, girls begin to prefer playing with other girls and boys with other boys

(Fagot, 1987; LaFreniere, Strayor, & Gauthier, 1984; Maccoby & Jacklin, 1987; Serbin, Moller, Powlishta, & Gulko, 1991). Three basic explanations have been advanced to explain the early emergence of play preferences for same-gender peers (Carter, 1987; Maccoby & Jacklin, 1987; Serbin, Moller, Powlishta, & Gulko, 1991). According to one explanation, *direct reinforcement*, children are reinforced by adults and possibly by other children for selecting same-gender playmates and engaging in gender-typed play, and therefore continue to do so. This explanation stems from social learning theory approaches to gender development (discussed in Chapter 5). The *cognitive consonance* explanation focuses on the idea that children prefer playmates who they perceive to be similar to themselves; as children begin to label themselves as female or male, they will also begin to selectively prefer same-gender peers. Finally, the *behavioral compatibility* explanation says that children prefer same-gender playmates because females and males have different play styles and prefer to be with children who share their play style.

In deciding among these alternatives, we need to consider three aspects of play: selecting gender-typed toys, engaging in gender-typed play interactions, and preferring same-gender playmates. And it must be remembered that these three explanations are not mutually exclusive; that is, all of them may be useful in understanding different aspects of gender-related play behaviors. Keeping this in mind, what is the evidence for each of these explanations?

Direct reinforcement

There is little evidence that adults reinforce play with same-gender peers or punish play with other-gender peers. However, adults do seem to reinforce gender-typed toy play. This research is discussed in detail in Chapter 5, on social learning theory approaches to gender development; here we shall consider only that research which bears directly on the question of toy choice and play. Research examining whether or not parents provide gender-typed toys for their children is somewhat inconsistent. Most researchers have found that parents do tend to give their children gender-typed toys (Etaugh, 1983; Rheingold & Cook, 1975; Snow et al., 1983), but a few researchers have not found a strong tendency in this direction (e.g., Fagot, 1978). Moreover, parents may be more likely to give gender-typed toys to boys than to girls. Most parents feel comfortable giving transportation toys and blocks to their daughters, but few are comfortable giving baby dolls, tea sets, and dress-up clothes to their sons.

We also need to consider why parents might give gender-typed toys to their children. Although it might be the case that parents base their toy selection on culturally accepted gender stereotypes, it is also possible that parents are responding to their children's toy preferences. Do parents provide gender-typed toys because children are asking for these toys? Robinson and Morris (1986) answered this question by examining the toys that children received for Christmas, and comparing the presents received to those the child had requested in their letters to Santa Claus. The majority of all toys requested by both boys and girls were gender typed. Moreover, of the gender-typed toys that children actually received, about 63% had been requested, whereas only about 37% of the non-gender-typed toys had been requested. So children choose gender-typed toys for themselves to a greater extent than parents choose gender-typed toys for their children. But why are children choosing gender-typed toys in the first place?

Although adults may not directly reinforce play with gender-typed toys (as we saw in Chapter 5), adults do play in different ways with boys and with girls, and these different types of inter-actions may subtly reinforce gender-typed toy choice and gender-typed play. Beginning in infancy and continuing through the preschool years, adults encourage more motor activity and more active play with boys than with girls, and they engage in more vocalization and face-to face interaction with girls than with boys (Etaugh, 1983; Fagot, 1987; Goldberg & Lewis, 1969; Maccoby & Jacklin, 1974). These different play patterns may lead to the selection of different types of toys. For example, it is easier to engage in large-scale motor activity with transportation toys than with tea sets, but tea sets encourage more quiet, face-to-face conversations (Caldera et al., 1989). In this way, although children may have many toys available to them, they may begin to select gender-typed toys preferentially because these toys allow for the kinds of interactions that have been reinforced. Of course, it is also possible that children are selecting particular types of toys and engage in particular types of interactions because of some internally generated preference for a particular style of play. That is, it may be that parents are responding to existing gender differences in their children rather than causing these differences to emerge.

Adults not only engage in different types of play interactions with boys and with girls; as we saw in Chapter 5, they also differentially reinforce different kinds of play behaviors displayed by boys and by girls. The study by Langlois and Downs (1980), discussed in Chapter 5, is a good illustration. As you may recall, mothers and fathers were asked to play with their 3- or 5-year-old child. Three types of toys were available in the playroom: masculine typed, feminine typed, and gender neutral. With boys, mothers actively rewarded cross-gender play; they were more likely to join in this kind of play and interact with their sons when playing with the feminine-typed toys. With girls, mothers showed no differential reward; they were equally likely to join in their daughters' play regardless of which toy the daughter selected. Fathers, in contrast, clearly reinforced gender-typed play and punished cross-gender play with both daughters and sons. That is, fathers were more likely to join in play with their children when interacting with gender-typed, rather than cross-gender toys.

Thus, boys may be getting mixed messages about appropriate play from mothers and fathers; mothers reinforce cross-gender play, whereas fathers reinforce gender-typed play. Girls, in contrast, seem to be getting relatively consistent messages. Both mothers and fathers reinforce gender-typed play with their daughters, although mothers do not clearly punish cross-gender play with daughters. It is important to note that none of the parents directly told their children what toys to play with or not to play with; the differential reinforcement was more subtle, taking the form of whether or not the parent joined in and praised the child's play.

Whereas the research on adults' reinforcement of gender-typed play has yielded complicated results, the research examining peer interactions is quite clear. Peers positively reinforce play with same-gender playmates and with gender-typed toys and, even more so, they punish cross-gender play (see Carter, 1987, for a review). For example, in the Langlois and Downs (1980) study, peer interactions between same-gender pairs of 3 and 5 year olds were also examined. When boys selected cross-gender toys, their playmates hit and ridiculed them. When girls selected cross-gender toys, their playmates ignored them. Thus, although the type of punishment is different for the different genders (we return to this issue later in the chapter), the message is clear: Don't play with cross-gender toys.

Similarly, Lamb and Roopnarine (1979) found that preschool children received positive reinforcement from their same-gender peers for engaging in gender-typed activities, although there was little evidence of punishment for engaging in cross-gender behaviors. Related to these findings, Martin (1989a) asked preschool and early school-age children to rate how much they would like various hypothetical children described in short stories. Some children were depicted as enjoying gender-typed play and others as enjoying cross-gender play. In addition, some of the hypothetical children were explicitly labeled tomboys or sissies. In general, children showed preferences for same-gender children over other-gender children, but children at both ages said they would dislike tomboys. Further, the older children but not the younger children said they would also dislike sissies. Clearly, children are sensitive to gender-"appropriate" behaviors and do not like peers who cross over the lines.

Fagot and Leinbach (1983) have demonstrated further the effectiveness of peer reaction to gender-appropriate play in a study of children ranging in age from 18 to 48 months. The children were observed for 4 hours a week during free play in their day care over a 1-year period. In general, both males and females received positive reinforcement from teachers for feminine-typed activities, such as artwork, and negative feedback for masculine-typed activities, such as large-scale motor play. Female peers also reinforced females for feminine-typed play.

Thus girls received positive reinforcement from both teachers and peers for engaging in gender-typed activities. However, male peers gave a good deal of negative feedback to boys engaging in feminine-typed activities and positive feedback for masculine-typed activities. So boys received mixed messages from teachers and peers. Which message do boys listen to? Fagot and Leinbach found that males were more sensitive to feedback from peers; teachers' negative feedback to masculine-typed activities had no effect on males' behaviors, but their peers' negative feedback to feminine activities had strong effects.

In general, then, the research indicates that adults may not consistently reinforce gender-typed toy choice but they do engage in gender-typed play interactions. Patterns of reinforcement for engaging in gender-typed play are somewhat complicated; mothers and teachers seem to reinforce both boys and girls for feminine-typed play, but fathers reinforce gender-typed play and punish cross-gender play with both daughters and sons. Peers, however, consistently and strongly reinforce gender-typed toy choice and play and punish cross-gender play. Thus there seems to be some evidence to support the idea that children engage in gender-typed play with same-gender playmates because they are reinforced for doing so. The question arises, however, as to why peers so strongly reinforce gender-"appropriate" play behaviors.

Cognitive consonance

One reason why gender-appropriate behavior may be so important in the peer group has to do with the way children come to understand gender as a concept. Much of this research is discussed in Chapter 6, on cognitive developmental theories of gender development. There, we saw that children of different ages understand what it means to be female or male in different ways. This understanding may also affect children's selection of gender-typed toys and same-gender playmates. In particular, it may be the case that as children first begin to label themselves consistently as female or male, sometime between 24 and 36 months of age, they begin to select for behaviors and playmates that are consistent with their own gender label.

Although this argument makes sense, the problem is that children begin to select gender-typed toys well before they are able to label gender consistently. Females begin to show preferences for dolls, soft animals, and dishes, and boys begin to show preferences for transportation toys, tools, and robots, as early as 12 months of age (Etaugh, 1983; Fagot, 1987; Snow et al., 1983). Many people have argued that these early preferences are due to parental socialization of toy choice, but as we just discussed, the research evidence is mixed. Although parental socialization surely plays a role in the early emergence of gender-typed toy choice, it does not seem to be the only factor. But cognitive consonance cannot be assumed to be operating this early in development either.

What about the emergence of preferences for same-gender playmates? Children begin to show a clear preference for same-gender playmates between their second and third birthdays. LaFreniere et al. (1984) conducted a 3-year longitudinal study examining play patterns in groups of children ranging in age from 1 to 6 years. For girls, there was a sharp increase in preference for same-gender playmates at about 27 months of age. At this point, girls selectively engaged in play with same gender peers about 65% of the time, and this preference remained stable over the course of the study. Boys showed a somewhat different pattern. Their preference for play with same-gender peers rose sharply at about 36 months of age and continued to increase over the age range studied, reaching a peak at which 75% of their play interactions were with same-gender peers.

In a similar study, Serbin et al. (1991) observed 26- to 40-month-old children several times a week for 4 to 7 months. At the earliest ages studied, there was a good deal of mixed-gender play, but even so, about 40% of the children selected same-gender playmates at a higher than chance level. More important, Serbin et al. also measured children's preferences for gender-typed toys, their ability to label gender consistently, and their knowledge of gender stereotypes (see Chapter 6 for a discussion of these measures). Interestingly, none of these measures was related to children's preferences for same-gender playmates. Children's developing knowledge about gender is not a critical factor in the selection of same-gender playmates. Further, children are not more likely to engage in gender-typed play when in same-gender play groups than when in mixed-gender play groups (Maccoby & Jacklin, 1987). Even when engaging in gender-neutral activities, such as swings and slides on the playground or puzzles in the play corner, children selectively play with same-gender peers. Thus it is not the case that children select same-gender playmates in order to engage in gender-typed activities.

But Serbin, Moller, Powlishta, and Gulko (1991) did find that children showed more advanced play, in the sense that the play was more cooperative and more socially skilled, when in same-gender groups than in mixed-gender groups. Jacklin and Maccoby (1978) also found that 33-month-old children showed more prosocial behavior (i.e., helping, cooperating) when with a same-gender peer than when with an other-gender peer.

Overall, there is not much evidence to support the cognitive consonance interpretation of gender segregation. Children's cognitive understanding of gender does not seem to be related to their preferences for either gender-typed toys or same-gender playmates. However, an interesting finding to emerge from this research is that children's play is more developmentally advanced when in same-gender groups than when in mixed-gender groups, and perhaps this can help explain gender segregation. Serbin et al. (1991) suggest that because play with same-gender peers is more advanced, it may be more intrinsically interesting and rewarding, and this is why children select same-gender play-mates. But it is not clear why play with same-gender peers would be more advanced. A possible answer comes from an examination of the third explanation of gender segregation.

Behavioral compatibility

Children may selectively prefer same-gender playmates because children of the same gender may share the same patterns or style of interaction (see especially Maccoby & Jacklin, 1987, for a detailed discussion of this idea). Basically, the idea is that males and females have gender-related ways of interacting socially, and therefore prefer to be with others of their own gender because they share this way of interacting.

Across many research studies two broad gender differences in styles of interaction have emerged. Males are more active and aggressive in their play than are females, and females are more nurturant and vocal in their play than are males (see Maccoby & Jacklin, 1987, and Pitcher & Shultz, 1983, for reviews). However, these differences do not emerge until about 3 years of age. At age 2, girls and boys are quite similar in their play styles (Fagot, 1987; Pitcher & Shultz, 1983). But keep in mind that at this early age, the majority of children's peer interactions are parallel play. It is as children begin to engage in more complex social interactions that differences in play style emerge. At this point, boys begin to engage in more aggressive behaviors with their peers than do girls; these behaviors include physical aggression, such as hitting and pushing, as well as verbal aggression, such as insults and teasing. Girls, in contrast, begin to engage in more nurturant types of behavior than do boys; they spend time grooming their female playmates and offer more compliments to their friends than do boys.

Related to these differences, boys also tend to play in large groups and to play outdoors, whereas girls are more likely to play indoors and in pairs. This, in turn, leads to additional differences in interactional styles as children grow older. Boy groups are more likely to have a leader than are girl groups, and their verbal interactions often focus on dominance issues. Girls have stronger conventions for turn taking during conversations than do boys, and they are more likely to reach consensus through discussion rather than through dominance. In general, boys use language to assert, to boast, and to take the floor; girls use language to create and maintain relationships and to express agreement (see, e.g., Lever, 1976; Maccoby & Jacklin, 1987; Sheldon, 1990).

Boys and girls also resolve conflicts in somewhat different ways. Boys initiate more conflicts than girls. More important, boys tend to use heavy-handed persuasion tactics, such as physical aggression and strong threats, to get their way. In contrast, girls tend to use conflict mitigation tactics, such as compromise, changing the topic, or clarifying the other's feelings in order to resolve a conflict (Miller, Danahar, & Forbes, 1986). Differences in conflict resolution appear as early as age 3. Sheldon (1990) examined spontaneously occurring conflicts in a play corner of a preschool. When 3-year-old girls enter a conflict situation, they try to resolve the conflict through compromise and clarification. Boys, in contrast, use a good deal of physical threat and force and appeal to higher order rules to get their own way. In characterizing the overall sense of the interaction, Sheldon claims that girls' agenda is to engage in mutual pretend play, and they use the play themes to resolve the conflict. Boys seem to oppose one another; they do not maintain the play theme but rather move into verbal and physical assaults and escalate the conflict.

Of course, it must be emphasized that, as with all gender differences, there is a great deal of variability among individuals. Not all boys show exactly the same pattern of play and social interaction, nor do all girls. Moreover, some of these style differences may be situation specific. That is, although girls tend to play indoors more frequently than do boys, when they do play outdoors, they are often as physically active as are boys (Fagot, 1987; Maccoby, 1988). Also, children, especially girls, will adjust their style to some extent depending on the gender of their playmate. Girls are more physically and verbally aggressive when playing with boys than when playing with girls (Pitcher & Shultz, 1983). Still, the general differences in interaction style are quite reliable; most boys and girls do seem to play in different ways most of the time.

Maccoby (1988; Maccoby & Jacklin, 1987) has argued quite convincingly that these different play styles lead to gender segregation. Girls may begin to avoid boys because they are uncomfortable with the higher levels of physical activity and aggression. Similarly, boys may begin to avoid girls because girls are too sedentary to fit with their own style. A good example of how this process might work comes from a study in which 36-month-old children were given access to a trampoline (as discussed in Maccoby, 1988). Pairs of girls took turns jumping up and down on the trampoline. Pairs of boys jumped up and down on the trampoline and on each other with little concern for turn taking. One can easily see how girls would not enjoy playing on the trampoline with boys, because their style of play is so different, and vice versa. Notice that this is so even though all the children are engaging in what is ostensibly the same activity, playing on the trampoline.

Further, differences in language use and conflict resolution would make it more difficult for children to engage in productive social interaction with other-gender playmates, and this would be especially true for girls. Because boys use language to dominate and to "take the floor," girls would find it difficult to communicate with boys. It would be particularly difficult for girls to "get the floor" during a conversation with boys, because girls are used to yielding the floor and have more conventionalized rules for turn taking. Girls would not want to interact with boys because boys are simply too rough and too dominant. Boys, on the other hand, would not want to play with girls because girls are too quiet and too yielding. It is interesting, in light of these arguments, that gender segregation is often heightened after situations in which girls and boys have interacted together. That is, after engaging in interaction in mixed-gender groups, children are even more likely to segregate by gender when given the choice than before, and this is especially true for girls (Maccoby & Jacklin, 1987). Thus gender segregation may occur because interaction with the other gender is somewhat aversive.

In sum, there is good evidence that boys and girls have different styles of play, and may choose same-gender playmates because these playmates are compatible with their own style. Moreover, because the play styles are compatible, children may be able to engage in more complex and advanced play and interaction in same-gender groups. But in mixed-gender groups, much of the interaction would break down as a result of conflicting styles, leading to less advanced play. But why do boys and girls differ in their play styles? Is it because of some biologically determined tendency to behave in certain ways, or is it because boys and girls have been socialized to interact in different ways? As with all gender differences, the answer is probably a complex interaction of these two possibilities.

Toward an explanation of gender differences in play style

We have already seen that adults do interact differently with boys and girls and that these differences begin in early infancy. During the very first weeks of life, parents engage in more face-to-face and vocal interaction with daughters than with sons (Goldberg & Lewis, 1969; Parke & Sawin, 1980; Power & Parke, 1982). This difference probably results from two factors. First, male infants, on average, are more active and more irritable than female infants. This would lead to male infants being held closer to the body for comforting, probably with the head held up to the parent's shoulder. This is obviously not a good position for face-to-face interaction. Female infants, on the other hand, are quieter and are able to sustain an awake, alert state earlier in development. This would allow for holding the infant in a cradling position, similar to one used for feeding, which is ideal for face-to-face communication. Thus the small biologically determined temperamental differences between male and female infants would lead to more vocal interaction with females than males.

At the same time, parental stereotypes and expectations about their male or female infants would also lead to more vocalization to females than males. Parents assume that females are more vocal and more interested in communication than are males, and they work harder to get their daughters to respond, with coos and gurgles, than their sons. Thus both biological differences and cultural expectations would lead to the same result: Females are engaging in more face-to-face communication than males from the very beginning of development. We can also assume that, in this way, females may be learning to value this kind of communication as well. With sons, both because they are more active to begin with and because of cultural stereotypes, parents tend to engage in more rough play even in infancy. Again, both biology and culture lead to the same result, and we can assume that males begin to value this kind of rough-and-tumble play.

Because parents and daughters have a history of sharing face-to-face communication, they may begin to select toys that allow for this same kind of communication: dolls, tea sets, and the like. With sons, toys that allow for rougher, more physically active play will be selected. Thus gender-typed toy choice results from a complex interaction. Males and females may begin with biologically influenced preferences for different kinds of interactions and activities (this idea is discussed in detail in Chapter 3), but we also need to consider how these tendencies have been shaped by parent–child interactions during infancy. As children come to interact with their peers, they will adopt the same interaction style that has been established with their parents. Girls will engage in more quiet, face-to-face play with a great deal of conversation, and boys will engage in more rough-and-tumble play with less verbal communication.

In addition, aggressive behaviors in boys are reacted to very differently than aggressive behaviors in girls, by both adults and peers. Somewhat surprisingly, adults intervene in boys' aggressive play much more frequently than in girls' aggressive play. For example, Fagot (1987) reports that preschool teachers responded to 41% of boys' aggressive acts but only 10% of girls' aggressive acts. Because most of these responses are negative, one might assume that boys would be getting more feedback about the inappropriateness of aggression, and therefore, would begin to display less aggression over time. However, one could also argue that because boys are receiving adult attention for aggression, even though negative, they continue to display these behaviors. Girls, on the other hand, tend to be ignored when they behave aggressively, and so these behaviors would tend to occur less and less frequently. Also recall that boys are more likely to change their behavior in response to peer feedback rather than teacher feedback (Fagot & Leinbach, 1983). How do peers respond to aggressive behaviors in boys and girls?

Serbin, Marchessault, McAffer, Peters, and Schwartzman (1991) examined this question in a study of children in fourth through sixth grade. They asked children to identify classmates who were very aggressive and then observed the behaviors of these children during free play. Girls who were perceived as aggressive by their classmates tended to spend more time in mixed-gender groups than girls not perceived as aggressive. These girls also displayed a relatively high rate of retaliatory acts. Moreover, classmates tended not to like aggressive girls. In contrast, boys perceived as aggressive received more attention from their peers than boys not perceived as aggressive, and they displayed high levels of motor activity. Most interesting, aggressive boys were extremely well liked by their peers. These results suggest that aggressive girls may be getting negative feedback from their peers, but that aggressive boys may be getting positive feedback from their peers.

Overall, then, small biological differences may come to be exaggerated by cultural stereotypes, leading to the reliable differences we see between boys' and girls' play interactions later in development. Further, both adults and children may differentially reinforce aggressive behaviors in boys and girls, leading to boys continuing to display more aggressive play behaviors than girls throughout childhood. The next question is what the long-term consequences are, if any, of these different play styles for children's and adults' developing relationships with others.

Friendship patterns

Children's friendships

Although preschool children clearly form emotional attachments to specific peers and show quite selective preferences for particular playmates over others (Howes, 1988), it is not until elementary school that they begin to form long-lasting friendships with peers based on mutual interests and affection (see Selman et al., 1977, for a detailed theoretical discussion). And, not surprisingly given the gender differences in play styles, these friendships are different for girls than for boys. In an intensive study, using both observation and questionnaires, Lever (1976) examined various aspects of school-age children's friendship and play patterns. During the elementary school years, children are quite gender segregated in their friendships; more importantly, school-age girls are much more likely to have a single best friend with whom they spend most of their free time than are boys. Female best friends, even this early in development, spend a good deal of time simply conversing with each other, sharing secrets, and talking about mutual interests. Although girls do play games, these seem to be secondary to the relationship itself. When conflicts arise, girls will drop the game in order to maintain harmony in the relationship. Boys, in contrast, play in groups and tend not to have a special best friend. Their activities tend to revolve around rule-governed games, especially team sports, and when conflicts arise, they are negotiated and settled in order to keep the game going. Boys tend not to engage in long or intimate conversations with their friends; vocal communication centers on discussion and negotiation of the game.

Examination of the actual content of conversations between female and male friends provides further evidence of gender differences. Tannen (1990) analyzed videotapes of same-gender best friends conversing. Female best friends in the second grade (about 8 years old) were already engaging in long, intimate conversations about personally significant events in their lives. Each girl listened attentively to her friend and provided support and encouragement. Second-grade boys, on the other hand, found little to talk about. They displayed extreme discomfort in this situation, and their topic of conversation centered on finding something to do. Similar patterns were obtained among sixth-grade same-sex best friends. By tenth grade, there were fewer gender differences; males were beginning to discuss issues and problems with their best friend; but between males, one friend tended to downplay or dismiss the other's problems, whereas between females, each friend provided support and understanding.

We can easily see how these patterns are related to the different play styles discussed earlier. As Lever (1976) argues, females and males are learning very different social skills in these different kinds of peer interactions. Boys are learning to negotiate conflict. They are also learning to be a "team member," to be part of a functioning group rather than taking all the glory for oneself. Moreover, because they play on different teams on different days, they are learning both to cooperate and compete with friends. Girls, in contrast, are learning more social relational skills – how to communicate one on one and the importance of listening. They are also learning to avoid conflict in favor of maintaining a relationship. Because they are not playing in large groups, they are not learning cooperation and competition in the same way that boys are. But, then, boys are not learning skills for developing intimacy with others.

Adolescence and the transition to adult friendships

As children grow older, and particularly as they enter adolescence, friendships take on a new meaning for them. They begin to move away from their parents and to establish an independent identity (see especially Erikson, 1968, and Marcia, 1980). Sometimes this takes the form of "adolescent rebellion" (e.g., Peterson, 1988). More often it involves developing deeper and more intimate relationships with peers, relationships that involve long, intensive discussions about inner feelings and experiences. Thus adolescent friendships often involve self-disclosure and self-scrutiny. Also, during adolescence, gender segregation greatly diminishes; in fact, adolescents become quite interested in forming more intimate relationships with members of the other gender. Some of these relationships will involve physical intimacy and romantic attachment (we discuss these kinds of relations in Chapter 8), but many others are friendships.

Given the differences we have already discussed in earlier play patterns and friendships, we can speculate that females and males will come into adolescence with different skills and possibly even different expectations about friendship. We might assume that females would have deeper, more intimate friendships involving more discussion of personal problems and emotions than do males. Males, in contrast, would be assumed to develop friendships based on shared interests (e.g., sports, academics), and that much of their time would be spent engaging in these mutual interests. In fact, this is exactly what the research demonstrates (Auckett, Ritchie, & Mill, 1988; Barth & Kinder, 1988; Caldwell & Peplau, 1982; Jones, Bloys, & Wood, 1990). Females report spending more time with their friends simply talking, especially about personal issues and problems, than males do. Females also stress the importance of emotion in their friendships. Female friends talk about emotions and disclose more about their own emotional lives than do male friends. Male friends, in contrast, spend most of their time together engaging in some form of activity, such as sports, rather than just talking. Moreover, when they do talk, they tend to converse about current events, sports, and personalities rather than about their own beliefs, values, and feelings.

As we mentioned, however, one thing that does change during adolescence is the formation of cross-gender friendships. Given the differences in females' and males' friendships, an interesting question is how cross-gender friends communicate. In general, males differentiate more between male and female friends than do females. More specifically, females report having deep intimate conversations with both their female and their male friends, but males report having these kinds of conversations significantly more often with their female friends than with their male friends (Auckett et al., 1988; Barth & Kinder, 1988; Caldwell & Peplau, 1982). Related to this, both males and females say they would go to a female friend over a male friend with a personal problem or for emotional and social support (Auckett et al., 1988). So, although males are capable of deep, emotional self-disclosure in friendships with females, they don't engage in this kind of friendship with other males.

Female friendships are also more long-standing than male friendships. Yet the degree of closeness and disclosure in a friendship is not related to how long the friends have known each other. Even for casual friends who have not known each other for long, females report deeper, more intimate relationships than do males. Similarly, it is not the case that as males know each other for longer, they begin to engage in more self-disclosure with their male friends (Barth & Kinder, 1988). Rather, it seems that females and males have different expectations about friendships. Females seem to view friendships as deep personal relationships. Males, on the other hand, seem to view friendships as more instrumental; friends are people to do things with. But note that when with female friends, males engage in more "feminine-typed" friendship patterns, but females do not engage in more "masculine-typed" friendship patterns when with male friends.

Thus it may be that males have difficulty in establishing close, intimate friendships and need a more expert partner, that is, a female, in order to do so. Again, looking back at early play and friendship patterns, we can see how this would happen. From the very beginning of social interaction females are engaging in conversation and are concerned with listening to others. Males engage in more group play centering on motor activity and so would not be learning the same kind of relational and communication skills as would females.

If this analysis is correct, then we would expect males who are less traditionally masculine and more androgynous to show more flexible friendship patterns (see Chapter 1 for a discussion of traditionalism and androgyny). Is it the case that androgynous people, and especially androgynous males, show different friendship patterns than more highly gender-typed individuals?

For females, it makes no difference whether they are traditionally feminine or androgynous; their friendships are close and intimate. Masculine-typed males show the typical male friendship pattern; their friendships tend to be instrumental. Androgynous males, however, do show more flexibility in their friendships. Although their friendships are not as deeply intimate as females' friendships, they are more involved with their friends than are more traditional males (Barth & Kinder, 1988). Androgynous males are also more expressive than traditional males. Expressivity is defined as the ease of communication with friends as well as the extent to which confidences are exchanged. Traditional males, in contrast, seem to have difficulty expressing themselves, and need a more expressive partner, whether a female or an androgynous male, to bring out emotionality and self-disclosure in the friendship (Narus & Fischer, 1982). Finally, androgynous males and females report feeling less lonely than do traditional individuals (Jones et al., 1990). So androgynous males may be better able to form close, intimate relations than are more traditional males.

Gender differences in friendship patterns continue throughout the life span. Females continue to place a greater emphasis on friendships and on confiding and sharing with friends than do males throughout adulthood. Moreover, females have more friends than do males, and this is especially true in old age. Males tend to name their spouse as their single closest friend, but women often name other close friends as well. Also, because women are more likely to be widowed than are males, in old age women are much more likely to have close friends outside their marriage than are males (see Wright, 1989, for a review).

Summary

By 2 or 3 years of age children begin to segregate by gender in their play, and this segregation seems to be more child-driven than adult-driven. Adults do not consistently reinforce gender-typed toy choice or play with same-gender peers, but peers clearly do. Perhaps most interesting, gender segregation seems to result from gender differences in play styles. These styles may be partly due to small biological sex differences, but they also emerge from differential social interactions that begin at birth. Girls enjoy quiet activity, involving face-to-face interaction, usually with one or two best friends. Boys enjoy more large-scale motor activity in large groups. Gender differences in early play interactions lead to clear and consistent gender differences in friendship patterns. Female friendships are deeper and more long-standing than are male friendships, and females engage in more self-disclosure in their friendships than do males. Intriguingly, males, and especially androgynous males, show feminine-typed friendship patterns in their cross-gender friendships, suggesting that males are capable of deep, intimate friendships but need a more expert partner to achieve such relationships.

8

Intimate relationships

We knew that there are consistent gender differences in male and female friendship patterns, but what about more intimate relationships? Do males and females differ in their experiences of sexual relationships? And what happens when they become mothers and fathers? Is the experience of parenthood the same for both sexes?

Puberty and the development of sexual relationships

Physical differences between the sexes that are present at birth are determined by sex hormones during the prenatal period, as discussed in Chapter 3. The other important stage at which physical sexual differentiation takes place is puberty. At puberty, the body changes from a child's to an adult's and becomes capable of reproduction. Once again, sex hormones control this process. The age at which puberty begins is influenced by genetic and environmental factors, including geographic location, ethnicity, emotional state, and nutrition (Hopwood et al., 1990).

During childhood, sex hormone levels are low in both males and females. The onset of puberty is associated with increased bursts of gonadotropin-releasing hormone from the hypothalamus (Buchanan, Eccles, & Becker, 1992; Hopwood et al., 1990). This causes an upsurge in the production of follicle stimulating hormone (FSH) and luteinizing hormone (LH) by the pituitary. In boys, these hormones cause the testes to produce testosterone, which is largely responsible for the development of male physical characteristics and reproductive function. In girls, increased levels of FSH and LH cause the ovaries to produce estrogen, which stimulates the development of a female body shape and the reproductive organs. Girls have male as well as female sex hormones, although at much lower levels than boys. It is the androgens produced at puberty that are responsible in girls for the growth of pubic and body hair. Just as girls have male sex hormones, boys have low levels of female sex hormones.

Girls usually enter puberty between the ages of 8 and 14. The development of breasts and a female body shape results from an increase in fatty tissue. This is followed by the growth of pubic and underarm hair. Puberty is also characterized by a growth spurt, development of the reproductive organs, and the start of menstruation. It is thought that girls need to attain a critical percentage of body fat before menstruation will begin (Fishman, 1980; Frisch & McArthur, 1974), and it is a low percentage of body fat that is believed to be responsible for the delay or absence of menstruation in girls with the eating disorder anorexia nervosa.

In boys, puberty begins 2 years later, on average, than in girls. Physical changes include growth of the penis and testes, as well as of pubic, body, and facial hair. During the growth spurt there is a rapid increase in height and in muscle tissue resulting in a male body shape. Boys also begin to ejaculate, and their voice deepens.

Both hormones and social factors affect the beginning of sexual activity in adolescents. The way in which biological and social factors interact to influence the development of sexuality has been examined by following more than 1,000 adolescents over a 2-year period (Udry, 1990). The study found that though the onset of interest in sex was associated with an increase in androgen levels in both boys and girls, the antecedents of sexual behavior differed between the sexes. For boys, initial involvement in sexual activity was highly dependent on hormones and not much affected by social influences. In contrast, girls' first involvement in sexual activity was much more influenced by social factors, such as whether or not their best friend had had sex, than by hormones.

In Western society, sexual activity has always been more acceptable for boys than for girls, and adolescent boys have been much more likely than adolescent girls to engage in sexual relationships. But the gap between the sexes has narrowed in recent years as more adolescent girls have become sexually active (Brooks-Gunn & Furstenberg, 1989). For most young people today, sexual intercourse first takes place during the teenage years. In a survey of 16 to 25 year olds in Los Angeles, the average age of first sexual intercourse was 14.9 years for boys and 15.9 years for girls (Moore & Erickson, 1985). Adolescents in Europe are slightly older when they first have sex. Recent surveys in the Netherlands (Straver, 1992) and West Germany (Schmidt, Lange, & Knopf, 1992) show that about 50% of 17 year olds have experienced sexual intercourse. Sexual activity with a partner of the same sex is experienced by about 10% of adolescents (DeLamater & MacCorquodale, 1979).

What characteristics do heterosexual males and females look for in choosing a sexual partner? In a study of more than 10,000 subjects in 33 countries, it was concluded that women prefer men who are able to provide for them, and men prefer women who are physically attractive (Buss, 1989). This research has focused on the identification of differences rather than similarities between the sexes. When characteristics such as kindness and sense of humor are considered, few sex differences emerge (Feingold, 1992; Goodwin, 1990), and it is these qualities that both heterosexual and homosexual men and women value most (Howard, Blumstein, & Schwartz, 1987). To a large extent, men and women seem to look for the same attributes in each other when choosing a sexual partner (Peplau & Gordon, 1985).

Male and female sexuality

It is often assumed that male and female sexuality are qualitatively different, and that men are much more interested in sex than are women. But just how different are the sexual experiences of men and women? The studies of Masters and Johnson (1966) did much to increase our understanding of the physiological changes that occur during sexual arousal, and demonstrated that in spite of differences in anatomy and reproductive function, men and women experience a similar pattern of sexual response.

Masters and Johnson monitored the physiological responses of men and women during sexual activity in the laboratory. From their observations, they outlined four stages of male and female sexual response: excitement, plateau, orgasm, and resolution. The *excitement* phase is characterized by an increase in blood flow to the genitals. This results in an erection in men, and in swelling of the external genitals as well as in lubrication and expansion of the vagina in women. The *plateau* phase is the stage of intense sexual arousal. In men, the penis undergoes further enlargement, and in women the clitoris retracts and the vaginal walls swell. *Orgasm* is similar for men and women, occurring when sexual tension builds to a point at which orgasm is felt to be inevitable and involving an intense pleasurable sensation accompanied by rhythmic contractions of the pelvic muscles. Although men ejaculate, the sensation of orgasm appears to be similar for males and females. When Vance and Wagner (1976) asked a panel of doctors and psychologists to decide whether a set of descriptions of the experience of orgasm was written by women or men, they found this hard to do, supporting the idea that orgasm feels very similar for the two sexes. During the *resolution* phase the body returns to an unaroused state. For men there is a refractory period after ejaculation during which time further ejaculation is impossible. This can last from a few minutes to several days, depending partly on age. Most women do not have a refractory period, and some women can have multiple orgasms, that is, one orgasm after another without loss of arousal.

One positive consequence of Masters and Johnson's research for women was the rejection of Freud's view that there are two types of female orgasm, an "immature" orgasm resulting from stimulation of the clitoris and a more superior "mature" orgasm resulting from sexual intercourse. Masters and Johnson demonstrated that orgasms are physiologically identical regardless of whether they result from clitoral or vaginal stimulation. They also showed that clitoral stimulation is important for the so-called vaginal orgasm, as the movement of the penis in and out of the vagina during sexual intercourse causes indirect stimulation of the clitoris. Although women have reported that an orgasm from direct clitoral stimulation can feel different from an orgasm experienced during sexual intercourse, Masters and Johnson's research has challenged the notion that the latter type is more desirable.

Not only are there strong similarities in sexual response between men and women but, contrary to common belief, women also seem to become just as aroused by erotic material as men. Heiman (1975) examined the physiological responses of men and women to erotic stories. In men, sexual arousal was monitored by means of a penile plethysmograph, a loop that is placed around the base of the penis to measure erection. In women, a probe with a photoelectric cell was inserted into the vagina to measure blood flow. Increases in erection in men and in vaginal blood flow in women provided objective measures of sexual arousal. The subjects also completed self-report measures of subjective feelings of arousal. Four types of story were presented: erotic – descriptions of heterosexual sex; romantic – descriptions of nonsexual affection; erotic-romantic – descriptions of sex and affection; and control – a couple engaged in conversation. Both men and women became most sexually aroused in response to stories containing sexually explicit material; neither men nor women responded sexually to the romantic story. However, about half of the women were unaware that they were sexually aroused. They showed evidence of physiological arousal as measured by the vaginal probe, but did not rate themselves as feeling aroused on the self-report measures. So though women respond as much as men do to erotic material, they are not always aware of their sexually aroused state.

Although men and women show similar patterns of sexual response, women are less likely than men to reach orgasm during sexual intercourse. In the first large-scale survey of sexual behavior, it was found that 30% of married women had never experienced an orgasm (Kinsey, Pomeroy, Martin, & Gebhard, 1953). Two decades later, it was still the case that a substantial minority (10% – 15%) of married women never or seldom reached orgasm (Hunt, 1974); and Hite (1976) found that only about 30% of women in her sample regularly had an orgasm during sexual intercourse without additional clitoral stimulation.

Gender differences also exist for masturbation. Kinsey et al. (1984, 1953) reported that only 58% of women compared with 98% of men had masturbated at least once. Similar findings were reported by Hunt (1974), with 63% of women and 94% of men having masturbated at least once. These surveys suffer from a number of methodological problems, particularly the use of samples that are unrepresentative of the general population, which makes it difficult to draw general conclusions from the findings. But they do provide information about sexual activity that cannot be obtained by other types of investigation. The Kinsey and Hunt surveys are thought to give reasonably accurate estimates of sexual behavior, although the subjects were probably more sexually active than average.

The Hite Report obtained a response rate of only 3% of a sample that was unrepresentative in the first place. The value of this survey lies in the detailed accounts of female sexuality that provided a new insight into women's sexual experiences. According to Hite (1976), the reason for women's difficulty in achieving orgasm during intercourse is not that women are less capable of orgasm than men, but that sexual intercourse often fails to give women the clitoral stimulation necessary for orgasm to occur. And because fewer women than men masturbate, particularly during the teenage years, women fail to learn about sexual responsiveness in this way. Cultural factors are important as well. Whereas it is considered acceptable for men to make sexual demands on women, women are not encouraged to voice their desires to men. So it is not surprising that women sometimes find it difficult to take an active role during sex and communicate their likes and dislikes to their partners. It seems that women's orgasm problems are a product of their passive sexual role (Barbach, 1975).

The double standards for sexual behavior in our society have negative consequences for men as well as women. As Zilbergeld (1978) has pointed out from his work with men experiencing sexual problems, a number of myths abound that put excessive pressure on men. These include "In sex, as elsewhere, it's performance that counts," "The man must take charge of and orchestrate sex," "A man always wants and is always ready to have sex," "Sex equals intercourse," and perhaps the most misguided of all "In this enlightened age, the preceding myths no longer have any influence on us"! Although a comparison of the Kinsey studies (1948, 1953) with that of Hunt (1974) shows that gender differences have diminished in some aspects of sexual behavior, such as participation in premarital and extramarital sex, there is still the expectation that men will play a more active sexual role than women in heterosexual relationships.

Sexual orientation

Sexual orientation refers to a person's preference for a sexual partner of the same or the other sex. In their survey of male and female sexual behavior, Kinsey et al. (1948, 1953) found that 4% of men and 2% of women were exclusively homosexual. They also reported that an additional 37% of men and 13% of women had had at least one homosexual experience after puberty that had led to orgasm. As a substantial minority of men and women had engaged in sexual relationships with partners of the same sex in addition to partners of the other sex, Kinsey suggested that sexual orientation should not be represented as the two categories of heterosexual and homosexual but as a

Table 8.1. *The Kinsey scale*

0. Exclusively heterosexual
1. Predominantly heterosexual, only incidentally homosexual
2. Predominantly heterosexual, but more than incidentally homosexual
3. Equally heterosexual and homosexual
4. Predominantly homosexual, but more than incidentally heterosexual
5. Predominantly homosexual, only incidentally heterosexual
6. Exclusively homosexual

Source: Kinsey, Pomeroy, and Martin (1948).

continuum ranging from exclusively heterosexual at one end to exclusively homosexual at the other. The scale is shown in Table 8.1.

Although this survey did much to highlight the diversity of sexual activity, it has been criticized for its emphasis on behavior rather than identity (Cass, 1990). For example, a person who engages only in heterosexual sex may identify as homosexual, and a person with a heterosexual identity may engage in homosexual sex, so it is misleading to use sexual behavior alone as an indicator of sexual orientation. Whereas some people identify as exclusively heterosexual or homosexual, others identify as bisexual and have a sexual orientation toward members of both sexes. The extent to which a preference for same-sex or other-sex sexual partners can change during one's lifetime is still debated. Some researchers argue that sexual orientation is determined early in life and does not change (Money, 1988), but this view is contradicted by studies that show that sexual behavior and identity may switch from heterosexual to homosexual and back to heterosexual (Sanders, Reinisch, & McWhirter, 1990).

Why is it that some people develop a preference for sexual partners of the other sex, some prefer same sex partners, and some like both sexes? The question that has traditionally been posed simply asks why some people become homosexual, seeing heterosexuality as normal and lesbianism and homosexuality as deviations from this norm. As we shall see in the following discussion, the view of heterosexuality as normal and homosexuality as deviant has had a major influence on the nature of research on sexual orientation that has been carried out. Biological explanations for sexual orientation have always been popular. Yet in spite of a large body of research, there is no firm evidence for any biologically based differences between heterosexual and homosexual men and women. The structure of the hypothalamus has been found to differ between heterosexual and homosexual men (LeVay, 1991); but why this brain difference occurs, and how it may influence sexual orientation, are questions that remain unanswered.

A recent study of homosexual men with twin brothers found that 52% of monozygotic co-twins were also homosexual, compared with 22% of dizygotic co-twins (Bailey & Pillard, 1991). Lesbian women with twin sisters have also been investigated by these researchers with findings similar to those of the homosexual men study (Bailey, Pillard, Neale, & Agyei, 1993). Of monozygotic co-twins, 48% were reported to be lesbian in contrast with 16% of dizygotic co-twins. Although the greater concordance between identical than non-identical twin pairs points to a genetic influence on homosexuality, this does not necessarily mean that a homosexual (or heterosexual) orientation is dependent on a specific genetic pattern. People with a similar genetic makeup have similar characteristics and, as a consequence, similar life experiences. As monozygotic twins are alike in a wide variety of ways, it is not surprising that this should also be the case for sexual orientation.

In line with these studies, Hamer et al. (1993) claim to have identified a genetic marker for male homosexuality. Of 40 pairs of brothers, both of whom were homosexual, 33 pairs were found to have a marker in a small region of the X chromosome. This suggests that there may be a specific gene, yet to be located, which is linked to male homosexuality. It does not mean, however, that the presence of this gene, if it exists, determines a homosexual orientation. Neither does it mean that all homosexual men possess the gene. After all, the marker was not found in 7 pairs of brothers. It remains for future research to replicate this finding and to answer the related questions of whether the gene is found in heterosexual men, or in lesbian women. From

Hamer's study alone, it cannot be concluded that there exists a gene that predisposes toward homosexuality.

No consistent differences in postnatal hormone levels have been identified between heterosexual and homosexual adults (Meyer-Bahlburg, 1984). It remains possible that prenatal hormones may play some part in facilitating the subsequent development of a heterosexual, bisexual, or homosexual orientation. However, as we have seen in Chapter 3, the existing evidence is based on a small number of studies and is extremely tentative. It is also important to remember that the proponents of the prenatal hormone theory themselves argue that sexual orientation cannot be determined by prenatal hormones alone, and that postnatal environmental factors are also influential.

Although a number of psychoanalytically oriented theorists consider homosexuality to arise from disturbed relationships with parents, empirical studies of the influence of parent–child relationships on the development of homosexuality have produced inconclusive results. A questionnaire was administered to psychoanalysts about the family relationships of their male homosexual patients (Bieber et al., 1962). Fathers of homosexual men were found to be hostile and/or distant and the mothers to be close-binding, intimate, and dominant. However, for psychoanalysts to have said otherwise would have meant contradicting some of the major teachings in their field. And gay men receiving therapy are not representative of gay men in general. With a nonpatient sample, Evans (1969) showed a similar pattern of a close mother and a detached father. However, rather different findings were reported by Bene (1965a), who found no evidence that homosexual men who were not in therapy were more likely to have been overprotected by, overindulged by, or strongly attached to their mother than heterosexual men. In a well-controlled large-scale study, no differences were identified in parental background between homosexual and heterosexual men who were low on neuroticism (Siegelman, 1974).

The differences in parental relationships between homosexual and heterosexual men found in earlier studies appear to be related to differences in neuroticism rather than to homosexuality per se. Studies of the mothers of lesbians have similarly failed to produce consistent findings, although some investigations have reported mothers of lesbian women to be more dominant than fathers, and that the fathers were viewed as inferior or weak (Bell, Weinberg, & Hammersmith, 1981; Bene, 1965b; Kaye et al., 1967; Newcombe, 1985).

A number of investigations point to a relationship between nonconventional gender role behavior in childhood and adult homosexuality. In a retrospective study, a striking difference in "sissiness" was found between homosexual and heterosexual men (Saghir & Robins, 1973). Sixty-seven percent of the homosexual men, in contrast to 3% of the heterosexual men, reported that as children they were considered to be sissies (had no male buddies, played mostly with girls, did not participate in sports). In a similar investigation, an inventory concerning childhood interest in cross-dressing, playing with dolls, preferences for affiliating with girls and older women, being regarded as a sissy by peers, and the nature of childhood sex was completed by heterosexual and gay men (Whitam, 1977). Of the gay men, 97% endorsed at least one of the six items as descriptive of their childhood experience, whereas 74% of the heterosexual men reported a complete absence of these behaviors in childhood.

Another retrospective study was carried out by Bell et al. (1981), who administered a battery of interviews and psychological tests to matched groups of 979 homosexual and 477 heterosexual men in the San Francisco area. The major difference between the two groups was in childhood gender conformity. Seventy percent of the heterosexual men had enjoyed ball games as children, whereas this was so for only 11% of gay men. Forty-six percent of the gay men and only 11% of the heterosexual men had liked traditionally feminine activities, such as playing house. Childhood cross-dressing occurred in 37% of the homosexual men compared with 10% of the heterosexual men. Even among "noneffeminate" gay men, dislike of boy's activities was the strongest predictor of adult homosexuality.

Comparable results emerge from retrospective research on childhood masculinity in girls. It was concluded from a summary of research findings that lesbian women differ from heterosexual women in having had greater tomboyish tendencies, more boys and fewer girls as playmates, and a greater childhood desire to be a boy (Safer & Reiss, 1975).

The validity of these studies has often been questioned, mainly because they are retrospective; adults' memories of their childhood are commonly influenced by their experiences while growing up. In particular, gay men and lesbian women may be more likely to identify behaviors that might have a bearing on their sexual orientation, whereas heterosexual men and women may not recollect, or admit to, cross-gender behavior as children.

To overcome the problem of selective recollection of childhood behavior, the relationship between gender role behavior in childhood and sexual orientation in adulthood has been investigated by longitudinal studies of children with gender identity disorder. These children express a strong desire to be the other sex, and characteristically engage in cross-gender behavior, including a marked preference for friends of the other sex. Zuger (1984) followed up 55 feminine boys who had been referred to a gender identity clinic in childhood or adolescence. Almost 73% identified as homosexual, 6.3% as heterosexual, and 20.8% of uncertain sexual orientation. Green (1987) carried out a prospective study of 66 feminine boys who had been referred to a clinic and a matched group of 55 nonfeminine boys. The average age of the boys when first seen was about 7 years. Two-thirds of both groups were followed up into early adulthood. Sixty-eight percent of the feminine boys developed a bisexual or homosexual orientation, compared with none in the control group, and 43% of the feminine boys were exclusively homosexual.

In considering these studies, it is important to remember that simply because an association exists between cross-gender behavior in childhood and homosexuality in adulthood, or because differences have sometimes been found in the patterns of parenting experienced by homosexual and heterosexual men and women, this does not mean that all or even most adults who identify as homosexual were unconventional in their gender role behavior as children or were raised by dominant mothers and distant fathers. The retrospective studies show that a substantial proportion of homosexual adults report no or few cross-gender behaviors as children, and that many had good relationships with their parents. The prospective studies examined homosexual men who, as children, had been referred to a clinic because of marked cross-gender behavior. They are not representative of the general population of adult homosexual men. So even if a lesbian or gay sexual orientation may sometimes be related to gender nonconformity in childhood or specific styles of parenting, it is clear that these factors do not provide a comprehensive explanation of why some people develop a homosexual, and others a heterosexual, sexual orientation.

The reasons for nonconventional gender role behavior in childhood are not known. Feminine boys did not differ from nonfeminine boys in the availability of male or female role models, although the feminine boys experienced greater father absence. And parents of feminine boys did not reinforce their cross-gender behavior, although mothers who initially approved of the feminine behavior had more feminine sons (Roberts, Green, Williams, & Goodman, 1987). In a study of "tomboys," no differences were found between masculine and feminine girls in terms of parent–child contact in the first 5 years of life or in the quality of parent–child relationships, although the masculine girls were reported to have a closer relationship with their father. The mothers of tomboys were more likely to have been tomboys themselves and were more accepting of tomboyish behavior on the part of their daughters. But because of their experience of bringing up a masculine daughter, these mothers may be more likely to recollect their own tomboyish behavior or be more accepting of tomboyish behavior than mothers of more traditional daughters (Green, Williams, & Goodman, 1982; Williams, Goodman, & Green, 1985). The girls have not been followed into adulthood.

So, although there seems to be a relationship between gender conformity and sexual orientation, the factors that contribute to gender nonconformity and to the relationship between childhood gender nonconformity and adult homosexuality are not understood. The link between boys' dislike of rough-and-tumble play and low levels of prenatal androgens and between boys' dislike of rough-and-tumble play and male homosexuality may provide a clue. It has been suggested that male homosexuality may result indirectly from low levels of prenatal androgens through the influence of androgen levels on rough-and-tumble play (Friedman, 1988; Green, 1987). Money (1988) also believes that it is through indirect effects on childhood gender role behavior that prenatal hormones may influence the development of adult sexual orientation. He suggests that boys who were exposed to low levels of prenatal androgens may show little aggressive behavior, causing them to be stigmatized in childhood, and that the stigmatization will influence them toward a homosexual orientation. This theory remains speculative, and there is no clear explanation of why boys who do not enjoy rough-and-tumble play should grow up to prefer male rather than female sexual partners.

What is clear is that no single factor has been identified as a determinant of whether a person will become homosexual, bisexual, or heterosexual. Instead, it seems that the pathways that lead from the prenatal period to adult sexual orientation are complex, and individuals experience a variety of biological and psychological as well as cultural influences at different stages of development. And just as in other aspects of human development, individuals are themselves active participants in this process (Cass, 1990). Some women, for example, adopt a lesbian identity and lifestyle as an active political choice (Kitzinger, 1987). People who identify as homosexual, like people who identify as heterosexual, differ greatly from each other, and so too it seems do the routes through which both homosexual and heterosexual men and women pass in the development of sexual orientation.

Motherhood and fatherhood

In spite of the trend toward the adoption of less traditional male and female roles by heterosexual couples, women are still largely responsible for running the home and caring for children, and men are primarily in charge of earning money and providing for the family. When both partners are employed, women's jobs are still seen as less important than men's, women do more housework than do men, and women have less say in financial and other family matters (Spitze, 1988; Steil, 1983). Even when wives earn more than their husbands and hold more prestigious jobs, the value placed on their career and their influence at home is less than that of husbands in a similar position (Steil & Weltman, 1991). And once men and women become parents, gender differentiation becomes considerably more marked. In the large majority of families, it is the woman who is most involved in child rearing even when she works outside the home.

For women, motherhood is seen as an important aspect of adult identity. It used to be thought that women had an innate desire to have children; that is, that women possessed a "maternal instinct" (Deutsch, 1945). More recent considerations of women's motivations for motherhood have focused on social and psychological explanations, particularly on the values associated with having children. These include

Adult status and social identity, which fulfill the need for acceptance as a responsible and mature adult member of the community

Primary group ties and affection, which fulfill the need to express affection and attain intimacy with another person, as well as to be the recipient of such feelings from someone else

Stimulation and fun, which fulfill the need to add the interest to life that children can provide

Expansion of the self, which fulfills the need to have someone carrying on for oneself after one's own death, as well as the need to have now growth and learning experiences to add meaning to life (Hoffman & Hoffman, 1973)

Women rate all of these values as more important than do men, except the need to achieve immortality through one's children, which men report to be more important than do women (Hoffman, Thornton, & Marris, 1978). We should keep in mind that parenthood is only one part of an individual's identity, and many people actively choose not to become parents.

Further evidence for the importance of motherhood for women's identity comes from an investigation of the reasons that women who are unable to have children give for wanting to become mothers (Woollett, 1991). These women wanted children in order to achieve a full adult status and feminine identity, to give them the opportunities that motherhood provides for establishing close relationships with others, and to overcome the negative image associated with childlessness. Because women's adult identity and status are so closely tied to motherhood, it is not surprising that the majority of women wish to become mothers, but, as we shall see in Chapter 12, the experience of raising children is not always a positive one and sometimes is a major source of conflict and distress.

Mothers have always been considered more important for the psychological development of their children than fathers. This partly stems from the view put forward by Bowlby (1951) that it is essential for mental health that the child should experience a warm, intimate, and continuous relationship with the mother. In the development of attachment theory, Bowlby (1969/1982) and Ainsworth (1982; Ainsworth, Blehar, Waters, & Wall, 1978) have focused on the child's relationship with the mother rather than the father. They argue that the child's principal attachment figure is usually the mother and that a secure attachment to her is important for the child's later social and emotional well-being. Empirical investigations of attachment have also focused on the mother–infant relationship because mothers are more involved than are fathers in the care of their children, because they are assumed to be more important for their children's development, and because they are easier to engage in research (Phares, 1992). With the growing interest in the role of fathers in child development in recent years, infant–father attachment has received increased attention (Lamb, 1986).

Most of the research on attachment in young children has used the Strange Situation Test, an observational technique devised by Ainsworth and Wittig (1969) to classify infants as securely or insecurely attached. This test begins with the mother and infant together in an unfamiliar room with toys and then proceeds through a series of different situations each lasting about 3 minutes – a stranger joins the mother and infant, the mother leaves the infant with the stranger, the mother returns, the baby is left alone, the stranger returns, and finally the mother returns. By analyzing the infant's responses to these different situations in terms of his or her exploratory activities, reaction to the stranger, reaction to separation, and reaction to being reunited with the mother, the child is catergorized as securely or insecurely attached. Studies that have examined children's attachments to their father as well as to their mother have used the Strange Situation Test first with one parent and then with the other. These studies have found a similar proportion of infants to be securely attached to the father as to the mother (Fox, Kimmerly, & Schafer, 1991).

Secure attachments have been shown to depend on the quality of interaction between the parent and the child (Ainsworth, 1979; Grossmann, Grossmann, Spangler, Suess & Unzer, 1985; Isabella, Belsky, & von Eye, 1989), so that infants whose parents are responsive and sensitive to their needs are more likely to become securely attached. Research has demonstrated that fathers are just as good as mothers at stimulating babies and responding to their needs (Parke, 1981). When mothers and fathers were observed feeding their baby, both parents talked to their infant more, touched their infant more, and looked more closely at their infant after infant vocalization. And fathers responded just as quickly and sensitively as mothers to their infant's signals of distress (Parke & Sawin, 1976). Fathers who engage in frequent social interaction with their babies and who respond readily and sensitively to them have strongly attached infants (Cox, Owen, Henderson, & Margand, 1992).

So fathers are as capable of parenting as mothers. But it remains the case that mothers are much more involved than fathers are with their children. It is not because fathers are incompetent and insensitive parents that they are less important attachment figures than mothers, but because in most cultures they interact with their children less (Bowlby, 1988). As Lamb (1986) points out, parenting skills are usually aquired "on the job" by both mothers and fathers, but as mothers are on the job more than fathers it is not surprising that as time goes on mothers become more experienced and sensitive to their children and fathers become less so. As a result, differences between mothers and fathers become more extreme.

The distinction between what fathers can do and what they actually do on a day-to-day basis has been examined by observing mother–infant and father–infant interaction in the home. The only activities that fathers engage in with their babies more frequently than mothers are reading and watching television (Belsky & Volling, 1987). Not only are fathers less available, but when they are at home they interact less with their infants and are less likely to provide basic care. And of the time that parents spend interacting with their babies, a much greater proportion of fathers' time is spent in playing, whereas a much greater proportion of mothers' time is spent in caregiving (Lamb, 1977). These differences remain as infants grow up. In childhood and adolescence, mothers still interact with their children more frequently and are more involved in caregiving, and fathers are more likely to engage in play and other recreational activities (Collins & Russell, 1991).

There has been much publicity recently about the "new father," who shares child rearing equally with the mother. But does he really exist? Although it appears that some fathers are more involved with their children than before, it is still mothers who take responsibility for most of their day-to-day care. Even when both the mother and the father are employed, fathers spend considerably less time with their children than do mothers and assume less responsibility for their care (Lamb, 1977; Lamb & Oppenheim, 1989). As Phoenix and Woollett (1991) put it, to know that a man is a father is generally less informative about how he spends his time and energies than to know that a woman is a mother.

Summary

Interest in sex is triggered in both males and females by the onset of puberty. The age at which teenagers first become sexually active depends not just on physical changes but on social factors as well, particularly for girls. The experience of sexual arousal and orgasm is similar for males and females, although women are less likely than men to achieve sexual satisfaction due to cultural pressures that mitigate against women taking an active sexual role. It is not known why some people develop a heterosexual and others a homosexual orientation. Although links have been identified between prenatal hormone levels, gender role behavior in childhood, and later sexual orientation, for the majority of people these factors may be unrelated to the preference for sexual partners of the same or the other sex. When men and women become mothers and fathers, gender role differences within their relationship become more marked. Though fathers are capable of performing a parenting role, primary responsibility for child care still falls to mothers.

9

Families

In recent years dramatic changes have taken place in the structure of the family. The traditional nuclear family, consisting of a heterosexual married couple and their 2.4 children and a father who goes out to work and a mother who stays at home, is becoming increasingly uncommon. Cohabitation has become an acceptable alternative to marriage, and, with one in three marriages ending in divorce, a growing number of children are being raised in stepfamilies or by a single parent. Today a high proportion of women with children go out to work, fathers have become more involved in the care of their children, children are being raised by homosexual parents, and families that would never before have existed are being created as a result of the new reproductive technologies.

As they grow up, children may experience a variety of family forms. After divorce, for example, they might first live alone with their mother. But she might remarry, and a stepfather will join the family home and possibly stepbrothers and -sisters as well. If both parents remarry, children will have two stepfamilies. They may live in one but visit the other, or spend half of the time in each. So whereas some children whose parents divorce remain with a single mother, others experience a much more complex network of family relationships than they ever did before. And just because children are raised by a single mother does not mean that they have experienced parental divorce. A growing number of women these days are opting for motherhood without marrying or living with the father of their child. How do these diverse and changing families influence the many facets of children's development? Is it the case, as is commonly believed, that traditional families are best? Or do children benefit from less rigid parental roles?

Maternal employment

The most common departure from the traditional family is where both parents go out to work. Although dual wage earner families are still widely considered to be bad for children, this view is not supported by research. School-age children with employed mothers do as well as, if not better than, children whose mothers are not employed in cognitive, social, and emotional development (Hoffman, 1979, 1989). Why is it that, contrary to expectations, the effects of maternal employment are potentially beneficial, rather than harmful, for children? Mothers who go out to work are, in general, more satisfied with life than mothers who remain at home. And studies that have examined the impact of maternal well-being for children of employed mothers show that satisfaction with their combined role has a positive effect not only on mothers' relationships with their children but on the children's adjustment and abilities as well (Hoffman, 1989).

As an increasing number of mothers are returning to work before their children reach school age, the consequences of maternal employment for infants and preschool children have become the focus of recent research. It has often been argued that young children's emotional bond with their mother would be disrupted by daily separations. Although there is little evidence to support this claim, the measures of infant–mother attachment used in early studies, such as crying on separation from the mother or willingness to approach an unfamiliar person, are now thought to be insensitive. Instead, reunion behavior following separation has been identified as the best indicator of quality of attachment.

Recent studies that have classified children as securely or insecurely attached according to reunion behavior suggest that more than 20 hours per week of nonparental care in the first year of life is associated with a heightened risk of insecure infant–parent attachment (Belsky, 1988). But the reunion behavior of infants attending day care may not mean the same as the reunion behavior of infants reared at home (Fox & Fein, 1990). And not all infants in this situation are at risk. Infants who receive excellent day care are unlikely to suffer adverse effects resulting from maternal employment. The outcome is less favorable for infants who enter day care before their first birthday, who receive poor alternative care, and who experience family or parenting problems as well. The specific family characteristics that make infants more vulnerable include feelings of anxiety or guilt by the mother, little involvement in child care by the father, and a poor marital relationship (Schachere, 1990). For the majority of preschool children, day care has no effect, either good or bad, on intellectual development, although there are clear benefits for disadvantaged children in day-care programs that specialize in cognitive enrichment (Belsky & Steinberg, 1978).

One aspect of development that is clearly influenced by maternal employment is sex role stereotyping. School-age children of working mothers, particularly girls, hold less traditional views of males and females than do children whose mothers remain at home (Hoffman, 1979, 1989). Even preschool children of employed mothers are less traditionally sex typed than children whose mothers do not go out to work (Weinraub, Jaeger, & Hoffman, 1988).

A number of longitudinal investigations of maternal employment during the child's early years have been carried out. These are of particular interest because they address the question of whether "sleeper" effects emerge, that is, whether the negative consequences of maternal employment only become apparent in later years. Studies that have followed children from infancy to middle childhood show no adverse effects of a mother going out to work. In an examination of 130 children from the age of 1 year until 7 years, no overall differences in cognitive functioning or emotional adjustment were found between children of employed and nonemployed mothers (Gottfried, Gottfried, & Bathurst, 1988). Employed mothers had higher educational aspirations for their children and the children were involved in more out-of-school lessons, and these factors had a positive effect on development.

The impact of maternal employment on attachment relationships has been investigated in 58 families, first when the child was aged 19 to 21 months and again at 5 to 6 years. No direct link was found between maternal employment and the security of children's attachment relationships at either preschool or school age (Goldberg & Easterbrooks, 1988). Once again, when children in these studies were found to be experiencing difficulties, these were related to inadequate alternative child care or poor family relationships. Longitudinal research provides further evidence that maternal employment does not, by itself, have a negative effect on the quality of mother–child interaction or child development. Interestingly, no consistent differences between boys and girls in psychological adjustment or intellectual ability in response to maternal employment have been identified.

Paternal involvement

One consequence of the increase in maternal employment is that some fathers have become more involved in household tasks and in the care of their children. This may help explain why children of employed mothers hold less stereotyped attitudes about sex roles than do children of nonemployed mothers (Hoffman, 1989). In families where the mother is employed, increased paternal involvement is associated with higher cognitive ability, academic achievement, and social maturity in both sons and daughters (Gottfried et al., 1988). But the reason for high paternal involvement is an important determinant of the outcome for children. Not surprisingly, children whose fathers choose to be involved benefit more than those with fathers forced by economic necessity to take an active role (Lamb, 1986; Russell, 1986).

A family type that, although still rare, has become more common in recent years is where the father takes equal responsibility for the care of children or where he becomes the primary caregiver while the mother goes out to work. In Sweden, families in which the father held primary responsibility for child care were compared with families in which the mother was the main caregiver (Lamb, Frodi, Hwang, & Frodi, 1982). (A change in Swedish law allowed either the mother or the father to take 9 months' paid leave from work after the birth of a child.) The parents were interviewed before their child was born, and at 3 months, 5 months, and 8 months after the birth. Parent–child interaction was observed at the 3-month and 5-month assessments. Nontraditional parents behaved in the same way toward their infants as did traditional parents. In both types of family it was the mothers who more frequently displayed affection, talked to, smiled at, held, and tended to the infant. So greater paternal involvement in child care did not change fathers' interactions with their infants. But in spite of their intentions, very few fathers had become primary caretakers, and those who did, had not done so for very long.

Studies of the effects of paternal involvement on the personality and cognitive development of preschool children have been carried out by Radin (1982) in the United States and Sagi (1982) in Israel, each using similar procedures. In both investigations volunteer families were divided into three categories according to whether the father was the primary caregiver, the mother was the primary caregiver, or the parents shared this role. High paternal involvement was associated with positive outcomes for children, such as increased intellectual performance, independence, and greater feelings of control. In addition, the children with involved fathers held less traditional attitudes about male and female roles. Does this mean that fathers make better parents than mothers? It seems not. The fathers who played a major role in the rearing of their children did so because they and their partners wanted to organize their family life in this way. As a result, family relationships were probably much warmer and richer than might otherwise have been the case, which would explain the positive outcomes for children (Lamb, 1986). In addition, these parents were highly educated, and were likely to have bright children whoever the primary caretaker had been.

Single parenthood

A different approach to the study of the role of fathers in child developmemt has been to examine families where the father is absent. Researchers have compared children raised by their mother alone with children in two-parent families, and have assumed that differences between these two groups are directly attributable to paternal influences. But the effects of the absence of a father are difficult to disentangle from those of the absence of one parent. It is important to keep this in mind when considering the following research findings.

Almost one-quarter of American families (Burns, 1992) and one-fifth of British families (Roll, 1992) are headed by a single parent, about 90% of whom are mothers. In studies of one-parent families, the father is most often the absent parent. Although much of the early research found that father absence had negative consequences for children's cognitive, social, or emotional development, the methods used were often inadequate, and the findings of the more carefully conducted studies tended to be inconsistent (Biller, 1974; Herzog & Sudia, 1973).

A major problem has been the failure to take account of factors that may be associated with father absence but not directly related to it. This is highlighted in a study of a nationally representative sample of families in the United Kingdom in which children in one- and two-parent families were compared (Ferri, 1976). Children in one-parent families were found to be less well adjusted than those with two parents. However, the children raised by a single parent experienced a number of disadvantages, such as lower social class, poor housing, and economic hardship. When these factors were taken into account, there was little difference in emotional adjustment between the two groups of children. So the absence of a parent in itself was not adversely related to the child's social adjustment. Instead, the poverty and social isolation that accompanied single parenthood had a negative effect. Similarly, large studies in the United States found no impairment in IQ for father-absent children after controlling for social class (Broman, Nichols, & Kennedy, 1975; Svanum, Bringle, & McLaughlin, 1982).

Another problem has been the failure to take account of the reason for becoming a one-parent family. In a comparison between children whose parents had divorced or separated and those who had lost a parent through death, a higher incidence of behavioral problems was found among the children who had experienced divorce or separation (Rutter, 1971). Discordant family relationships rather than the loss of a parent were responsible for the children's difficulties.

It has often been argued that the lack of a father as an identification figure or role model will result in atypical sex role behavior in children, particularly for boys. For this reason much of the research on father absence has focused on children's sex-typed behavior. Again, the empirical findings are contradictory and inconclusive (Biller, 1974; Herzog & Sudia, 1973; Stevenson & Black, 1988). Most children raised by a single mother show typical sex role development, but there may be a slight effect on some behaviors and attitudes. Father-absent boys of preschool age tend to show less stereotyped choices of toys and activities. Older father-absent boys appear to be more stereotyped in their behavior than their father-present age-mates. This effect is strongest for aggressive behavior, however, which is common among boys who have experienced parental divorce.

Divorce

Parents whose marriage breaks down are commonly advised to stay together for the sake of their children. But research on the psychological adjustment of children whose parents are in conflict suggests that a bad marriage may have more negative consequences for the children than divorce. A number of studies have examined this issue, the most noteworthy of which is the longitudinal investigation by Hetherington and her colleagues (Hetherington, 1988, 1989; Hetherington, Cox, & Cox, 1982, 1985). Children of divorced parents in mother-custody families were compared with children of nondivorced parents at 2 months, 1 year, 2 years, and 6 years following divorce using a variety of observational, interview, and rating scale measures of the children's behavior at home and at school. It was found that in the first year the children from divorced families showed more behavioral problems. They were more aggressive, demanding, and lacking in self-control than their counterparts in nondivorced families. By 2 years following divorce, the girls had adapted to their situation and had a positive relationship with their mother, providing she had not remarried. The boys, although slightly improved, still showed problems in adjustment and difficulties in their relationship with their mother. In comparison with boys in nondivorced families, they were more antisocial, aggressive, and noncompliant both at home and at school and showed difficulties in friendships and social adjustment.

By the time of the 6-year follow-up, some of the mothers had remarried, so that the children were living with their mother and a stepfather. The mothers who had not remarried continued to have good relationships with their daughters and difficult relationships with their sons. This pattern was reflected in the children's behavior. The daughters were functioning well, whereas the boys were more likely than boys in nondivorced families to be noncompliant, impulsive, and aggressive. In families where the mother had remarried, however, the situation was rather different. After the early stages of remarriage, the boys had fewer problems than boys in nonremarried families. If the stepfather was supportive, boys developed a good relationship with him.

The girls, on the other hand, had more difficulties with family relations and adjustment than girls whose mothers had not remarried, and continued to reject their stepfather however hard he tried to develop a good relationship (Vuchinich, Hetherington, Vuchinich, & Clingempeel, 1991).

Wallerstein and her colleagues (Wallerstein & Blackeslee, 1989; Wallerstein, Corbin, & Lewis, 1988; Wallerstein & Kelly, 1980) also carried out a longitudinal study of the effects of divorce on children from the time of the parents' separation until 10 years later. A number of methodological problems with this research have led to an overestimation of the incidence and severity of psychological disturbance in children whose parents divorce (Elliot, Ochiltree, Richards, Sinclair, & Tasker, 1990). The sample was obtained by offering counseling in return for participation, which, in spite of the authors' attempts to exclude children with psychological disturbance, is likely to produce a group of children who were experiencing more difficulties than children in other divorcing families. Moreover, a comparison group of nondivorced families was not included, so that it is not possible to be sure that any problems experienced by the children resulted directly from the divorce. At 5 years following divorce, it was reported that 37% of the children were moderately to severely depressed. At the 10-year follow-up, the problems were found to persist in the form of underachievement, worry, loneliness, anger, and difficulty in forming relationships. Although boys and girls showed similar levels of psychological distress 5 years after the separation, 10 years later girls showed greater evidence of emotional difficulties than did boys.

Although it is generally believed that the effects of divorce are more severe for boys than for girls, not all of the evidence points to that conclusion. The effects of marital dissolution on children's well-being have been examined using a large, nationally representative sample (Allison & Furstenberg, 1989). Reports were obtained from parents, teachers, and the children themselves. In line with other studies, it was shown that marital dissolution had pervasive and long-lasting negative effects on problem behavior, psychological distress, and academic performance. There was no evidence, however, that boys were more at risk than girls. A review of the divorce studies has attempted to resolve the issue of whether boys react more negatively than girls (Zaslow, 1988, 1989). It appears that boys do not respond more negatively under all circumstances. Instead, more negative reactions in sons are likely if they are living with a mother who does not remarry. Girls fare worse than boys in families with a stepfather or where the father has custody.

When intense marital conflict continues after divorce, it can have a more harmful effect than when it occurs in intact families (Hetherington, 1988, 1989). Wallerstein and Kelly (1980) also found that the children with difficulties were those whose parents remained in conflict after divorce, and concluded that whether or not children's problems diminish is a function of whether or not divorce improves parental relationships. The quality of the child's relationship with parents is also an important determinant of the child's psychological adjustment. Children who have good postdivorce relationships with their parents are less likely to suffer negative effects following divorce (Hess & Camara, 1979; Hetherington, 1988).

Overall, in the long run it is not a good idea for parents to remain in a conflicted marriage for the sake of the children, as marital discord is associated with more adverse outcomes for children than divorce, although it is worse for children when parents divorce and remain hostile than when they stay together and remain hostile. A good relationship between the child and the parents can go some way toward protecting the child from the psychological problems that can result from the experience of parental divorce.

Homosexual families

In the 1970s there was a rise in the number of lesbian mothers who applied for custody of their children at the time of divorce. These mothers had married and had children before establishing a lesbian relationship. In the majority of cases, custody was refused on the grounds that the children would show atypical gender development as a result of their exposure to unusual models of sexual behavior, and that they would develop behavioral or emotional problems due to teasing, ostracism, or social disapproval by peers. More recently, attention has been drawn to the controversial issue of whether lesbian mothers should be allowed to foster or adopt children. Following the court cases a number of empirical investigations of the consequences for children of being raised by a lesbian mother were carried out. Little is known about children raised by gay fathers. When a gay father divorces, courts almost always award custody to mothers in preference to fathers.

Studies of lesbian families have compared children in lesbian households with children in households headed by a single heterosexual mother. These two types of family are alike in that the children are being raised by women without the presence of a father, but they differ in the sexual orientation of the mother. Thus any differences that exist between children in lesbian and heterosexual families may be attributed to the mother's sexual orientation.

This research has examined the two areas of child development that have been the focus of concern in custody cases – gender development and psychiatric disorder (Falk, 1989; Golombok, Spencer, & Rutter, 1983; Hoeffer, 1981; Kirkpatrick, Smith, & Roy, 1981; Mandel, Hotvedt, Green, & Smith, 1986; Patterson, 1992). The gender identity of children in lesbian families is in line with their physical sex, and no differences in sex role behavior have been found between the two types of family for either boys or girls. In fact, an examination of preferred toys, games, activities, and friendships found the children in both types to be quite traditional. This was in spite of the lesbian mothers' preference for a more equal mixture of masculine and feminine toys for their sons and daughters than the heterosexual mothers, who preferred more sex-typed ones. Assessments of psychiatric state showed no differences between children with lesbian and heterosexual mothers, and the incidence of disorder was similar to that found for children in heterosexual two-parent families. In addition, there were no differences in the quality of the children's friendships between children raised in the two types of household.

These investigations have a number of limitations. First, a

large majority of the children spent the early part of their life in a heterosexual family, so that the research findings do not allow any conclusions to be drawn about the development of children raised in lesbian families from birth. Second, the studies are of school-age children. One of the main issues in custody cases involving a lesbian mother is whether the children will themselves become homosexual. As negative attitudes toward lesbian women and gay men still prevail in our society, this is generally considered by the courts to be an undesirable outcome. In fact, adults raised as children in lesbian families are no more likely than adults raised in heterosexual families to identify as lesbian women or gay men (Tasker & Golombok, 1992). It is also worth remembering that almost all lesbian and gay adults grew up in heterosexual families. The third difficulty with existing studies is that all of the mothers were volunteers, so it remains possible that they are not representative of lesbian mothers in general. However, similarities among the findings of studies, which have been carried out in diverse geographic locations and have included families from a wide variety of backgrounds, give some confidence in the generalizability of the conclusions. Taken together, the studies give no evidence to support the claim that children raised by lesbian mothers will show gender identity confusion, cross-gender behavior, a homosexual orientation, or psychological difficulties as a direct result of their upbringing.

New reproductive technologies

In recent years a growing number of families have been created as a result of the new reproductive technologies. The most high tech of these is in vitro fertilization (IVF) in which the woman's egg is removed from her ovary, fertilized in the laboratory with male sperm, and the resulting embryo returned to her womb. The first IVF child, Louise Brown, was born in England in 1978 (Edwards & Steptoe, 1980), and IVF has now become an accepted treatment for infertility in many countries. Donor insemination (DI) is used when the man is infertile, and involves insemination of the mother with sperm collected from a donor. This procedure is usually performed at a medical clinic using an anonymous donor who has contributed to a sperm bank. Egg donation refers to a woman donating an egg that is then fertilized by the father's sperm. The embryo is then placed in the mother's womb to produce a pregnancy. Although egg donation is similar to sperm donation insofar as both procedures involve the donation of gametes, they differ in two important ways. First, an egg donor is more likely to be a friend or relative of the recipient than a sperm donor. Second, the donation of eggs, unlike the donation of sperm, is an intrusive procedure. In some cases both the egg and sperm may be donated (embryo donation). When a woman hosts a pregnancy for another woman, this is called surrogacy. Usually the host mother is inseminated with the father's sperm, but sometimes an embryo is implanted in the host mother's womb.

The new reproductive technologies are not, in fact, all new, and some do not even involve technology. Artificial insemination was first conducted more than 200 years ago, and has been widely available as a treatment for male infertility for several decades. It is not a highly technical procedure and can be successfully carried out without the assistance of the medical profession. Similarly, surrogacy does not involve sophisticated techniques. The surrogate mother usually undergoes the normal procedure for donor insemination using the father's sperm. What the new reproductive technologies have in common is that they separate sex from procreation, they involve some kind of external intervention in order for a woman to have a child, and they challenge traditional beliefs about what it means to be a family.

Families may be created by the new reproductive technologies in a number of ways, and the social and genetic parents are not always the same:

The child may be genetically related to both parents, as with IVF using the father's sperm and the mother's egg.

The child may be genetically related to the mother but not the father, as with donor insemination or IVF using donor sperm.

The child may be genetically related to the father but not the mother, as with IVF using egg donation.

The child may not be genetically related to either parent, as with IVF using embryo donation.

This latter group of children are similar to adopted children in that they are genetically unrelated to both parents, but differ in that the parents experience a pregnancy and develop a relationship with the child from birth. In the case of surrogacy the child may be genetically related to neither, one, or both parents, depending on the use of a donated egg and/or sperm. As Einwohner (1989) points out, it is possible for a child to have five parents – the egg donor, the sperm donor, the birth mother, and the two people the child knows as mother and father. In addition, lesbian women have become mothers through donor insemination, and gay men have become fathers through surrogacy. As many lesbian and gay parents live with a partner, these children often have two parents of the same gender. All of these new types of family raise important questions about the psychological consequences for children (Golombok, Bhanji, Rutherford, & Winston, 1990).

A major issue has been the effect on children of originating from donated gametes and thus being genetically unrelated to one or both social parents. It has been suggested that a missing genetic link between the child and one or both parents may pose a threat to the relationship between the parents and the child. This has led to much debate about whether or not children conceived by gametes should be told of their origins and, if so, whether or not the actual identity of the donor should also be disclosed (Daniels & Taylor, 1993; Haimes, 1990). Doctors have generally advised couples to keep the child's origins secret. This serves to protect the father from having to openly admit his infertility. It is thought by some that, if told, the child will become confused about his or her identity and may feel that a parent who is not genetically linked is not a real parent. Those who believe that the child should be told argue that it is the secrecy that may undermine family relationships. Clamar (1989) argues that secrecy about genetic origins has a powerful and destructive effect on the life of every family member, separating those who know (the parents) from those who do not (the child). A child conceived by gamete donation may thus feel deceived by the parents.

Because adopted children are genetically unrelated to their parents, their experiences are relevant to the question of whether children born as a result of gamete donation should be told about their origins. Sants (1964) introduced the term *genealogical bewilderment* to refer to the confusion about their identity that has been described by some adult adoptees. It is now generally believed that adopted children wish to know about their genetic parents, and that openness improves rather than threatens family relationships. A strongly negative response to information about their background is more likely to come from children who accidentally discover that they are adopted than from children who grow up knowing the truth. Secrecy about gamete donation is now being challenged on the grounds that adoptive children benefit from information about their biological parents, and in some countries new laws allow information about the donor to be made available to the child.

But there remains a discrepancy in attitudes between professionals and the parents themselves on the issue of secrecy. Although there are generally accepted stories in our society to explain adoption, none exists for in vitro fertilization or gamete donation, making it difficult for parents to tell their children about the way in which they were conceived. The parents often fear that the children will respond negatively to being told about their origins and that the child will reject them. In a recent study in the United Kingdom it was found that only 32% of egg recipients and 12% of sperm recipients were in favor of the child being told how he or she had been conceived (Bolton, Golombok, Cook, Bish, & Rust, 1991). A higher percentage of egg recipients were in favor of telling because some of the egg donors were friends or relatives of the parents. In New Zealand, only 22% of couples receiving donor insemination thought that the children should be told (Daniels, 1988). It remains for future research to inform us about the consequences of telling or not telling children about their method of conception. Snowden (1990), reporting on interviews with a small number of young adults who had been told that they had been conceived by donor insemination, found no evidence to suggest that they had been traumatized by this information, were unsure of their identity, or that the father–child relationship had been damaged. It is also important to determine the psychological effects for the child of being given identifying information about the donor, or growing up in contact with a relative or friend of the family who has acted as a surrogate mother or donated a gamete.

An issue that has caused a great deal of controversy is whether single heterosexual or lesbian women should be allowed access to the new reproductive technologies, particularly donor insemination. Opponents believe that the child would be at risk for psychological problems. For single heterosexual mothers it has been argued that the lack of a father together with the use of an anonymous donor is likely to lead to difficulties for the child. Concern has also been expressed about the suitability of a woman who is not involved in an intimate relationship with a man to be a mother. No studies of the development of children conceived by donor insemination to single heterosexual mothers have yet been carried out. A small, uncontrolled investigation of 10 single women requesting donor insemination (cited by Fidell & Marik, 1989) found that an important reason for opting for this procedure was to avoid using a man to produce a child without his knowledge or consent. Donor insemination also meant that they did not have to share the rights and responsibilities for the child with a man to whom they were not emotionally committed. Although rare, women who have never experienced a sexual relationship with either sex have also been given donor insemination (Jennings, 1991). These so-called virgin births have given rise to a great deal of public outcry.

Lesbian women have been refused access to donor insemination on the grounds that they would not provide an appropriate family environment for the child. Particular concerns have been that the child would have two mothers, the child would not be genetically related to one mother, and the donor would be unknown to both mothers. An investigation of lesbian families created as a result of donor insemination has shown that lesbian mothers are less secretive about the child's genetic origins than heterosexual parents of children conceived by donor insemination, and are less likely to perceive the donor as a threat to family relations (Brewaeys, Ponjaert-Kristoffersen, Van Steirteghem, & Devroey, 1993).

The same researchers are currently carrying out a longitudinal investigation of the development of children conceived by donor insemination to lesbian mothers. This is of interest for a number of reasons. First, the children are being raised in a lesbian family from birth. In existing studies of lesbian families most of the children spent their early life in a heterosexual family, so that the consequences of growing up in a lesbian family from the outset are not known. Second, the study involves a new type of lesbian family where the couple planned to have children together. In previous studies the children were born before the couple met. Third, the mothers are open about the way in which the child was conceived. This research will help answer many questions about children growing up in new kinds of families.

Selection for parenthood

Although the right to parenthood is generally upheld in our society, in cases where intervention is necessary for a man or woman to have a child, some form of selection usually occurs. The most widespread use of selection for parenthood has been for adoption. Typically, it is young, two-parent, heterosexual, married couples with a wife who is prepared to give up work to look after the child who are most likely to be allowed to adopt, particularly if they wish to adopt a healthy baby rather than an older child with physical or emotional problems. More recently, criteria for access to the new reproductive technologies have been under debate. The extent to which families created by the new reproductive technologies are accepted by society depends on how much they resemble the traditional family; IVF with the social father's sperm and the social mother's egg is more acceptable than IVF with gamete donation, and donor insemination involving a single parent or surrogacy where the social mother does not give birth to the child are the least acceptable of all (Haimes, 1990). As a result, surrogacy and the provision of new reproductive technologies to single heterosexual or lesbian women are not widely practiced.

It has been suggested that everyone requesting access to the new reproductive technologies should be screened for their suitability as parents. Recommendations have been made that clinics should assess psychological functioning, social functioning, the marital relationship, and social support, as well as insight into the ramifications of donor insemination, before accepting a couple for treatment (Humphrey, Humphrey, & Ainsworth-Smith, 1991; Stewart, Daniels, & Boulnois, 1982). Although the traditional family is no longer the norm, it seems likely that screening, if instituted, would favor this type of family. But the psychological research discussed in this chapter suggests that the development of children in families created as a result of the new reproductive technologies is likely to depend not so much on family structure as on the quality of family relationships. In considering the issue of selection for parenthood for those requesting some form of assisted reproduction, we should ask ourselves how many *natural* parents would qualify.

A further consequence of the reproductive technologies is that gender selection is now a possibility. The sex of the fetus can be determined using amniocentesis, and the pregnancy terminated if the fetus is not of the desired sex. Or male and female sperm can be separated, and artificial insemination used to select the sex of the child. Given the preference for boys rather than girls in most cultures of the world, the widespread use of sex-choice technology would result in fewer women than men (Ullman & Fidell, 1989). The outcome of this fundamental change to society is difficult to imagine. It seems likely, however, that the experiences of boys and girls as they grow up would be even more different from each other than they already are today.

Summary

The demise of the nuclear family has brought with it a variety of alternative family forms. It is widely believed that the greater the deviation from the traditional family, the more negative the consequences for children. But whether the mother is employed, the father is absent, or two mothers are present does not, by itself, determine the outcomes, good or bad, for child development. It is the factors that accompany these diverse family forms, such as the quality of parent–child relationships and of alternative child care, that play a crucial role. Apart from less stereotyped beliefs about gender roles among children in nontraditional families, family structure has little impact on gender development.

10

School

In 1912, the U.S. government mandated compulsory education, giving females and males equal access to publicly funded schooling. Yet to this day, males attain higher levels of education than do females, despite the fact that there are no gender differences in general measures of intelligence. Moreover, males are more likely to be admitted to colleges and universities than are females with the same qualifications, and males are overwhelmingly more likely to enroll in mathematics and science courses and to pursue careers in those areas than are females (see Eccles, 1987, and Stockard, 1980, for reviews). In this chapter we discuss why these inequities in education exist. We begin by examining teacher–student interaction in the classroom. We then turn to a discussion of gender differences in particular academic areas. Specifically, we examine gender differences in mathematics and science and in language arts; gender differences both in ability and expectations for success and failure are assessed. We end the chapter with a discussion of the values females and males place on academic achievement, and the relationship between academic achievement and self-esteem.

Teacher–student interaction

As we saw in Chapter 7, on play and friendships, boys are more aggressive and rambunctious than girls. Although this may be appropriate behavior on the playground, it is not appropriate in the classroom. And, indeed, boys pose a greater behavior problem in the classroom than do girls (Stake & Katz, 1982; Stockard, 1980). Boys are referred for serious behavioral problems in the classroom up to 10 times more often than are girls. Even within the range of normal behaviors, teachers reprimand boys significantly more often than girls. Interestingly, though, teachers also praise boys more often than girls. Overall, boys are simply receiving more teacher attention than are girls.

Gender differences in teacher–student interaction begin extremely early. In observations of a preschool classroom, Cherry (1975) found that teachers engaged in more verbal interaction with 4-year-old boys than with 4-year-old girls. This is a particularly surprising finding because girls have a history of engaging in more social interaction with their parents beginning as early as infancy (Caldera, Huston, & O'Brien, 1989; Goldberg & Lewis, 1969). Perhaps girls have a difficult time bidding for an adult's attention when in a large group. This difficulty may be related to gender differences in verbal interaction discussed in Chapter 7, on play. In mixed-gender groups, girls have some trouble gaining the floor, but boys are able to do so, and this ability serves them well in a classroom environment.

Boys continue to receive more teacher attention throughout the grade school years. During the early elementary school years, boys receive more praise and more criticism than girls, and this is true for both explicit verbal feedback and more implicit non-verbal feedback, such as nods and eye gaze (Simpson & Erikson, 1983). By the time children reach fourth or fifth grade, the pattern changes somewhat. Of course, we need to consider how the structure of classroom interactions changes across this developmental period. During the early school years teachers spend a good deal of time on behavioral management, but by the end of elementary school, children have been socialized into the classroom environment, and the majority of teachers' feedback focuses on academic work (Brophy & Everston, 1978; Eccles, Midgeley, & Adler, 1984). By this time, there are few differences in overall amount of praise given to boys and girls (Dweck, Davidson, Nelson, & Enna, 1978; Stake & Katz, 1982), but there is some suggestion that teachers may still reprimand boys more than girls (Stake & Katz, 1982).

Although gender differences in overall amount of praise and criticism seem to diminish over the elementary school years, a closer look at exactly what boys and girls are being praised and criticized for reveals some intriguing differences. Boys are praised for their knowledge and for giving the right answer; girls are praised for obedience and compliance. In contrast, boys are reprimanded for misbehavior, but girls are reprimanded for not giving the right answer (Dweck et al., 1978; Stockard, 1980). Some examples from an actual first grade classroom help illustrate (from Good & Brophy, 1987, pp. 596–597). During this lesson, the children are learning about the four seasons:

Teacher: Carol, do you remember how many seasons we have in a year?

Carol: Three

Teacher: No, we wrote more stories than just three – think for a minute

Carol: Four

Teacher: All right, now can you name them for me?
Carol: Fall, winter, summer . . .
Teacher: Didn't you write four stories?
Carol: I don't remember
Teacher: (Forcefully and with some irritation) You may have
            to go back and write them again. Who knows the
            fourth season? . . . John you answer.
John: Fall, winter, spring and summer
Teacher: Good thinking

Notice in this example that the teacher reprimands Carol for
not knowing the answer, and then turns to John to provide the
correct answer. And when he does, the teacher explicitly praises
him. Later in the lesson, the teacher talks about weather and
holidays associated with each of the seasons:

Teacher: What is another word for the fall season? Lynne?
Lynne: Halloween?
Teacher: I didn't ask you to give me a holiday, a word
Lynne: I can't think of it
Teacher: I'm going to write it on the board and see if Bobby
            can pronounce it for me.
Bobby: (no response)
Teacher: This is a big word Bobby. I'll help you.

Here, we see that Lynne is criticized for giving the wrong
answer, but then, when the teacher writes it on the board, she
doesn't allow Lynne to read the word. The teacher turns to
Bobby to provide the correct response. When Bobby doesn't
respond, rather than asking another child, as the teacher did with
Lynne, the teacher encourages and helps Bobby to give the right
answer. The implicit message is that Lynne didn't know the
answer but Bobby did.

By the time children are in fourth and fifth grade, 90% of
positive feedback given to boys is for their intellectual performance, but less than 80% of praise given to girls is for intellectual
performance. In contrast, less than one-third of the negative
feedback given to boys is based on intellectual performance, but

more than two-thirds of the negative feedback given to girls is for poor performance (Dweck et al., 1978). From this pattern of praise and criticism, boys may be learning that they are smart, even if not very well behaved. Girls, on the other hand, are learning that they may not be very smart, but that they can get rewards by being "good."

Perhaps surprisingly, given these patterns of interaction, girls receive higher grades throughout formal schooling than do boys, and girls like school more than boys do. Yet, beginning in early adolescence, boys begin to score higher than girls on standardized achievement tests, especially in math and science (see Eccles, 1987, for a review). And keep in mind that these gender differences in grades and achievement tests emerge even though there are no overall gender differences in intelligence. So an intriguing puzzle emerges: Why do boys begin to outperform girls academically beginning in adolescence? Does this pattern mean that boys have greater ability than girls in particular academic disciplines? If not, what other factors can explain this discrepancy?

Gender differences in academic ability

Following from cultural stereotypes about gender, boys are believed to excel in math and science, and girls in language arts, such as reading and writing (e.g., Eccles, 1987; Hyde & Linn, 1988). Several issues need to be addressed in evaluating the truth of these beliefs. First, are there, in fact, gender differences in ability in these areas? Second, how are these beliefs communicated to students, and how do students come to evaluate their own academic performance? Finally, what are the long-term implications of these gender differences for academic achievement and career choice?

Gender differences in language ability

A great deal of research has demonstrated that females outperform males in language arts. Females read earlier than do males, have fewer reading problems, and respond more easily to reading instruction (see Allred, 1990, and Hyde & Linn, 1988, for reviews). Girls also spell more words correctly and recognize more correctly spelled words than do boys during the grade school years (Allred, 1990). Further, these differences seem to persist throughout schooling; females continue to outperform males on measures of vocabulary and reading comprehension through high school (Hogrebe, Nest, & Newman, 1985).

In a comprehensive analysis of 165 studies examining gender differences in verbal abilities, Hyde and Linn (1988) concluded that females do show a small advantage over males. However, this difference is so small as to be unimportant. Essentially, if we think about all the factors that might contribute to an individual's verbal abilities, gender plays a small role in allowing us to predict how an individual will perform. Thus, although there is a statistically significant effect of gender on verbal abilities, when it comes to predicting behavior in the real world, Hyde and Linn argue, gender will not be an important factor.

Gender differences in math and spatial ability

The question of gender differences in mathematical ability has probably generated more research and more controversy than almost any other topic concerning gender. In 1980, Benbow and Stanley published an article demonstrating that males outperform females on standardized tests of mathematical ability. Notably, the gender difference was only evident among the highest achieving boys and girls. For children of moderate and low ability, there were no reliable gender differences. Still, Benbow and Stanley proposed a biological explanation of the obtained gender difference. Essentially, they argued that there was a "math gene" that was linked to sex. As you might imagine, this conclusion generated an explosion of research and debate on the meaning of males' superior mathematical ability. Over the ensuing years, researchers have argued over various explanations for the gender gap in math (see especially Eccles, 1987, Halpern, 1992, and Walkerdine, 1989, for reviews). Are gender differences in mathematical ability biologically based, or do they arise from differences in socialization experiences? While the debate has raged, few researchers have questioned whether or not a gender gap in mathematical ability actually exists.

Recently, Hyde, Fennema, and Lamon (1990) analyzed more than 100 research studies examining gender differences in mathematical ability. Overall, males do outperform females, but the gender difference is extremely small. Moreover, when one considers these effects in terms of the age of the participants in the studies, females show a slight superiority over males until early adolescence, when males begin to outperform females, especially in mathematical problem solving. There are no gender differences in computational skills. Hyde et al. conclude that, like gender differences in verbal abilities, gender differences in mathematical abilities are so small as to be unimportant in understanding individual variation in math achievement. Perhaps most important, the gender differences in math performance have been decreasing over the past decade. Therefore, any gender differences that do exist cannot be fully accounted for by biological differences, as this is too short a period of time for biology to change. Rather, gender differences in math achievement must be at least partly the result of cultural beliefs and differential socialization of females and males.

Still, we cannot conclude that biology plays no role at all. In particular, gender differences in spatial ability do seem to have some biological influences, and spatial ability is an important component of mathematical skills. Spatial abilities include such skills as spatial orientation and mental rotation. An example of a spatial orientation task is the embedded figures test, in which the subject is required to find a geometric shape embedded in a more complex design. In mental rotation tasks subjects must imagine how a shape would change in orientation as it moves through space. Spatial orientation and mental rotation skills facilitate comprehension of abstract mathematical concepts used in geometry, trigonometry, and calculus.

There are clear and reliable differences in spatial performance favoring males (see Baennenger & Newcombe, 1989, and Halpern, 1992, for reviews). Moreover, spatial ability seems to be related to measures of physical masculinity, such as pubertal maturation (Baennenger & Newcombe, 1989). In fact, there is some evidence that a minimum amount of testosterone is necessary at puberty for the development of good spatial skills (Halpern, 1992). So differences in spatial ability may be at least partly biologically determined. Yet Baennenger and Newcombe found that the magnitude of the gender difference has been diminishing over time, as did Hyde and Linn for math abilities. Again, biology alone cannot explain the gender difference. We need also to look at cultural and social factors.

Baennenger and Newcombe (1989) point to the fact that males grow up in more spatially complex environments than do girls. Boys play outdoors, and are given more freedom to explore large environmental spaces. Boys also play with more spatially complex toys, such as building and construction toys. And, indeed, studies have shown that these kinds of spatial experiences are related to later spatial ability. Male superiority on spatial tasks is most likely due to a complex interaction between small biological differences and larger gender differences in socialization experiences. But it is important to keep in mind that though these gender differences exist, they are extremely small and account for very little of the actual variation among individuals.

Gender differences in computer literacy

Related to mathematical education is computer education. Although computers are beginning to be integrated in virtually all aspects of the curriculum, they are still heavily associated with math and technological training. Beginning in elementary school, boys interact with computers more than do girls (Hawkins, 1985); computer games are aimed at males, and overwhelmingly more boys than girls attend computer camps. Twice as many males as females enroll in computer courses in high school, and by college, three times as many males select computer courses than do females (Stasz, Shavelson, & Stasz, 1985). Moreover, even when females do interact with computers, they do so for different reasons than do males. Boys use computers for programming and spatial games; females use computers for writing.

Moreover, boys are significantly more likely to use computers during free time than are girls (Hawkins, 1985). Although the research indicates clear gender differences in interest in and use of computers, little research has addressed possible differences in computer-related abilities.

Gender differences in science

Females enroll in substantially fewer science courses than do males, beginning in high school and continuing through college (see Steinkamp & Maehr, 1983, for a discussion). And in this academic domain, in contrast to language arts and mathematics, there are substantial gender differences in ability. In an analysis of 42 studies examining gender differences in science ability, Becker (1989) found that males significantly outperform females. Moreover, this gender difference occurs at all grades examined, and there has been no decrease in the gender difference over time. Gender differences are largest for physics and biology, with only small or insignificant gender differences for geology, chemistry, and earth sciences. Although this is the one academic domain in which the strongest gender effects have been found, no one has posited a biological explanation for this difference. Rather, most researchers agree that the gender gap in science is attributable to differences in socialization.

Summary of gender differences in academic ability

Although there is widespread belief that males are superior in mathematical abilities and females are superior in verbal abilities, in fact the research has shown very small differences in these areas. Careful statistical analyses across hundreds of studies have demonstrated that gender differences in ability in math and language are so small as to be virtually nonexistent for all practical purposes. Only in the domain of science have substantial gender differences been demonstrated. Yet, even though males and females do not differ greatly in their actual academic abilities, it is certainly the case that females enroll in significantly fewer advanced mathematics and science courses especially at the college level, that females report liking mathematics and science less than males do, and females believe mathematics and science to be less useful in their lives than do males (Eccles, 1987; Raymond & Benbow, 1989; Steinkamp & Maehr, 1983).

Mathematics has been described as a "critical filter" for later occupational choices (Sells, 1973). If females do not take advanced math courses, they will not be able to pursue many of the higher paying, prestigious occupations in medicine, engineering, and computer science. Thus it becomes critically important to understand why females are not selecting math and science in their educational choices. If it is not because they are less able to perform in these areas than are males, then we need to look to other factors. In particular, we need to consider how cultural values about math and science are communicated to students by teachers and parents and how students themselves come to perceive their own abilities in these areas.

Before discussing the relevant research, it is important to point out that this is an area in which gender stereotypes have played an influential role in defining the important research questions. Although a great deal of research has been done on gender differences in verbal abilities, very little has been aimed at understanding why males do not pursue education in the language arts. In contrast, there is a vast literature on why females do not pursue education in math and science. This discrepancy is partly due to our shared cultural belief that math and science are more important than verbal skills. Perhaps this is because, in reality, math and science open the way for more prestigious occupations. But it might also be the case that math and science are more highly valued because they are seen as masculine. In any case, in the remainder of this chapter, we consider various explanations of why females do not choose math and science courses to the same extent that males do.

Attitudes and attributions concerning academic performance

Eccles (1983, 1987; Eccles & Wigfield, 1985) has presented a comprehensive model of why females do not pursue mathematics and science either in education or occupational selection. She argues that we need to consider several critical factors leading to these choices. First, we need to consider how individuals perceive the options open to them; in making a choice, individuals tend to consider only a subset of their actual options. How do females and males perceive their educational and career options? Second, individuals' choices will be mediated by their expectations of success or failure. If individuals believe they will fail at a given task, they will be less likely to opt for that task. Conversely, individuals will be more likely to choose tasks in which they believe they will be successful. Do females and males differ on which tasks they believe they will succeed or fail at? Related to this, we need to consider the subjective value of the task. How does the task relate to the individual's self-concept? For example, if one perceives oneself as nurturant, then tasks that confirm that self-concept will be more valuable than tasks that are unrelated to nurturance. Fourth, we need to examine the perceived cost of the task. If individuals believe that they are likely to fail at a task and that the failure experience will be devastating, they are even more unlikely to engage in that task than if failure is perceived as unimportant. Finally, all of these factors need to be considered in light of different socialization experiences for females and males. Selecting options, one's expectations of success or failure, the subjective value of the task, and the perceived cost of the task are all communicated to individual students by teachers and parents.

Expectations of teachers and parents

We have seen how teachers interact differently with girls and boys in the classroom, and some of these differences seem to have implications for students' developing understanding of their academic abilities. But are teachers communicating messages specifically about math and science?

First and foremost, although the overall majority of public school teachers are female, more males than females teach math and science (Stockard, 1980). This alone might convey the message that math and science is a male domain. However, there is mixed evidence on whether math teachers differentially interact with students based on gender. Some research has found no differences in the amount of praise or criticism teachers direct to boys and girls in junior high and high school math classes (Heller & Parsons, 1981), whereas other research has found that junior high and high school boys receive more praise and more criticism in math classes than do girls (Eccles-Parsons, Kaczala, & Meece, 1982). Further, the more praise and criticism boys receive about their math performance, the more sure they are about their mathematical abilities; but there are no relations between praise and criticism in the classroom and girls' beliefs about their math abilities (Eccles-Parsons, Kaczala, & Meece, 1982). Across studies, boys predict that they will receive higher grades in their current math class than do girls, and boys also predict that they will receive higher grades in future math classes than do girls (Eccles, 1983; Eccles-Parsons, Meece, Adler, & Kaczala, 1982; Keller & Parsons, 1981). Overall, then, although there may or may not be gender differences in how math teachers treat boys and girls, it is certainly the case that girls are not responsive to positive feedback about their math abilities in the same way as boys are, and girls do not expect to do as well in math courses as boys do.

Male students receive more praise and more criticism than female students do in both physics and chemistry classrooms (Jones & Wheatley, 1990), a pattern similar to findings in general elementary classrooms. Male students also call out more answers than do female students, and teachers accept answers called out by male students more often than answers called out by female students. So females receive less teacher attention in science classrooms than males, and their responses are not as well received.

In sum, teachers may be communicating gender-typed messages about science, but the evidence from math classrooms is mixed. If math teachers are not communicating gender-typed expectations, why do we see such clear gender differences in students' expectations? A great deal of research demonstrates that parents may facilitate gender-typed notions about math in their children. As early as kindergarten, mothers expect their daughters to do well in reading and their sons to do well in math (Lummis &

Stevenson, 1990), and parents continue to expect their sons to do well in math through elementary school (Entwistle & Baker, 1983). How might these kinds of parental expectations be communicated to children and come to affect their actual performance in math?

Yee and Eccles (1988) asked mothers and fathers of low, average, and high ability junior high school math students to fill out questionnaires regarding their child's math performance. There were no overall gender differences in math ability in this sample of children. Yet mothers of girls thought that their children were less talented in math than did mothers of boys. Further, mothers believed that their daughters had to work harder than their sons to do well in math. Mothers rated effort as the most important factor in their daughter's math success, but they rated talent as most important for their sons. Fathers showed the same pattern as mothers. Additionally, fathers believed that their sons were not doing as well as they could be in math (i.e., not living up to their potential), but they believed their daughters were doing quite well.

Clearly, parents have very different expectations for their daughters and their sons, and when their children succeed in math, parents attribute this success to very different causes. In this way, males and females may be learning very different things about their math ability from their parents, even when they are performing at comparable levels. Parents who believe that their children are not that able in math and have to work hard to do well have children who have low math self-esteem and low confidence in their mathematical abilities (Eccles-Parsons, Adler, & Kaczala, 1982). It is not simply a question of whether one succeeds or fails on a given task. The reasons or attributions for that success or failure also matter. Girls are learning that their success is due to effort and hard work, whereas boys are learning that their success is due to talent and ability.

Attributions and expectations of success and failure

The attributions we make about the causes of our successes and failures are critical in determining our understanding and evaluation of these outcomes (see Weiner, 1985, for an overview of attribution theory, and Wittig, 1985, for a review of attribution theory as related to gender). Attributions can be made to either internal or external factors. Internal factors include ability and effort; external factors include luck and task ease or difficulty. Let us consider internal factors first.

If we attribute success to ability, then we will have a positive self-concept and expect to do well on future tasks of the same type. On the other hand, if we attribute success to effort, then future success depends heavily on how much effort we will be willing or able to expend. Failure attributed to lack of ability is most debilitating; if we do not have the ability to perform this task, then certainly we can expect to fail in the future. Failure attributed to lack of effort is mixed; if we are willing or able to expend more effort, we might succeed on future tasks. Notice, however, that there is a trade-off: The less ability one has in a particular domain, the more effort one must exert in order to succeed. Thus attributions to greater effort often carry information about lesser ability level as well.

If we attribute success to luck or task ease, external factors, we may or may not succeed in the future, depending on whether these factors occur again. But it is not under our control. Failure attributed to lack of luck or task difficulty helps preserve the self-concept ("It is not my fault I failed"), but also provides no predictability for the future. External factors are not under the individual's control, and attributions to these factors carry no predictive information about future performance. How might these patterns of attributions for success and failure influence gender differences in academic performance, and how are they related to expectations and beliefs about math performance?

Initial research on attributional patterns indicated that when females succeed on a task, success is attributed to external factors, such as luck and task ease. In contrast, males' success is attributed to ability. Failure is also attributed to external factors for females, but to lack of effort for males (e.g., Deaux & Emswiller, 1974; Feather, 1969). Moreover, these patterns are the same whether subjects are asked to judge another person's performance or their own (Sweeney, Moreland, & Gruber, 1982; Wittig,

1985). Females are perceived as having little control over their performance, whereas males are perceived as having a great deal of control.

But, as Deaux and Emswiller (1974) argue, these patterns might be a function of the kind of task that the individual is performing. Deaux and Emswiller asked subjects to rate the performance of males and females under two conditions. In one condition subjects were led to believe that the task being performed was "feminine," and in the other condition, they were led to believe it was "masculine." The individual performing the task was actually a confederate of the experimenter, and performance was equal in all conditions. Yet, when subjects rated successful performance in the masculine task condition, males were rated as more able, and females were rated as lucky. For the feminine task, there were no differences; all performances were rated as due to ability. So when females succeed on feminine tasks, their success is perceived as due to internal ability factors, but when they succeed on masculine tasks, it is due to luck. Males' success is attributed to ability regardless of the type of task being performed.

This differential pattern is extremely interesting because mathematics is very strongly stereotyped as masculine (e.g., Eccles, 1987; Hyde, Fennema, Ryan, Frost, & Hopp, 1990). As we already discussed, parents attribute sons' math performance to talent or ability, but daughters' math performance is attributed to hard work. Although effort is an internal attribution, it is a very different kind of internal attribution than ability; one needs to exert more effort in those areas in which one has less ability. How do students perceive their own successes and failures?

In general, females attribute success in mathematics to luck more than do males, and males attribute success in mathematics to ability more than do females, and this pattern seems to begin as early as first grade. Elementary school boys perceive themselves as having higher ability in math than girls, but girls believe they are more capable than boys in music and social skills (Wigfield et al., 1989). Moreover, elementary school girls express more anxiety about math than do boys, but they also express more anxiety than do boys about being socially accepted.

Differential beliefs about math performance continue throughout high school. High school girls attribute both success and failure in math to effort or lack thereof; boys attribute success in math to ability, and failure to lack of effort (Eccles-Parsons, Meese, Adler, & Kaczala, 1982; Ryckman & Peckham, 1987). In contrast, for language arts, both boys and girls attributed success to ability and failure to lack of effort, so it is not the case that females simply have lower academic self-esteem overall than males (Ryckman & Peckham, 1987). Boys also express more interest in math than girls, whereas girls express more anxiety about math than boys (Meese, Wigfield, & Eccles, 1990). Clearly, we see a more debilitating pattern of attributions and beliefs about math performance for females than males, but no gender differences for the "feminine" domain of language arts.

In fact, in reviewing more than 70 studies examining attributional patterns, Hyde, Fennema, Ryan, Frost, and Hopp (1990) concluded that males have a more positive attitude toward math and higher confidence in their mathematical ability than do girls. Not surprising, then, males are more likely to attribute their success in math to ability, and girls are more likely to attribute their success in math to effort and luck.

Attributions and theories of intelligence

Dweck (1986) has extended these attributional patterns to explain why females may be less motivated than males to enroll in advanced math courses. It is a somewhat complicated model based on an individual's understanding of what intelligence is. Essentially, Dweck has found that some people believe that intelligence is a fixed quantity, something you either have or do not have. She labels this the *entity* theory of intelligence. Individuals who hold this theory believe that you are either smart or you're not and no amount of hard work can make you smarter. In contrast, some people hold an *incremental* theory of intelligence. They believe that intelligence is something that grows and that the harder you work and the more you learn, the smarter you get.

Students who hold the entity theory of intelligence are motivated to perform well, but they are only concerned with the performance and not with increasing learning or competence. After all, they believe they can't get any smarter than they already are; no amount of effort will increase their intelligence. Thus students who hold the entity theory will be motivated to choose tasks that they already do well rather than more challenging tasks in which they will most likely fail at first. Students who hold the incremental theory, in contrast, are motivated to learn and to increase competence. They will seek challenging tasks because even if they cannot perform them at first, they believe hard work and effort will allow them to gain the ability to perform them well in the future. This process is summarized in Table 10.1.

An interesting wrinkle to this model is that girls are more likely to hold the entity theory of intelligence than are boys. Girls are more likely to believe that there is nothing they can do if and when they fail at a task. Dweck further argues that the entity theory is particularly debilitating for math. Because mathematics involves learning whole new sets of concepts (e.g., algebra, geometry), it is extremely likely that at first, children will have some difficulty understanding the material. Because girls hold the entity theory, when they initially fail at math, they will attribute it to lack of ability and begin to avoid this domain. Boys, in contrast, who are more likely to hold the incremental theory of intelligence, will attribute failure to lack of effort and work harder to gain mastery. When they later succeed, boys will attribute this success to their increased competence and ability. Integrating Dweck's model with the findings from the attributional research, we see a pattern where females are likely to attribute their success in mathematics to effort, but at the same time believe that this effort will not increase their actual ability to perform math tasks in the future. Even females who succeed in math will not necessarily predict future success, and will therefore begin to avoid this academic domain.

Overall, then, the research indicates that females and males make different attributions concerning their academic successes and failures, particularly in mathematics. These different attributions may be related to different underlying conceptions about

Table 10.1. *Achievement goals and achievement behavior*

Theory of intelligence	Goal orientation	Confidence in present ability	Behavior pattern
Entity theory (Intelligence is fixed)	→ Performance goal (Goal is to gain positive judgments/avoid negative judgments of competence)	If high but If low	→ Mastery-oriented Seek challenge High persistence → Helpless Avoid challenge Low persistence
Incremental theory (Intelligence is malleable)	→ Learning goal (Goal is to increase competence)	If high or low	→ Mastery-oriented Seek challenge (that fosters learning) → High persistence

Source: Dweck (1986). Reprinted by permission of the American Psychological Association.

what intelligence is; certainly these differential attributions will lead males to continue to choose math courses, but will probably discourage females from doing so.

A cautionary word needs to be said about gender differences in attributional patterns. A great deal of the research on this issue relies on individuals publicly reporting the reasons why they believe they succeeded or failed on a task. It is possible that females are less likely to attribute success to ability than are males because females see this as bragging. Heatherington, Crown, Wagner, and Rigby (1989) examined the consequences of males and females boasting about their personal achievements. High school students rated characters in stories that were portrayed as very successful. Half of the characters were female and half were male, and characters were either successful in popularity and student government or in science and music. Finally, the characters were portrayed as either bragging about their achievements or being somewhat humble. In general, boastful characters were seen more negatively than humble characters, but this was especially true for female characters. Moreover, this effect held regardless of the domain of success. Females may not publicly attribute success to ability because they have learned that boastful females are particularly negatively evaluated by their peers. Future research should try to disentangle whether females really believe their own attributions or whether they are simply being modest because of the social consequences of immodesty.

Gender differences in academic values

The final aspect of Eccles's (1987) model that we shall consider is the value that females and males place on various academic disciplines. Closely related to this question is the relationship between academic achievement and self-concept. As discussed in many other chapters in this book, females seem to have a relationally oriented self-concept and males have an individuated self-concept. Females seem to define themselves in terms of their social relationships, whereas males seem to define themselves in terms of their individual achievement; and this difference may become particularly strong during adolescence as individual identity becomes an important psychological issue (see Roberts, Sarigiani, Peterson, & Newman, 1990, for a discussion). If we relate these differences to the classroom environment, it becomes clear that classrooms favor an individuated concept. Competition, not cooperation, is the norm. And indeed, more academically successful students are less cooperative than their less successful peers. Girls are more cooperative than boys in third grade, but by fifth grade, there is no longer a gender difference (Engelhard & Monsaas, 1989). Girls may be learning to act more competitively in the highly individualized, competitive school environment.

But girls may still continue to value interpersonal relations more than academic achievement. Male college students assign a higher value to mathematics than do female students, but female students assign a higher value to literature and prosocial concerns than do male students (Feather, 1988). Further, results of sophisticated statistical modeling suggest that for females, their personal commitment to prosocial values led to their academic orientation away from math and toward literature. For males, positive valuation of math was predicted by personal values of control and intellectual orientation. So gender differences in interpersonal versus intellectual orientation may lead to gender differences in academic achievement.

Similarly, math ability is highly related to overall self-esteem for males, but not for females (Singer & Stake, 1986; Skaalvik & Rankin, 1990; Wentzel, 1988). That is, males see high performance in math in particular, and academics in general, as important to their sense of self-worth, but females do not. Not surprisingly, then, females are less likely to value math as an academic discipline than are males, and they are less likely to see math as important for their ultimate career and life goals.

Summary

In this chapter we have explored gender differences in the classroom and in academic achievement. Gender differences in teacher –student interaction emerge as early as preschool, with teachers giving more attention to males than to females. Moreover, males seem to be praised for knowledge and females for obedience; on the other hand, males are reprimanded for disobedience and females for lack of knowledge. Given this pattern, it is perhaps not surprising that males tend to attribute their academic success to ability and females to either effort or luck. It is important to keep in mind in interpreting these findings that there are no gender differences in overall intelligence.

When we turn to specific academic disciplines, the picture gets a bit more complicated. Although a great deal of research has investigated gender differences in language and math abilities, in fact, the differences are so small as to be negligible for all practical purposes, with the possible exception of males' superiority in certain science domains. Yet it is the case that males like math and science more than females and that they enroll in substantially more math and science courses than do females. Further, males are more likely to attribute their success in math to ability, whereas females are more likely to attribute their success in math to effort. These differences may be exaggerated by the fact that females tend to believe in the entity theory of intelligence, and therefore may believe that they will not be able to get any better in math no matter how hard they try. These patterns of attributions may discourage females from enrolling in advanced mathematics courses.

At the same time, females value interpersonal and prosocial concerns more so than males and may gain more self-esteem from academic disciplines that allow them to pursue these goals. For males, in contrast, self-esteem is highly related to academic success, especially in math. Taken together, all of these research findings provide converging evidence for why females do not choose math, even though by all objective measures they are as capable in math as are males.

11

Work

As we saw in Chapter 10, a great many gender differences in the classroom may contribute to continuing gender differences in career choice and achievement. Although the political changes of the late 1960s and early 1970s have led to substantially greater numbers of women entering and remaining in the labor force, it is still the case that women are extremely underrepresented in high-prestige, high-salaried occupations. Whereas nearly 40% of managers in the United States are women, most are to be found at the lower levels of management, and women who hold top management jobs in large organizations are an extremely small minority (U.S. Department of Labor, 1989). When women do obtain senior management posts, these tend to be in female-dominated occupations. Further, women are still paid less than men even when performing the same job (see Stockard & Johnson, 1992, for a review). The barrier preventing women from obtaining top management jobs has been aptly described as a "glass ceiling" because it clearly exists and yet cannot be seen.

Two general forms of explanation have been advanced to explain continuing gender differences in career attainment. The first focuses on personality characteristics, such as assertiveness and achievement motivation. These *person-centered* explanations assume that gender differences in career aspirations and outcomes are due to individual differences between women and men. The second type of explanation focuses on the influence of societal and institutional structures. These *situation-centered* explanations emphasize issues of discrimination in the evaluation of work and in the hiring and promotion of women and men into particular occupations. In this chapter we consider how each of these explanations contributes to our understanding of gender differences in career choice.

Person-centered explanations

Achievement motivation and fear of success

A major factor contributing to a person's career aspirations is the need to achieve. Some people are extremely motivated to pursue a particular career path, for reasons of prestige, power, money, or interest. Others simply are not as motivated to achieve in the workplace. Early research by McClelland and his associates (McClelland, 1961; McClelland, Atkinson, Clark, & Lowell, 1953) documented that individual differences in the need to achieve could be reliably measured by asking people to tell a story about a somewhat ambiguous picture. For example, one picture depicts an older woman and man sitting at a kitchen table, and a younger man standing by the open door. When asked to tell what is happening in this picture, some people produce stories that are high in "achievement imagery" in that they focus on career goals, aspirations, and sometimes conflict. Moreover, McClelland's research has shown that a high need to achieve, as measured by this kind of achievement imagery, is related to an individual's actual aspirations and achievement-related behaviors in the world: High need to achieve individuals attain higher levels of education and enter and succeed in higher prestige occupations than do low need to achieve individuals.

Perhaps not surprisingly, the early work on need to achieve

included only male subjects. The few studies that did include females found that need to achieve could not be reliably measured in the same way as it was for males, but few researchers worried about this problem; after all, at that historical time period, women were not assumed to have any achievement needs beyond family and home. With the political changes that began in the mid-1960s, however, women's career achievement became an increasingly important question.

In 1972, Matina Horner published a seminal paper that presented a fundamentally new way of conceptualizing women's achievement motivation. She argued that women were placed in an untenable situation in having to choose between career and family. Whereas men could be successful in the workplace and still pursue family and home goals, this was not true for women. A woman who was successful in the workplace, especially if she was in a traditionally male occupation, faced many negative consequences stemming from a perceived loss of femininity. In Horner's studies, female subjects were presented with stories about hypothetical women succeeding in traditionally male careers such as medicine (remember that in the mid-1960s, medicine was still overwhelmingly male dominated) and asked to describe the story character. The majority of subjects told stories that contained a great deal of negative imagery, centering on the character's loss of important relationships, loneliness, and inability to find a suitable romantic partner.

For example, in one study, when asked to complete a story about Anne, who is in the top of her medical school class at the end of first-term finals, 65% of female subjects told stories focusing on negative consequences. Often, subjects would rework the story to make Anne more traditional. In a typical story, Anne deliberately lowers her grades the following term; she soon drops out of medical school and marries and raises a family. Some female subjects even told extremely negative and somewhat bizarre stories about Anne's character deficits. For example, one subject responded:

> Anne is recollecting her conquest of the day. She has just stolen her ex-friend's boyfriend away.... She is sitting in a

chair smiling smugly because she has just achieved great satisfaction from the fact that she hurt someone's feelings. (p. 172)

Another subject responded:

Anne is at her father's funeral. There are over 200 people
there. She knows it is unseemly to smile but cannot help
it.... Her brother Ralph pokes her in fury but she is uncontrollable.... Anne rises dramatically and leaves the room,
stopping first to pluck a carnation from the blanket of flowers
on the coffin. (p. 172)

Clearly, the women in these stories are seen in extremely
negative terms. Based on these findings, Horner argued that
women experience a *fear of success*. Although women may want
to succeed in the workplace, they are afraid that career success
will mean failure in terms of home and family goals. Success in
nontraditional careers may even be associated with pathological
personality attributes.

Horner's ideas generated a great deal of interest, both within
psychology and in the mass media (see Henley, 1985, for a
review). But while the idea of fear of success is provocative, the
research findings have been mixed. Two lines of evidence suggest
that fear of success cannot fully explain females' lower career
aspirations and achievements. First of all, many studies find little
evidence of fear of success. This may be because Horner's original
findings were not reliable, or because with the political changes
occurring over the last 20 years, women no longer feel the same
conflict between career and home. Second, researchers criticized
Horner's original work on two methodological grounds. One,
Horner studied only female subjects, and two, Horner elicited
stories only about females pursuing nontraditional careers.

In a study designed to examine these issues, Cherry and Deaux
(1978) asked both female and male subjects to respond to stories
about a female succeeding in a traditionally female career (nurse),
a female succeeding in a traditionally male career (doctor), and a
male succeeding in each of these careers. Negative imagery was
associated with either a male or a female pursuing a nontradi-

tional career. Interestingly, whereas males and females showed equal amounts of negative imagery toward a male character pursuing a traditionally female career, males showed substantially more negative imagery to a female pursuing a traditionally male career than did females. More recent research confirms that males attribute more fear of success to characters crossing traditional gender lines than do females (O'Connell & Perez, 1982). So fear of success is not a "female phenomenon," but may be more appropriately conceptualized as fear of negative consequences for crossing gender lines in choosing a career.

Are there, in fact, negative consequences for pursuing a nontraditional career? Pfost and Fiore (1990) asked college students to read a series of stories about male and female characters succeeding at traditional or nontraditional careers. They then asked the subjects to select the character that would be the most desirable romantic partner, the most desirable other-sex friend, and the most desirable same-sex friend. In general, characters choosing traditionally male careers were seen as the least desirable romantic partners by both male and female subjects. But female characters pursuing masculine careers were selected the least often as romantic partners and least often as either same-sex or other-sex friend. Women seem to suffer greater negative consequences for pursuing nontraditional careers than do men, and these kinds of real-world consequences may nudge women into choosing traditional careers.

Another reason why females may continue to choose traditional careers is because they do not believe they can succeed in more male-dominated occupations. We have seen in Chapter 10 that females select out of certain occupations early in their education by not pursuing math and science courses. Related to this, females may believe that they do not have the necessary personal skills for certain occupations. In particular, high-powered jobs, which are traditionally male, are seen as requiring assertiveness and feelings of competency. College women who consider themselves more assertive and more able are more likely to select nontraditional careers than are women who consider themselves less assertive and less able (Nevell & Schlecker, 1988; Rotterg, Brown, & Ware, 1987).

In a somewhat more detailed study, Bridges (1988) asked college students to imagine that they had been working in a particular job for a number of years and to rate their expected performance. The jobs were either traditionally female (e.g., dietitian), traditionally male (e.g., astronomer), or neutral (e.g., X-ray technician). In general, females had higher expectancies of success in the traditionally female careers than in either the neutral or traditionally male careers. Males, in contrast, assumed that they would be performing well regardless of the gender typing of the occupation.

Thus, although women do not seem to experience fear of success in quite the way that Horner described, it does seem to be the case that women as well as men assume negative consequences for pursuing nontraditional careers, and women in particular may feel that they are not capable of performing well in traditionally male careers.

Note that research on career choice and achievement has centered on the selection of and success in traditionally male occupations. But perhaps we need to question this conceptualization of achievement. From the initial research, it was simply assumed that the motivation to achieve would be related to career goals, and that achievement could be defined as the competitive urge for power and prestige. Thus this is another area of psychological research where the male model has been taken as the norm, and females are evaluated according to this standard. There are at least two problems with this conceptualization. First, there may be alternative means of achievement that are not based on competition, and second, there may be other arenas of life in which individuals have achievement goals.

Gender differences in achievement and leadership styles

Lipman-Blumen, Handley-Isaksen, and Leavitt (1983) have proposed that individuals may differ in *style* of achievement. That is, some individuals may achieve through power assertion and competition, whereas others may show a more relational achieving style centering on interpersonal relationships and cooperation. Not surprisingly, given much of the research reviewed throughout this book, Lipman-Blumen et al. argue that males have a tendency to show a direct, competitive achievement style and women a relational, cooperative achievement style. This is not to argue that males are better suited to particular achievement situations such as high-powered, high-prestige occupations. Women can achieve just as much, but they may accomplish their goals in somewhat different ways. In studying both men and women managers, Lipman-Blumen et al. found that the actual levels of achievement may be equal but that the style varied somewhat according to gender. Research on differing achievement styles is extremely important in demonstrating, first, that achievement may be much more complex than originally conceptualized, and second, that women may show different but equally successful achievement patterns as do men.

One way in which different achievement styles may be expressed in the workplace is through differing styles of management and leadership. Leadership styles have been classified in a number of ways, including "job centered versus employee centered," "task oriented versus interpersonal," and "democratic versus autocratic." Interestingly, the various classifications all correspond to male and female stereotypes. Managers who are job centered, task oriented, and autocratic emphasize employees' performance, goals, and deadlines and maintain responsibility for decision making. Employee-centered, interpersonal, and democratic managers focus on employees' personal needs, develop strong interpersonal relationships, and delegate decision making and responsibility. Given the pervasive gender stereotypes of the assertive, dominant male and the understanding, sympathetic female, it is not surprising that women managers are expected to be employee centered, interpersonal, and democratic in their style of leadership, and their male counterparts to be job centered, task oriented, and autocratic.

But how much do these expectations reflect reality? Eagly and Johnson (1990) have tried to answer this question by conducting a meta-analysis of a large number of studies comparing the leadership styles of men and women. They did not find that women are more concerned with interpersonal relationships and that men are more task oriented. However, women do appear to be more democratic, allowing their subordinates to participate in decision making, whereas men adopt a more autocratic style. But rather than having a negative effect, Korabik (1990) has argued that women's more democratic approach contributes significantly to managerial effectiveness.

Why might we see gender differences in achievement and leadership styles? In a comprehensive study exploring this question, Farmer (1985) examined what background factors influence three aspects of adolescent girls' and boys' achievement motivation: their level of career aspiration; their need to master new knowledge; and their commitment to their chosen career. In general, boys had higher mastery needs than did girls, but girls had higher career aspirations than did boys. More important, very different variables were related to achievement motivation for boys and girls. The best predictor of achievement motivation for boys was competitiveness. But for females, higher achievement motivation was related to independence, a low commitment to homemaking, and especially, high teacher support. Similarly, the strongest predictor of career aspiration in female college students was the support and mentoring of female teachers. Surprisingly, friends had little influence on motivation or career choice, but the perceived support of the father was related to a nontraditional career choice (Hackett, Esposito, & O'Halloran, 1989).

The pattern of results suggests that teachers, and especially female teachers, may play a more important role in the development of females' achievement motivation than of males' achievement motivation, and may account for why women's style tends to be more relationally oriented. But why are role models more important for achievement development in females than in males? Perhaps it is because females are more dependent on feedback for evaluating their own performance. For example, Roberts and Nolen-Hoeksema (1989, Experiment 1) asked male and female college students to imagine giving an important job-related presentation, after which they receive either positive or negative feedback from their boss. The subjects are then asked to judge their presentation performance, their ability to give presentations in the future, and their general job competence. Females were more affected by the feedback than were males. Specifically, when given negative feedback, females assumed that they would not perform well in the future either on the particular task or in general. Males, on the other hand, did not think that current feedback predicted future performance.

In a second study, Roberts and Nolen-Hoeksema (1989, Experiment 2) asked college students to perform a pattern tracing task. Some subjects were given positive feedback about their performance, some were given negative feedback, and some were given no feedback at all. All subjects were then asked to judge how well they thought they had performed. Importantly, there were no differences between males and females in the no-feedback condition, indicating that self-evaluation on this task was similar for both genders. However, when given negative feedback, females underestimated and males overestimated how well they had performed. Thus females may be more sensitive to feedback, and especially to negative feedback, than are males. And therefore females may depend more on teacher support, and teacher support may become a more important factor for females' achievement motivation than for males.

Gender differences in achievement goals

Another concern in understanding gender differences in achievement focuses on the arena in which achievement is measured. Although career aspirations are certainly important, there are other aspects of life in which people may wish to achieve various goals. For example, most people want to have a harmonious family life, and in fact, the majority of college students claim that personal relationships are more important to them than are career goals (Hammersla & Frease-McMahon, 1990). Given the research on friendships discussed in Chapter 7, we can assume that females are better able to achieve affiliative needs than are males. The question is whether females and males place differential value on different achievement needs in making life choices.

Females are more likely to consider coordination of home and work in making a career decision than are males (Paludi, 1991).

It is certainly the case that females continue to bear the burden of home and child care even in dual-earner families (Douthitt, 1989). Females also rate interpersonal opportunities as more important in choosing a career than do men (Strange & Rea, 1983). In any case, more research is certainly needed in order to understand the ways in which different kinds of achievement needs are expressed and coordinated in the selection and pursuance of particular occupations.

Changes in females' achievement motivation over time

Given that so much has changed over the last 15 to 20 years in females' access and penetration into traditionally male occupations, females' achievement aspirations may be changing as well. Paludi (1991) interviewed 80 women ranging in age from 20 to 80 years about their career aspirations and opportunities. In general, younger women were more competitively oriented than older women. All women expressed concern over coordination of work and family, and even the youngest women were reluctant to compromise personally important social values in order to achieve career success. Women's career strivings also showed a substantial increase when their children left home. So though younger women may be more competitive than older women, we are still seeing conflict between home and family affecting contemporary women's career aspirations.

A critical question in evaluating change over time is whether these changes are due to individual growth and development or to societal changes. In examining this question, Harmen (1981, 1989) has been following the same group of women over time, as well as women coming of age in each new decade. In an initial study, Harmen documented the career goals and attainments of a group of women who began college in 1968. These women were contacted again in 1974, 2 years after they were scheduled to graduate, and during a particularly stormy historical period. Only about half of the women had actually obtained a college degree by 1974, and 15% of these women were working on or had obtained a graduate degree. Seventy-one percent of the women were employed in 1974, 45% were in their career of choice, and the vast majority of all women were in traditionally female careers. Sixty-three percent were married, and 73% saw marriage with children as the ideal life. Although 55% rated career and family as equally important, 35% rated family as more important than work. In terms of the actual jobs that the women considered in 1968 compared to 1974, there was some increase in business-related occupations, but the overwhelming majority of women aspired to traditional careers.

In 1981, Harmen (1989) again contacted these women, and also studied a group of freshman women in 1983. All of the women in both groups expected to receive their degree when they began college, but only about 60% of the older women had actually achieved this goal. Both groups of women also expected to be in the work force for most of their lives. Although there was some increase in nontraditional career aspirations among the younger women, the majority of women at both ages were pursuing traditional careers. Even with all of the political changes of the past two decades, there seems to be little change in women's career aspirations.

In sum, gender differences in achievement motivation and career aspirations may account for some aspects of differential representation of gender in specific occupations. In particular, women tend to experience more conflict between career goals and relationship and family goals than men. Related to this, women may suffer more negative personal consequences of pursuing a nontraditional career than do men. Further, women seem to be more sensitive to negative feedback in evaluating their own performance than are men, and may also feel inadequate to perform well in traditionally male careers. But this is only part of the answer to why most women do not pursue nontraditional careers. To understand this phenomenon fully, we need to consider the structure of the workplace and women's roles within organizations.

Situation-centered explanations

In order to succeed in a career, one must first be hired and then evaluated positively by the employer. Is there any evidence that females and males are differentially hired and evaluated in traditional and nontraditional careers?

Access discrimination

Many researchers have argued that women are not hired into jobs that they are qualified for simply because of their gender. This kind of bias has been labeled *access discrimination*, because it bars access into an occupation based on a presumably irrelevant characteristic. In a review of research investigating the occurrence of access discrimination, Martenko and Gardner (1983) find mixed evidence. Although a few studies have found unequivocal evidence of access discrimination based on gender, several other studies find discrimination to be much more complex. Factors such as education and experience may be more important than gender in the hiring decision, but it also seems to be the case that different qualifications are important for females than for males in obtaining jobs. Whereas education and appearance seem to be the most important factors in the decision to hire a female, motivation, ability, and interpersonal skill seem more important for males.

In an extensive study examining how hiring decisions are made, Glick, Zion, and Nelson (1988) asked upper-level managers and business professionals to decide who they would interview for various jobs. The subjects were sent a cover letter and a résumé for applicants for a traditionally male job (sales manager in a heavy machinery shop), a traditionally female job (dental secretary), or a gender-neutral job (administrative assistant). The résumés varied both the gender and the personal information about the applicant. Some of the male and some of the female applicants displayed traditionally masculine interests (they had worked in a sporting goods store, they were a varsity team captain) and other applicants displayed traditionally feminine interests (they had worked in a jewelry store, they were a member of the pep squad). In general, the evaluators rated the applicants with more traditionally masculine interests as more masculine, and vice versa. However, regardless of previous experience and expressed interests, males were most likely to be selected to be interviewed for the traditionally male job and females were most likely to be selected to be interviewed for the traditionally female job. Gender alone plays an important role in deciding who to interview, regardless of other kinds of individuating information.

Perception and evaluation of work

It is clear that traditionally male occupations are accorded more prestige than traditionally female occupations (Paludi & Strayer, 1985; Powell & Jacobs, 1984). However, people in nontraditional careers are also accorded less prestige than those pursuing traditional career goals, so that women in nontraditional careers have less status than men in those same occupations. Moreover, as the number of women entering a given occupation increases, the prestige level of that occupation decreases. Also of interest, the prestige level of occupations varies as a function of earning power for males, but there is no systematic relationship between money and prestige for females (Powell & Jacobs, 1984).

Even when performing the exact same work, females are evaluated more poorly than males. Paludi and Strayer (1985) asked college students to evaluate a series of articles on politics, education, and the psychology of women. Half the subjects were led to believe that the articles had been written by a female, and half that they had been written by a male. Overall, both male and female students responded less favorably to the articles when they thought they were written by a female, even though the articles were exactly the same. How might these kinds of biases operate in the workplace?

For one thing, attitudes toward women in senior positions are often negative, with women being viewed as less capable of performing their job effectively than their male counterparts (Alban-Metcalfe & West, 1991; Nieva & Gutek, 1981; O'Leary, 1974; Terborg, 1977). This is especially true when women show stereotypically masculine leadership styles (Eagly, Makhijani, & Klonsky, 1992). Additionally, there is a pervasive belief that women do not possess the appropriate personality traits and leadership skills necessary for the job, and this belief is reflected by the preference of both male and female employees for a male supervisor. For example, Frank (1988) asked business students to evaluate hypothetical male and female managers. Male managers were rated more effective, more decisive, more demanding, more knowledgeable, and more distant than female managers, especially by male students. Male students rated female managers as more unsure, more incompetent, and weaker than male managers; female students rated female managers more communicative, more understanding, friendlier, and more democratic than male managers. Even though females rated female managers somewhat positively, more than two-thirds of both the males and females claimed they would prefer working for a male manager than a female manager, and assumed that others would feel the same way.

Women are also believed to be less committed to their careers than are men. And females' marital status seems to play a role in how they are perceived in the workplace (Etaugh & Petroski, 1985). Married women are seen as more reliable, more secure, more influential, and more attractive than are single women. Most interesting, single women are not seen as more career oriented or as more professionally competent than married women, which Etaugh and Petroski interpret as reflecting the "pervasive negative stereotype of unmarried women" (p. 337).

Clearly, women in the workplace are not perceived to be as competent as men in the workplace. Indeed, one explanation of why so few women achieve high management positions hinges on gender differences in personality. Early theorists argued that the characteristics believed to be associated with a successful manager are those that are generally attributed to men rather than women – aggressiveness, competitiveness, forcefulness, independence, and rationality – and that women fail to reach senior positions because they have been socialized to show characteristics and behaviors that are in conflict with those expected of leaders within organizations (Hennig & Jardin, 1977; O'Leary, 1974; Schein, 1973, 1975). In contrast to this widespread belief, however, the large number of studies that have addressed this question have found few differences between the characteristics of men and women managers (Brenner, 1982; Gregory, 1990; Steinberg & Shapiro, 1982). And women managers themselves do not believe they are different from male managers. Rather they see themselves as equally ambitious, controlling, forceful, and creative (Alban-Metcalfe & West, 1991).

Overall, women's work is simply not perceived as well as men's work. Traditionally female careers are not accorded as much prestige as traditionally male careers, and even when women are in traditionally male careers, they are not perceived as well as men in those same positions. Clear and pervasive negative stereotypes of women managers prevail in the workplace, despite the fact that there are few empirically demonstrated gender differences. Moreover, by focusing on differences between the characteristics of men and women to explain different achievement patterns, we fail to consider the differential influence that an organization may have on the attitudes and behavior of its male and female employees.

Roles within organizations

Kanter (1977) argues that we need to consider the organizational context in which men and women work. Organizational structures rather than women's personalities are responsible for the differential achievements and experiences of men and women within organizations. Women fail to show the characteristics associated with successful managers because of their low status within organizational hierarchies. According to Kanter, if women held more senior posts with greater power and opportunity, then they would show the same behavior and attitudes as do their male colleagues. Kanter also argues that an increase in the proportion of women in senior management positions would reduce gender stereotyping in organizations. Research addressing this theory has produced contradictory findings. Although there is some empirical support for Kanter's proposition that a higher proportion of women would result in higher levels of achievement (Heilman, 1980; Izraeli, 1983; Sprangler, Gordon, & Pipkin, 1978), it has also been found that contact with male colleagues decreases as the proportion of women increases (South, Bonjean, Corder, & Markum, 1982). As O'Leary and Johnson (1991) point out, increasing the number of women in power is not likely to be effective unless there is also a change in the perception of their suitability for these posts.

It is now generally agreed that the differential experiences of men and women in organizations cannot simply be explained by the lower proportion of women in senior positions. Rather, much of the differential treatment of male and female managers results from gender stereotyping in the workplace (Fagenson, 1990; Gregory, 1990; Riger & Galligan, 1980). The higher value placed on men and on male characteristics within organizations and in the wider society must be taken into account (Fagenson, 1990; Gregory, 1990).

Related to this perspective is the concept of *sex role spillover*, a term Gutek and her colleagues coined to refer to the carryover of gender-based expectations of behavior into the workplace (Gutek & Cohen 1987; Gutek & Morasch, 1982; Nieva & Gutek, 1981). This phenomenon is particularly apparent where one sex is greatly outnumbered by the other, so that characteristics such as aggressiveness and competitiveness are highly valued in male-dominated jobs, and nurturance and passivity are associated with jobs dominated by women. Gutek and Cohen (1987) argue that because the sex role of the gender in the majority spills over into the work role of the occupation, when women are in the minority they are perceived as women "in a man's job" and are treated differently as a result. Incongruence between sex role and work role also occurs for men in female-dominated jobs, but this situation is uncommon. As the authors point out, this is probably because men have little to gain from being in the minority in low-status "women's work." When men do work in traditionally female occupations, they are usually in senior positions and thus highly valued.

Stress and support in the workplace

Because women are in the minority in high-prestige, high-paying occupations, they face special problems in the workplace. First of all, women are often excluded from networking, the informal process whereby their male colleagues make contact with each other to transmit information and provide favors (Kanter, 1977). It is also more difficult for women to find mentors (more senior colleagues who support them and help them in their career) than it is for men. Women, like men, have been found to benefit from mentoring in terms of both job success and job satisfaction (Burke & McKeen, 1990; Noe, 1988). Women in upper management are thus not only at a disadvantage in terms of advancement within the organization, but because of their lack of acceptance and support, they are also more likely than senior male managers to feel isolated and lonely (O'Leary & Johnson, 1991). Moreover, women have to deal with the additional demands of running a home, and are much less likely than their male colleagues to have children (Alban-Metcalfe & West, 1991; Davidson & Cooper, 1983). Sexual harassment is also a major problem for women, particularly when they are in the minority (Gutek, 1985; Gutek & Morasch, 1982).

The difficulties of being female in a male-dominated organization present a major source of stress for women managers. In an investigation of occupational stressors and their effects, Davidson and Cooper (1984) found that women managers experienced significantly higher levels of pressure at work and significantly higher rates of physical and psychological symptoms of stress than did their male colleagues. This was particularly true for women at junior and middle levels of management, who reported high levels of pressure associated with discrimination and prejudice and who felt under pressure to perform better at their job than their male counterparts. In fact, recent studies of women holding middle to top management positions have found that gender stereotyping within the organization is still perceived by women to be the most significant barrier to the top (Andrew, Coderre, & Denis, 1990; Carr-Ruffino, 1991).

Summary

The reasons why women are still so underrepresented in high-status, high-paying jobs are complex. Although women do not experience fear of success as originally conceptualized by Horner, they do experience conflict between career and relationship goals, perhaps more so than men. Women are also less sure of their abilities in traditional male domains, and are more sensitive to negative feedback than are males, and this pattern may make it particularly difficult for women to pursue nontraditional careers.

But even those women who choose nontraditional careers face many obstacles. Women may find it harder even to get interviewed for certain jobs, and once hired, their work may be evaluated more poorly than their male colleagues'. Women in managerial positions are generally perceived more negatively than their male counterparts, and women lack the support systems of networking and mentoring available to men. Perhaps most telling about the perception of women and work is that research has focused almost exclusively on women pursuing nontraditional careers. This fact alone indicates that traditional "women's work" is not considered important, exciting, or fulfilling.

12

Psychopathology and emotion

It is not just in the workplace that women experience psychological difficulties. Women are generally more at risk for psychiatric disorder than are men. Whether we look at rates of
admission to psychiatric hospitals, outpatient referrals to a psy-
chiatrist or psychologist, the prescription of tranquilizing or
antidepressant drugs, or community surveys of people who
have not sought treatment, the conclusion is the same: At least
twice as many women as men receive a diagnosis of psychiatric
disorder (Briscoe, 1982; Gove, 1980; McGrath, Keita, Strickland,
& Russo, 1990; Nolen-Hoeksema, 1987; Weissman & Klerman,
1985).

In this chapter we examine why the rate of psychiatric disorder in women is double that of men. First, we look at biases in the diagnostic process and ask whether women really are more psychologically disturbed than men, or whether they are just more likely to be given a psychiatric disorder diagnosis. We then consider the explanations for women's greater vulnerability to disorder than men. We explore whether it is aspects of women's lives or their biological makeup that puts them at risk. Finally, we look at gender differences in vulnerability to stress and in the experience and expression of emotion, and examine whether differences in the socialization of emotions in girls and boys can help us to understand gender differences in disorder in childhood and adult life.

The diagnostic process

One explanation put forward to account for the gender difference in psychiatric disorder is that the difference is not real but simply reflects biases in the process of diagnosis. In a classic study, male and female psychiatrists, psychologists, and social workers were asked to indicate which adjectives on a sex role questionnaire best described a "mature, healthy, socially competent adult man," a "mature, healthy, socially competent adult woman," and a "mature, healthy, socially competent adult person" (Broverman, Broverman, Clarkson, Rosenkrantz, & Vogel, 1970). There was agreement between the characterizations of the healthy adult man and the healthy adult person; both were described as competent, independent, and objective. However, a healthy adult woman was considered to be not at all like a healthy adult person. Instead, she was described as emotional, submissive, and conceited. This study was extremely revealing about clinicians' stereotypes of psychologically healthy men and women and suggested that women are more likely to receive a psychiatric disorder diagnosis than men.

In recent years, mental health professionals have become less stereotyped in their beliefs about what constitutes appropriate male and female behavior. In a replication of the Broverman et al. investigation, psychiatrists were asked to identify the items on a sex role questionnaire that best described optimal psychological functioning in a male or a female patient (Kaplan, Winget, & Free, 1990). No differences were found between the descriptions of male and female patients, with the majority of psychiatrists rating a mixture of masculine and feminine characteristics as optimal for both men and women.

What these studies do not tell us is whether clinicians' diagnoses really are affected by the gender of their patients. Research on this issue suggests not only that women are likelier than men to be diagnosed as having a psychiatric disorder, but also that the type of diagnosis often has more to do with the patient's gender than the patient's symptoms. This bias operates in the opposite direction for men, resulting in failure to diagnose psychiatric disorder when it exists.

Much of the evidence for a greater prevalence of disorder among women has come from community surveys. Because these surveys are conducted with general population samples rather than patients who have consulted a doctor, they are thought to give a "true" estimate of gender differences in psychiatric disorder. But a major problem with these studies is that they have focused on the mild symptoms of distress that are common among women rather than such symptoms as heavy drinking that are common among men, and so have produced an overestimate of gender differences in rates of disorder (Newmann, 1984). When a doctor is approached for help, women are again likelier than men to receive a psychiatric disorder diagnosis. Even among patients who do not have a psychiatric disorder according to standard criteria, doctors are more likely to diagnose disorder in women than in men (Marks, Goldberg, & Hillier, 1979; Redman, Webb, Hennrikus, & Gordon, 1991).

The type of diagnosis made is also influenced by the gender of the patient. Generally, women are likelier to be diagnosed as anxious or depressed, and men as alcoholic or having a personality disorder. Cultural factors may, to some extent, be responsible; alcoholism may be more common among men, and anxiety and depression more common among women, because of social pressures that operate against women drinking excessively and men showing emotional distress (Nolen-Hoeksema, 1987).

But gender differences in psychiatric disorder are not simply a reflection of real differences in types of disorder. Clinicians' diagnostic judgments are influenced by their beliefs about gender differences in particular disorders, so that female patients are more likely to be diagnosed as depressed even when the available diagnostic information points to a different diagnostic category, and male patients may fail to be diagnosed as depressed even when they show typical symptoms (Lopez, 1989; Potts, Burnham, & Wells, 1991).

Two hundred and ninety psychiatrists were asked to diagnose the same two patients according to standard diagnostic criteria. At the time of the study, both patients were being treated for schizophrenia. When the patients were described as white men or when no information was provided about their gender, 56% of the psychiatrists gave schizophrenia as their diagnosis, but when the patients were described as women, only about 20% of the psychiatrists diagnosed schizophrenia. And when the researchers examined diagnoses other than that of schizophrenia, they found that almost 50% of the male psychiatrists diagnosed depression when the patients were described as women (Loring & Powell, 1988). So even when symptoms are identical, depression is likelier to be diagnosed in women than in men. This gender bias was not so clearly apparent among female psychiatrists, showing that diagnosis is influenced not only by the gender of the patient but also by the gender of the clinician.

It has been argued that a gender bias is built in the psychiatric diagnostic classification system itself and that this further increases the likelihood of women being diagnosed with certain disorders. Although difficult to test, it does seem to be the case that the criteria used to define certain diagnostic categories are likelier to be met by women than by men, suggesting that the more that women adhere to traditionally female roles, the likelier they are to be diagnosed as psychiatrically disturbed (Busfield, 1982; Kaplan, 1983; McGrath et al., 1990; Williams, 1984).

The high rates of psychiatric disorder among women have also been attributed to women's greater ability to recognize emotional problems and to their greater willingness and opportunity to seek help. Although these factors may be of some importance, the available evidence suggests that they make only a small contribution to the marked gender difference that exists between men and women with psychiatric disorder (Nolen-Hoeksema, 1987; Radloff & Rae, 1979; Weissman & Klerman, 1985; Williams, 1984). One criterion for histrionic personality disorder, for example, is uncontrollable sobbing on minor sentimental occasions.

Gender roles

Many researchers believe that the gender difference in rates of psychiatric disorder is real, and that the higher prevalence of disorder among women is a direct result of experiences in women's lives. One reason for this view is that gender differences in psychiatric disorder are greatest among married people, suggesting that women's high rates are associated with their roles within marriage (Gove, 1972; Gove & Tudor, 1973). Various aspects of women's marital roles are thought to be detrimental to mental health. Women are often restricted to the roles of housewife and mother, whereas men are likelier to have both family and work as sources of satisfaction. Further, when women are employed they commonly combine low-status work outside the home with low-status housework. Gove predicted that rates of mental illness would be higher for married women than married men but the same for unmarried women and men. Although the prediction for married men and women was confirmed from studies of patients receiving psychiatric treatment, unmarried men showed *higher* rates of psychiatric disorder than did unmarried women (Gove, 1972, 1979; Gove, Hughes, & Style, 1983; Gove & Tudor, 1973). This finding led to the widely cited conclusion that marriage is more beneficial for husbands than for wives. Although later studies of community samples cast doubt on Gove's finding that single men are more at risk for psychiatric disorder than are single women (Williams, 1984), single people are generally more likely to experience psychiatric disorder than are married people (Gove et al., 1983; Wood, Rhodes, & Whelan, 1989). This is true for women as well as men.

Why is it that differences in rates of mental illness between men and women are greatest among married people? Recent research has focused in greater detail than before on the link between marital status and mental illness, and has demonstrated that it is the quality of the marital relationship rather than simply whether or not a person is married which determines mental health (Fowers, 1991). It seems that a poor marital relationship has greater negative consequences for women than for men. Women in distressed marriages are more depressed than either happily married or unmarried women (Aneshensel, 1986), and almost half of all women in unhappy marriages are depressed compared with less than 20% of men (Weissman, 1987).

Although married women are likelier to experience psychiatric disorder than do their husbands, they are also likelier to report greater happiness and life satisfaction; women differ from men in positive as well as negative well-being. This has been attributed to women's greater sensitivity to and expression of emotional experiences, particularly regarding emotional aspects of close relationships (Wood et al., 1989). So marriage is not necessarily better for men than for women. Instead, it seems that unhappy marriages are more likely to result in psychiatric disorder for women than for men, but that women benefit more from happy marriages than do men.

Are women who work outside the home less at risk for psychiatric disorder than women who are not employed? Employment benefits the mental health of many women, particularly unmarried women and married women who choose to be employed (Repetti, Matthews, & Waldron, 1989). This is largely due to the social support that women receive in the workplace. Employment has even been found to reduce the negative effects of marital strain on women's mental health (Aneshensel, 1986; Kandel, Davies, & Davies, 1985). And though it has often been suggested that women with children who are employed may be more at risk for disorder than those engaged in full-time child care, because of the pressures involved in combining work and home roles, this appears to be untrue. Mothers at home with young children are more at risk for psychiatric disorder than those who go out to work, particularly working-class women whose home circumstances are stressful and who lack social support (Brown & Harris, 1978; Cleary & Mechanic, 1983; Kandel et al., 1985; Parry, 1986). It is the circumstances under which women are mothers and workers that determine the effects on mental health. Not surprisingly, working women benefit more from employment if their husbands contribute to child care or housework (Kessler & McRae, 1982; Ross & Mirowsky, 1988).

When men adopt women's roles, they too become anxious and depressed. In a survey of the use of tranquilizers and antidepressants, the most common treatments for emotional problems, the usual pattern of twice as many women as men taking medication was found in traditional families. But in non-traditional families where the woman went out to work and the man stayed home, men were just as likely as women to be taking psychotropic drugs (Cafferata, Kaspar, & Bernstein, 1983).

The mechanisms by which women's roles lead to disorder can be explained by learned helplessness theory (Radloff, 1975; Radloff & Rae, 1979). According to this theory, individuals who do not have control over negative events in their lives are likely to develop feelings of helplessness that result in depression, particularly if they tend to explain negative events in a pessimistic way (Abramson, Seligman, & Teasdale, 1978; Seligman, 1975). Radloff argues that women, because of their unequal position in society, are more likely than men to feel helpless and thus become depressed. Although learned helplessness theory has not yet been tested directly in relation to gender differences in psychiatric disorder, it offers a promising approach to increasing our understanding of the negative emotional consequences of women's traditional roles.

Hormones

A rather different explanation of women's vulnerability to mental illness is that female hormones are responsible. Hormones have been implicated because emotional problems in girls increase around the time of puberty, and because it is widely believed that women are more prone to depression and other psychiatric symptoms in the premenstrual period, after childbirth, and during menopause, each of which is characterized by changes in hormone levels (Nolen-Hoeksema, 1987). But there is no consistent evidence to support this claim. Social factors play a much more important role than hormones do in negative mood in adolescent girls (Brooks-Gunn & Warren, 1989). And though some women do report premenstrual mood and behavior changes, including depression, anxiety, irritability, insomnia, and lack of energy, these symptoms are generally not as severe as those of clinical depression (Hamilton, Parry, & Blumenthal, 1988; McGrath et al., 1990). Investigations that have obtained daily ratings of mood throughout the menstrual cycle, rather than retrospective reports of premenstrual symptoms, have found little increase in depression during the premenstrual period (Hamilton et al., 1985).

Although many women experience the "baby blues" within a few days of childbirth, this syndrome generally involves only mild depression and most women recover very quickly. Postnatal depression does not begin until several weeks after the birth, and the symptoms are much more severe and longer lasting than those of the baby blues. The much smaller proportion of women who develop postnatal depression were often depressed before giving birth, suggesting that factors other than changing hormone levels are involved (Nolen-Hoeksema, 1987). And though hormonal changes associated with menopause have often been linked with depression because of the rise in rates of psychiatric disorder among women in their late 40s and 50s, studies have shown that the increase in psychiatric symptoms occurs in women who are still menstruating (McKinley, McKinley, & Brambilla, 1987). It is the changes in women's lives around that time, such as children leaving home or having to care for aging parents, rather than hormonal changes, that appear to contribute to the increased rates of psychiatric disorder in women as they reach middle age.

So psychiatric disorder in women cannot be attributed to normal fluctuations in female hormone levels. It remains possible that abnormal hormonal functioning may be responsible. But investigations of the effects of abnormal hormone levels on mood have produced contradictory results, and as yet no clear explanation exists of the mechanisms by which hormonal abnormalities result in psychiatric disorder (Nolen-Hoeksema, 1987).

Gender differences in vulnerability to stress

In childhood, psychiatric disorder is more common among boys than girls (Offord et al., 1987; Rutter, Tizard, & Whitmore, 1970). The most frequently occurring boyhood disorders are conduct disorder and attention deficit disorder. Conduct disorder describes a wide range of antisocial behaviors, such as stealing, lying, fighting, and other destructive, disobedient, or aggressive behaviors (Baum, 1989; Martin & Hoffman, 1990). Children with attention deficit disorder (now called attention deficit hyperactivity disorder in the psychiatric classification system) have difficulty in concentrating and are impulsive and overactive. They often have problems in settling to a task or even sitting still, and tend to shift from one activity to another (Barkley, 1990; Whalen, 1989). One rare disorder that is more common among boys than girls and that is of particular relevance to this book, is gender identity disorder (see the discussion in Chapter 8). Children with this disorder express an intense desire to be the other sex, and persistently engage in cross-sex behavior (Zucker & Green, 1992).

In spite of the greater overall prevalence of psychiatric disorder among boys, from early childhood girls are likelier than boys to show emotional difficulties, particularly anxiety disorder. This can involve anxiety about separation, either from parents or the home environment, anxiety associated with contact with unfamiliar people, or more generalized excessive worry or fear (Last, 1989; Miller, Boyer, & Rodoletz, 1990). The prevalence of childhood depression is similar for boys and girls (Fleming, Offord, & Boyle, 1989).

It is when children reach adolescence that girls become more vulnerable to disorder than do boys. Although this reversal may be partly explained by a decrease in boys' behavioral difficulties, it is largely due to an increase in girls' emotional problems, particularly depression, during the transition from childhood to adolescence (Brooks-Gunn & Petersen, 1991; Cairns, Cairns, Neckerman, Ferguson, & Gariepy, 1989; Forehand, Neighbors, & Wierson, 1991; Links, Boyle, & Offord, 1989; Rutter, 1986). Symptoms of depression include feeling sad or blue, loss of interest in usual activities, insomnia, changes in appetite, and poor concentration. Girls are also much likelier than boys to develop eating disorders in adolescence, such as anorexia nervosa, which involves extreme weight loss following refusal to eat, and bulimia, in which excessive overeating is accompanied by vomiting, over-exercise, or the use of laxatives to counteract binge eating (Attie, Brooks-Gunn, & Petersen, 1990).

Why is it that young boys are more at risk for psychiatric disorder than young girls, but by adolescence, the situation is reversed? One explanation is that the reversal in rates of psychiatric disorder between males and females is due to a reversal in vulnerability to stress. In a follow-up study of children from 1 to 3 years old, boys were found to be more vulnerable than girls to the effects of family stress, and the outcome for boys who experienced stressors such as marital discord or maternal depression was conduct disorder (Earls & Jung, 1987). Emery and O'Leary (1982) obtained a similar finding. Although the boys and girls in their sample were equally aware of and equally exposed to marital discord, only the boys showed marked behavioral problems. Boys were also found to be more vulnerable than girls to parental divorce, as well as other stressors, such as the birth of a sibling (Rutter, 1983). It has been proposed that under difficult family circumstances, parents may be less tolerant of boys' more active and aggressive behavior. Consequently, parents may treat their sons more severely than their daughters, resulting in more behavioral problems for boys than for girls (Earls, 1987). Rutter (1985) has also suggested that distressed parents may interact differently with boys and girls, and pointed to the finding that parents who are in severe conflict are more likely to quarrel in front of their sons than their daughters.

As children reach adolescence, girls begin to react more negatively to stress than do boys. Simmons, Burgeson, Carlton-Ford, and Blyth (1987) investigated the impact of major life transitions on more than 4,000 adolescents and found that girls experienced greater difficulties. In particular, adolescent girls were more sensitive than adolescent boys to problems in peer group relations and to changes in body shape. But why is it that boys are more vulnerable to stress than girls in childhood, and girls become more vulnerable than boys in adolescence? The answer to this question may lie in the differential socialization of emotion in boys and girls.

Gender differences in emotional socialization

A possible explanation for gender differences in pathology is that females and males deal with emotions and emotional problems in different ways. One of the most pervasive gender stereotypes is that females are more emotional and, by extension, are more emotionally vulnerable than males (see, e.g., Brody, 1985, Malatesta & Haviland, 1985, and Zahn-Waxler, Cole, & Barrett, 1991, for reviews). More specifically, women are seen as expressing more happiness, more sadness, and more fear than men, but men are seen as expressing more anger than females (Fabes & Martin, 1990; Zahn-Waxler et al., 1991). Even children as young as 3 years of age believe these gender stereotypes about emotions (Birnbaum & Cheminski, 1984). Emotion stereotypes surely play a role in how parents socialize their children's understanding and expression of emotional experience. Although part of emotional experience is undoubtedly based on physiological processes (e.g., Ekman, 1984; Izard, 1977), most researchers agree that the way in which emotions are understood, interpreted, and expressed are culturally influenced, and the cultural norms for emotional expression are learned through socialization (e.g., Gordon, 1989; Lutz & White, 1986). Are parents socializing emotions differently with sons and with daughters, and, if so, how might these gender differences influence gender differences in psychopathology?

Infants are born with the ability to display emotional expressions of happiness, fear, anger, disgust, and sadness (Malatesta et al., 1989). Moreover, infants display these emotional expressions in the appropriate contexts; they look sad when caregivers leave them and happy when they return; they show disgust upon eating an unappetizing food, and they display anger when frustrated. Importantly, in the first few months of life, there are no gender differences in emotional expression (Malatesta et al., 1989), but it is the case that adults believe that male and female infants express emotions differently (Fabes & Martin, 1990). And these beliefs seem to influence the ways in which adults interact emotionally with young infants.

Mothers display more emotional expressions and more intense emotional expressions to daughters than to sons. Moreover, they are more likely to match their sons' emotional expression by mirroring the same expression, but with daughters, they are more likely to express a different emotion than the one the infant displays. Overall, female infants are being exposed to a greater variety of more intense emotions than are male infants. And by 7 months of age, female infants are beginning to express emotion more frequently, and a greater variety of emotions as well, than are males (Malatesta & Haviland, 1985; Malatesta et al., 1989).

As children continue to develop and start to use language, they begin to talk about themselves and their experiences. Most children are able to label at least some emotions by 18 months of age, and become increasingly able to talk about their own emotions, others' emotions, and the causes and consequences of emotions throughout the preschool years (see Bretherton, Fritz, Zahn-Waxler, & Ridgeway, 1986). And similar to the findings on mothers' emotional expressions with daughters, parents use more emotional language with daughters than with sons beginning as early as 18 months of age, well before there are any gender differences in children's use of emotional language (Dunn, Bretherton, & Munn, 1987; Kuebli & Fivush, 1992).

There are also gender differences in the way parents talk about specific emotions with daughters and with sons. Both mothers and fathers talk more about sadness with preschool daughters than with sons, but they talk more about anger with sons than with daughters (Fivush, 1989, 1991; Kuebli & Fivush, 1992). Moreover, when anger is discussed with preschool daughters, mothers often end the conversation by trying to reestablish a harmonious relationship between the child and the person who made her angry. With sons, in contrast, mothers do not focus on restoring harmony. Rather, sons are more likely to bring up a retaliatory act against the person who made them angry than are daughters, and mothers seem to accept retaliation as an appropriate response to anger (Fivush, 1991).

The pattern of findings suggests that emotional socialization begins very early in life. Parents not only engage in more face-to-face vocal interaction with female infants than with male infants, but these interactions are more intensely emotional with females than with males. And the same pattern continues as children develop and begin engaging in verbal conversations with their parents about emotions. Moreover, preschool girls are already talking about emotions more than preschool boys (Dunn et al., 1987; Kuebli & Fivush, 1992), although there are few gender differences in basic understanding or recognition of different emotions during childhood (see Brody, 1985, for a review).

In addition to gender differences in emotional language, there are also gender differences in emotional behavior that emerge at an early age, particularly in empathic and caregiving behaviors. By the second year of life, girls are more likely to exhibit distress at parental conflict than boys and are more likely to try to come to the aid of an ailing or sad parent than are boys (e.g., Robinson, 1989; see Zahn-Waxler et al., 1991, for a review). This pattern continues throughout childhood. As we saw in Chapter 7, on play and friendships, girls are more distressed by conflict and work harder to avoid or resolve conflict than do boys. What might account for this gender difference?

As just discussed, in talking about anger with their preschool children, mothers are more likely to try to resolve angry feelings by restoring harmony with daughters than with sons. Related to this, when disciplining children for transgressing against another child, parents are more likely to focus on the other child's feelings with daughters than with sons (e.g., Zahn-Waxler et al., 1991). These patterns of discussion and discipline may foster females' attunement to others' distress. Notice how this pattern of empathic concern for others is related to Chodorow's (1978) and Gilligan's (1982) discussions of females being socialized to be more relationally oriented than males (see Chapter 4).

We can also speculate about how these early patterns of emotional socialization might lead to adult gender differences in emotional understanding and emotional vulnerability. At a general level, because females are socialized to be more attuned to emotions, they may learn to pay more attention to both their own and others' emotional states. As adults, women rate emotions as more important than do men (Allen & Haccoun, 1976), and as discussed more fully in Chapter 7, female friends spend more time talking about emotions and personal problems than do male friends. A pattern of focusing on emotions may lead to women being more vulnerable to emotional disorders than are men. And more specifically, the kinds of emotions that parents focus on with their children may influence the kind of emotional vulnerability that is experienced. Because parents focus more on anger and retaliation with sons than with daughters, males may be more prone to externalizing disorders, such as conduct disorders and alcoholism, than females. And because parents focus on sadness with daughters more than with sons, females may learn to focus on sadness, leading to greater vulnerability to depression. In fact, a current model of depression suggests that women may experience depression more than men because women tend to ruminate on sad experiences more than men do (Nolen-Hoeksema, 1987). Clearly, the ways in which boys and girls come to understand and interpret the emotional experiences beginning very early in life, will come to influence their understanding of emotions as adults, and possibly also the way in which emotional difficulties will be expressed.

Summary

In this chapter we have examined whether women are more psychologically disturbed than men. Although the evidence that women are likelier than men to be diagnosed as having a psychiatric disorder because of biases in the diagnostic process is compelling, this alone does not account for the rate of psychiatric disorder in women being double that of men. Women's roles rather than their hormones are responsible for their increased vulnerability. Mothers who are not employed and who are bringing up young children in adverse home circumstances are most at risk, particularly if they have a poor relationship with their partner and lack other sources of social support. In addition, developmental differences in reactions to stress and emotional socialization may help explain gender differences in adult psychopathology.

13

Conclusions

In this book we have discussed various aspects of what it means to grow up male or female. And, as we have seen, there are many ways in which gender plays a critical role in development. In this last chapter we try to bring together the threads that have been running throughout our discussions and to present a coherent picture of gender development.

Before we begin, it is imperative to emphasize three things. First, because this book is about gender development, we have focused on the ways in which females and males differ from infancy through adulthood. But it should be borne in mind that there are also great similarities between the genders. There are few if any gender differences in most cognitive skills and abilities. Males and females have similar sensory systems and perceive the world, both visually and auditorially, in similar ways. Males and females have similar memory abilities; the development of the ability to store and retrieve information is quite orderly and quite similar in both genders. As we have seen, language and mathematical abilities are virtually the same for females and males, despite stereotypes to the contrary. And males and females display similar abstract problem-solving skills and are similar in their conceptual skills. There are few if any gender differences in the ways in which parents express affection and love to their children, and boys and girls show similar overall patterns of emotional attachment to their caregivers. Thus, in thinking about the development of gender, keep in mind that boys' and girls' development is as similar as it is different.

Just as important, not all girls are alike, nor are all boys alike. Not only are there differences between girls and boys, but there are differences within groups of girls and within groups of boys. An individual girl might show a typically "male" pattern of play and friendship behavior, for example, or an individual boy might do quite poorly in math and believe he has no mathematical ability. The differences we have discussed in this book are *group* differences, averaged across large numbers of girls and boys. But each individual is unique and will display a unique developmental pathway. Finally, virtually all of the research we have discussed has focused on white, Western cultures. Clearly, gender may be understood in different ways in different cultures, and we need to be extremely cautious about generalizing beyond the populations studied. In thinking about the conclusions we can draw from our review of the literature, it is important to remember all of these limitations.

Still, the research indicates that in order to have a complete theory of development, we need to take gender into account. How can we best conceptualize gender development? What aspects of gender-related behaviors and beliefs change with age, and why? Throughout this book we have seen that gender development is a complex interaction among biological gender differences; cultural belief systems as expressed both in stereotypes and behaviors and in institutionalized structures such as school and the workplace; and, equally important, the child's own developing understanding of gender and what it means to be female or male.

Gender development originates from the moment of conception. When a female egg unites with a male sperm to form an XX or XY chromosome pair, males and females embark upon different developmental pathways. The most far-reaching effect of our genetic makeup is the determination of physical sexual characteristics. Our physical appearance as male or female has a powerful influence on how we perceive ourselves and are perceived by others, and it is central to the development of gender identity. Also beginning before birth is the production of sex hormones, which lay the foundation for some aspects of later gender role behavior. Sex hormones do not determine gender development, however. At most, it seems that prenatal sex hormones may facilitate the development of gender role behavior in a male or female direction when postnatal experiences are compatible.

Once born, from the very first day of life, boys and girls are treated differently. Parents perceive boys to be stronger and rougher than girls, and girls to be more delicate and prettier than boys, although there is little evidence that infants vary along these dimensions. In fact, simply labeling an infant as male or female elicits somewhat different interpretations of the very same infant behavior from an adult. Parents hold boys closer to the body than they do girls, and they spend more time verbalizing and cooing to girls than to boys. Although parents may be acting on their stereotypes of male and female behavior, they may also be responding to temperamental differences between male and female infants. Because males are somewhat more irritable than girls, they may need closer body contact for comfort. Because girls can stabilize their state a bit better than boys, parents can hold them cradled along the forearm, a position ideally suited to face-to-face communication. So here we see how parental beliefs and biological differences combine to produce differences in parent–daughter and parent–son interactions.

Interestingly, infants begin to show preferences for sex-typed toys as early as 12 months of age, although the research on parental sex typing of toy play during infancy is somewhat mixed. Again, although parents are most likely engaging in some sex typing of their infant's play behaviors, many of these preferences seem to come from the infant's own temperamental disposition. These early emerging differences, which are already an interaction between biology and culture, set the stage for what is a critical period in gender development, the preschool years. It is during this time that children first begin to understand for themselves what it means to be male or female, and gender concepts become increasingly important and increasingly stereotyped from age 2 through 5.

In addition to learning the physical differences, by age 3 children already know many of the cultural stereotypes associated with gender. This is probably not too surprising given how pervasive gender stereotypes are in our culture, permeating children's literature, television, and, of course, parents' and teacher's beliefs. Preschool children are usually extremely stereotyped and rigid in their beliefs about gender, and this seems to be true regardless of family values. It seems that at this point in development, the child's own need to make sense of the world overrides other information. And because preschool children are not yet capable of sophisticated and flexible thought, they are only able to understand gender in rigid fashion.

It is also during the preschool years that gender differences in play begin to emerge more consistently. By age 3, most children greatly prefer to play with same-sex peers when given a choice, and play patterns of female and male groups diverge. We see large differences in toy choice, and parents' differential reinforcement of their children's sex-typed toys and activities is strongest at this age. Peers also become important socializing agents, and peers, because they are so gender typed in their beliefs, strongly reinforce gender-typed behaviors. It is almost as if once the child realizes that gender is an important way of categorizing individuals, gender becomes extremely important.

There is little doubt that parents interact with their preschool daughters and sons differently. Parents engage in more face-to-face, communicative play with daughters and more rough-and-tumble play with sons. Again, this develops from earlier patterns of play and communication, which, in turn, result from interactions between biology and culture. Parents also subtly reinforce girls for staying close to adults and for helping around the house. In conversations with their preschool children, parents talk more about sadness with girls and more about anger with boys, although they talk more about emotions overall with girls than with boys. Through all of these avenues, girls are learning to stay close and emotionally related to other people, and boys are learning to be independent and emotionally less open.

These patterns continue through the middle childhood years. Friendships between girls tend to be close and intimate, involving one-on-one communication, whereas boys tend to play rule-governed games in large groups. As children begin to think about moral issues, we see the influences of these patterns as well. Girls are more relational and care oriented in their moral reasoning than are boys, especially when thinking about moral issues in their own lives. Boys tend to think about moral issues in terms of individual rights and principles of justice. These patterns have their effects in the classroom. Boys are somewhat more competitive than girls. Teachers also respond to boys and girls differently, praising boys for getting the right answer, but praising girls for being obedient and working neatly.

Further, once gender identity becomes firmly established in middle childhood, the modeling of same-sex individuals as a process for acquiring sex-typed behavior takes on greater importance than during the preschool years. As we have seen, preschool children do not necessarily imitate models of the same sex as themselves. Instead, they learn the behaviors that are typical for both males and females through observation, and model only those behaviors they consider to be appropriate for their own sex regardless of whether it is performed by a woman or a man. So preschool girls are more likely to imitate a male model who behaves in a traditionally feminine way than a female model who behaves in a traditionally masculine way. By the time children reach middle childhood and understand that gender will not change as a function of behavior or time, they begin to show an active preference for models of the same sex as themselves so as to learn behaviors that are consistent with their gender identity.

Intriguingly, girls know more about gender than do boys, yet boys are more sex typed than are girls. Girls not only know more about gender in general, they know more about the male gender stereotype than boys know about the female gender stereotype. At the same time, girls are more flexible in their beliefs about gender than are boys and will imitate male role models to a greater extent than males will imitate female models. Gender differences in gender knowledge can be partly attributed to differences in socialization and prevailing cultural values. It is simply more acceptable for girls to engage in cross-sex-typed behaviors, such as playing with cars and trucks, than for boys to engage in cross-sex-typed behaviors, such as playing with baby dolls and dressing up. There is no simple explanation for this. But certainly males, and by extension, stereotypically male behaviors, are seen more positively in our culture. And males also hold more power than females. Therefore, it is more advantageous for females to know about males than it is for males to know about females.

With the advent of puberty, biological factors again come to the forefront. Along with the physical changes that take place at this time, adolescents begin to experience sexual feelings and to form intimate relationships. Although the development of sexuality is an important feature of adolescence for both boys and girls, the beliefs and expectations that govern sexual behavior are different for the two sexes. Greater social sanctions operate against girls engaging in sexual relationships. Girls are also thought to be less interested in sex and to experience sex differently. The research evidence suggests, however, that in the absence of social constraints, women's and men's interest and involvement in sexual relationships would not be substantially different.

Adolescence is also a time of forming close, intimate friendships, and the relational patterns of interacting that females show through childhood continue through this period. Female friendships continue to be deeper, more intimate, and more emotionally disclosing than male friendships. Males, who tend not to engage in intimate relationships in childhood, now begin to have more emotionally disclosing relationships as well, but most often these relationships are with females.

During adolescence one also begins to consider one's future role as an adult. Most adolescents are still fairly traditional; females tend to aspire to home and family and, if a career is considered, it is most often a traditionally female career. Again, these choices may stem from females' concerns with caring for other people. Males are also gender typed in their career aspirations, almost always selecting traditionally male careers. It is also at this point in development that we begin to see divergence in academic performance. Although females are equally able to perform mathematics as males, females begin to select out of mathematics courses, and believe that they are not capable of mathematical reasoning. These choices will later limit females' career opportunities.

As men and women enter the work force, career paths continue to diverge. Traditionally female work is less valued than traditionally male work, and even when women are performing the same job as men, they are evaluated more negatively and paid less money. Although a growing number of women are now in management positions, it is still the case that few hold top jobs. Moreover, women and male managers experience organizational life rather differently. Being in the minority often excludes women from informal communication networks that benefit their male colleagues, and additional domestic responsibilities place greater demands on women than on men.

It seems to be the case that the increasing number of young women entering the work force has been accompanied by a shift toward more egalitarian roles within heterosexual relationships. However, when women and men become mothers and fathers, differences in family roles and responsibilities clearly emerge. Although men are just as able as women to care for their children, mothers are more involved in parenting than fathers. And even when fathers are at home with their children, they interact with them less often than do mothers.

Interestingly, although motherhood is greatly valued by women and contributes toward a positive sense of identity, the restrictiveness of the traditionally female roles of wife and mother puts women at increased risk of psychiatric disorder. In spite of the pressures involved in combining work and family life, women who are employed benefit from social relationships in the workplace and experience greater emotional well-being than women who do not work outside the home.

Overall, then, the patterns of interaction we see emerging in infancy are maintained throughout the life span. Females are more relationally oriented than are males, and this orientation affects virtually all aspects of development. Moreover, although females and males do not differ greatly in terms of basic cognitive abilities, it may be the case that a relational orientation will lead females to select into or out of particular cognitive domains, such as mathematics and science.

Given the evidence that gender differences are at least partly biologically based, is it the case that these differences are inevitable? We think not. First, although there are slight biological differences between infant males and females, it is certainly true that these differences can be exaggerated or diminished by the prevailing cultural beliefs. That is, cultures determine which aspects of behavior will be deemed important, and through socialization and institutional structures, will communicate to each developing member of the culture the appropriate norms of behavior.

Second, we are already seeing many changes in gender-related behaviors, especially over the last 20 years. More women are entering the work force, and more women are entering traditionally male jobs. Family structures are changing as well. Families today encompass a much broader range of relationships and roles than the more traditional families of the past. It is no longer the norm for children to be raised by a mother and father who are married to each other or who remain married until the children leave home, and where the father goes out to work while the mother stays at home. Instead, children are being raised in a variety of family types, including dual-career families, one-parent families, and stepfamilies, and may move from one type of family to another as they grow up.

Does this mean there might come a time when gender is not an issue in developmental psychology? Probably not. Although the stereotypes about what it means to be female or male may evolve and change, it is the case that females and males are somewhat different. Different cultures and different times may note and value these differences in different ways, but all cultures in all times have categorized people by gender. Our task as developmental psychologists is to understand how gender interacts with children's developing understanding of their world and themselves. We must also remember that gender development results not simply in gender differences but, more importantly, in gender inequalities. The understanding of gender development in childhood is central to the understanding of gender inequality in adult life.

References

Abramson, L. Y., Seligman, M. E. P., & Teasdale, J. D. (1978). Learned helplessness in humans. Critique and reformulation. *Journal of Abnormal Psychology, 87,* 102–109.

Ainsworth, M. (1979). Attachment as related to mother–infant interaction. In J. Rosenblatt, R. Hinde, C. Beer, & M. Busnel (Eds.), *Advances in the study of behavior.* Orlando, FL: Academic Press.

(1982). Attachment: Retrospect and prospect. In C. M. Parkes & J. Stevenson-Hinde (Eds.), *The place of attachment in human behavior.* New York: Basic Books.

Ainsworth, M., Blehar, M., Waters, E., & Wall, S. (1978). *Patterns of attachment: A psychological study of the strange situation.* Hillsdale, NJ: Erlbaum.

Ainsworth, W., & Wittig, B. A. (1969). Attachment and exploratory behavior of one-year-olds in a strange situation. In B. M. Foss (Ed.), *Determinants of infant behavior.* London: Methuen.

Alban-Metcalfe, B., & West, M. A. (1991). Women managers. In J. Firth-Cozens & M. A. West (Eds.), *Women at work.* Milton Keynes, U. K.: Open University Press.

Allen, J. G., & Haccoun, D. M. (1976). Sex differences in emotionality: A multidimensional approach. *Human Relations, 29,* 711–722.

Allen, L. S., Hines, M., Shryne, J. E., & Gorski, R. A. (1989). Two sexually dimorphic nuclei in the human brain. *Journal of Neuroscience, 9,* 497–506.

Allison, P. D., & Furstenberg, F. F. (1989). How marital dissolution affects children: Variations by age and sex, *Developmental Psychology, 25,* 540–549.

Allred, R. A. (1990). Gender differences in spelling achievement in grades 1 through 6. *Journal of Educational Research, 83,* 187–193.

Andrew, C., Coderre, C., & Denis, A. (1990). Stop or go: Reflections of women managers on factors influencing their career development. *Journal of Business Ethics, 9,* 361–367.

Aneshensel, C. S. (1986). Marital and employment role-strain, social support, and depression among adult women. In S. E. Hobfoll (Ed.), *Stress, social support, and women.* Bristol, PA: Hemisphere.

Ashmore, R. D. (1990). Sex, gender, and the individual. In L. A. Pervin (Ed.), *Handbook of personality theory and research*. New York: Guilford.

Ashmore, R. D., DelBoca, F. K., & Wohlers, A. J. (1986). Gender stereotypes. In R. D. Ashmore & F. K. DelBoca (Eds.), *The social psychology of female–male relations: A critical analysis of central concepts* (pp. 69–119). New York: Academic Press.

Attie, I., Brooks-Gunn, J., & Petersen, A. C. (1990). A developmental perspective on eating disorders and eating problems. In M. Lewis & S. M. Miller (Eds.), *Handbook of developmental psychopathology*. New York: Plenum.

Auckett, R., Ritchie, J., & Mill, K. (1988). Gender differences in friendship patterns. *Sex Roles, 19*, 57–66.

Baennenger, M., & Newcombe, N. (1989). The role of experience in spatial test performance: A meta-analysis. *Sex Roles, 20*, 327–343.

Bailey, J. M., & Pillard, R. C. (1991). A genetic study of male sexual orientation. *Archives of General Psychiatry, 48*, 1089–1096.

Bailey, J. M., Pillard, R. C., Neale, M. C., & Agyei, Y. (1993). Heritable factors influence sexual orientation in women. *Archives of General Psychiatry, 50*, 217–223.

Bakan, D. (1966). *The duality of human existence*. Chicago: Rand McNally.

Baker, D. P., & Entwistle, D. R. (1987). The influence of mothers on the academic expectations of young children: A longitudinal study of how gender differences arise. *Social Forces, 65*, 670–694.

Bandura, A. (1977). *Social learning theory*. Englewood Cliffs, NJ: Prentice Hall.

(1986). *Social foundations of thought and action: A social cognitive theory*. Englewood Cliffs, NJ: Prentice Hall.

Barbach, L. (1975). *For yourself: The fulfillment of female sexuality*. New York: Doubleday.

Barkley, R. A. (1990). Attention deficit disorders: History, definition, and diagnosis. In M. Lewis & S. M. Miller (Eds.), *Handbook of developmental psychopathology*. New York: Plenum.

Barth, R. J., & Kinder, B. N. (1988). A theoretical analysis of sex differences in same-sex friendships. *Sex Roles, 19*, 349–363.

Bartlett, F. F. C. (1932). *Remembering: A study in experimental and social psychology*. Cambridge: Cambridge University Press.

Basow, S. A. (1992). *Gender stereotypes and roles*. Pacific Grove, CA: Brooks/Cole.

Bauer, P. A. (1993). Memory for gender-consistent and gender-inconsistent event sequences by 25-month-old children. *Child Development, 64*, 285–297.

Baum, C. G. (1989). Conduct disorders. In T. H. Ollendick & M.

Hersen (Eds.), *Handbook of child psychopathology.* New York: Plenum.

Baumrind, D. (1986). Sex differences in moral reasoning: Response to Walker's (1984) conclusion that there are none. *Child Development, 57,* 511–521.

Becker, B. J. (1989). Gender and science achievement: A reanalysis of studies from two meta-analyses. *Journal of Research in Science Teaching, 26,* 141–169.

Beere, C. A. (1990). *Gender roles: A handbook of tests and measures.* San Francisco: Jossey Bass.

Bell, A. P., Weinberg, M. S., & Hammersmith, S. K. (1981). *Sexual preference: Its development in men and women.* Bloomington: Indiana University Press.

Belsky, J. (1988). Infant day care and socioemotional development: The United States. *Journal of Child Psychology and Psychiatry, 29,* 397–406.

Belsky, J., & Steinberg, L. D. (1978). The effects of day care: A critical review, *Child Development, 49,* 929–949.

Belsky, J., & Volling, B. L. (1987). Mothering, fathering, and marital interaction in the family triad during infancy: Exploring family system's processes. In P. W. Berman & F. A. Pedersen (Eds.), *Men's transitions to parenthood: Longitudinal studies of early family experience.* Hillsdale, NJ: Erlbaum.

Bem, S. (1974). The measurement of psychological androgyny. *Journal of Consulting and Clinical Psychology, 42,* 155–162.

(1977). On the utility of alternate procedures for assessing psychological androgyny. *Journal of Consulting and Clinical Psychology, 45,* 196–205.

(1981). Gender schema theory: A cognitive account of sex typing. *Psychological Review, 88,* 354–364.

(1989). Genital knowledge and gender constancy in preschool children. *Child Development, 60,* 649–662.

Benbow, C. P., & Stanley, J. C. (1980). Sex differences in mathematical ability: Fact or artifact? *Science, 210,* 1262–1264.

Bene, E. (1965a). On the genesis of male homosexuality: An attempt at clarifying the role of the parents. *British Journal of Psychiatry, 111,* 803–813.

(1965b). On the genesis of female homosexuality. *British Journal of Psychiatry, 111,* 815–821.

Berenbaum, S. A., & Hines, M. (1992). Early androgens are related to sex-typed toy preferences. *Psychological Science, 3,* 202–206.

Best, D. L., Williams, J. E., Cloud, J. M., Davis, S., Robertson, L., Edwards, J., Giles, H., & Fowles, J. (1977). Development of sex-trait stereotypes among young children in the United States, England and Ireland. *Child Development, 48,* 1375–1384.

Bieber, I., Dain, H., Dince, P., Drellick, M., Grand, H., Gondlack, R.,

Kremer, R., Rifkin, A., Wilber, C., & Bieber, T. (1962). *Homosexuality: A psychoanalytic study*. New York: Basic Books.

Biller, H. B. (1974). *Paternal deprivation*. Lexington, MA: Heath.

Birnbaum, D. W., & Cheminski, B. E. (1984). Preschooler's inferences about gender and emotionality: The mediation of emotionality stereotypes. *Sex Roles, 10*, 505–511.

Bleier, R. (1984). *Science and gender: A critique of biology and its theories of women*. Oxford: Pergamon.

Block, J. H. (1973). Conceptions of sex-roles: Some cross-cultural and longitudinal perspectives. *American Psychologist, 28*, 512–526.

   (1976). Issues, problems, and pitfalls in assessing sex differences: A critical review of "The psychology of sex differences." *Merrill-Palmer Quarterly, 22*, 283–308.

   (1978). Another look at sex differentiation in the socialization behaviors of mothers and fathers. In J. A. Sherman & F. L. Denmark (Eds.), *The psychology of women: Future directions in research*. New York: Psychological Dimensions.

   (1983). Differential premises arising from differential socialization of the sexes: Some conjectures. *Child Development, 54*, 1335–1354.

Boldizar, J. P. (1991). Assessing sex typing and androgyny in children. *Developmental Psychology, 27*(3), 505–515.

Boldizar, J. P., Kilson, K. L., & Deemer, D. K. (1989). Gender, life experiences and moral judgment development: A process oriented approach. *Journal of Personality and Social Psychology, 57*, 229–238.

Bolton, V., Golombok, S., Cook, R., Bish, A., & Rust, J. (1991). A comparative study of attitudes towards donor insemination and egg donation in recipients, potential donors and the public. *Journal of Psychosomatic Obstetrics and Gynaecology, 12*, 217–228.

Boston, M. B., & Levy, G. D. (1991). Changes and differences in preschoolers' understanding of gender scripts. *Cognitive Development, 6*, 417–432.

Bowlby, J. (1951). *Maternal care and mental health*. Geneva: World Health Organization.

   (1969/1982). *Attachment and loss. Vol. 1: Attachment*. New York: Basic Books.

   (1988). *A secure base: Clinical applications of attachment theory*. London: Routledge.

Brabeck, M. M. (1987). Gender and morality: A response to Philibert and Sayers. *New Ideas in Psychology, 5*, 209–214.

Bradbard, M. R., & Endsley, R. C. (1983). The effects of sex-typed labeling on preschool children's information seeking and retention. *Sex Roles, 9*, 247–272.

Brenes, M. E., Eisenberg, N., & Helmstadter, G. C. (1985). Sex role development of preschoolers from two-parent and one-parent families. *Merrill-Palmer Quarterly, 31* (1), 33–46.

Brenner, O. C. (1982). Relationship of education to sex, managerial status, and the managerial stereotype. *Journal of Applied Psychology, 67,* 380–383.

Bretherton, I., Fritz, J., Zahn-Waxler, C., & Ridgeway, D. (1986). Learning to talk about emotions: A functionalist perspective. *Child Development, 55,* 529–548.

Bretl, D. J., & Cantor, J. (1988). The portrayal of men and women in U.S. television commercials: A recent content analysis and trends over 15 years. *Sex Roles, 18,* 595–609.

Brewaeys, A., Ponjaert-Kristoffersen, I., Van Steirteghem, A. C., & Devroey, P. (1993). Children from anonymous donors: An inquiry into heterosexual and homosexual parents' attitudes. *Journal of Psychosomatic Obstetrics and Gynaeology.*

Bridges, J. S. (1988). Sex differences in occupational performance expectations. *Psychology of Women Quarterly, 12,* 75–90.

Briscoe, M. (1982). *Sex differences in psychological well-being. Psychological Medicine.* Monograph Supplement I.

Brody, L. R. (1985). Gender differences in emotional development: A review of theories and research. *Journal of Personality, 53,* 102–149.

Broman, S. H., Nichols, P. L., & Kennedy, W. A. (1975). *Pre-school IQ: Parental and early development correlates.* Hillsdale, NJ: Erlbaum.

Brooks-Gunn, J., & Furstenberg, F. F. (1989). Adolescent sexual behavior. *American Psychologist, 44,* 249–257.

Brooks-Gunn, J., & Petersen, A. (1991). Studying the emergence of depression and depressive symptoms during adolescence. *Journal of Youth and Adolescence, 20,* 115–119.

Brooks-Gunn, J., & Warren, M. P. (1989). Biological and social contributions to negative affect in young adolescent girls. *Child Development, 60,* 40–55.

Brophy, J. E., & Evertson, C. M. (1978). Context variables in teaching. *Educational Psychologist, 12,* 310–316.

Broverman, I., Broverman, D. M., Clarkson, I. E., Rosenkrantz, P. S., & Vogel, S. R. (1970). Sex role stereotypes and clinical judgments of mental health. *Journal of Consulting and Clinical Psychology, 34,* 1–7.

Brown, G. W., & Harris, T. (1978). *Social origins of depression: A study of psychiatric disorder in women.* London: Tavistock.

Buchanan, C. M., Eccles, J. S., & Becker, J. B. (1992). Are adolescents the victims of raging hormones: Evidence for activational effects of hormones on moods and behavior at adolescence. *Psychological Bulletin, 111,* 62–107.

Burke, R. J., & McKeen, C. A. (1990). Mentoring in organizations: Implications for women. *Journal of Business Ethics, 9*, 317–332.

Burns, A. (1992). Mother-headed families: An international perspective and the case of Australia. *Social Policy Report, 4*(1), 1–24.

Busfield, J. (1982). Gender and mental illness. *International Journal of Mental Health, 11*, 46–66.

Buss, D. (1989). Sex differences in human mate preferences: Evolutionary hypotheses tested in 37 cultures. *Behavioral and Brain Sciences, 12*, 1–49.

Bussey, K. (1986). The first socialization. In N. Grieve & A. Burns (Eds.), *Australian women: New feminist perspectives*. Melbourne: Oxford University Press.

Bussey, K., & Bandura, A. (1984). Influence of gender constancy and social power on sex-linked modeling. *Journal of Personality and Social Psychology, 47*, 1292–1302.

(1992). Self-regulatory mechanisms governing gender development. *Child Development, 63*(5), 1236–1250.

Cafferata, G. L., Kaspar, J., & Bernstein, A. (1983). Family roles, structure and stressors in relation to sex differences in obtaining psychotropic drugs. *Journal of Health and Social Behavior, 24*, 132–143.

Cairns, R. B., Cairns, D. R., Neckerman, H. J., Ferguson, L. L., & Gariepy, J. (1989). Growth and aggression: 1. Childhood to early adolescence. *Developmental Psychology, 25*, 320–330.

Caldera, Y. M., Huston, A. C., & O'Brien, M. (1989). Social interactions and play patterns of parents and toddlers with feminine masculine and neutral toys, *Child Development, 60*, 70–76.

Caldwell, M., & Peplau, L. (1982). Sex differences in same-sex friendship. *Sex Roles, 8*, 721–732.

Calvert, S. L., & Huston, A. C. (1987). Television and children's gender schemata. In L. S. Liben & M. L. Signorella (Eds.), *Children's gender schemata: New directions for child development* (No. 38, pp. 75–88). San Francisco: Jossey-Bass.

Carr-Ruffino, N. (1991). U.S. women: Breaking through the glass ceiling. *Women in Management Review and Abstracts, 6*, 10–16.

Carter, D. B. (1987). The roles of peers in sex role socialization. In D. B. Carter (Ed.), *Current conceptions of sex roles and stereotyping* (pp. 101–121). New York: Praeger.

Carter, D. B., & Levy, G. D. (1988). Cognitive aspects of early sex-role development: The influence of gender schemas on preschoolers' memories and preferences for sex-typed toys and activities. *Child Development, 59*, 782–792.

Cass, V. C. (1990). The implications of homosexual identity formation for the Kinsey model and scale of sexual preference. In D. P. McWhirter, S. A. Sanders, & J. M. Reinisch (Eds.), *Homosexuality/*

heterosexuality. Oxford: Oxford University Press.

Cherry, F., & Deaux, K. (1978). Fear of success or fear of gender-inappropriate behavior. *Sex Roles, 4,* 97–101.

Cherry, L. (1975). The preschool teacher–child dyad: Sex differences in verbal interaction. *Child Development, 46,* 532–535.

Chodorow, N. J. (1978). *The reproduction of mothering: Psychoanalysis and the socialization of gender.* Berkeley: University of California Press.

Clamar, A. (1989). Psychological implications of the anonymous pregnancy. In J. Offerman-Zuckerberg (Ed.), *Gender in transition: A new frontier.* New York: Plenum.

Cleary, P. D., & Mechanic, D. (1983). Sex differences in psychological distress among married people. *Journal of Health and Social Behavior, 24,* 111–121.

Colby, A., Kohlberg, L., Gibbs, J., & Lieberman, M. (1983). A longitudinal study of moral development. *Monographs of the Society for Research in Child Development, 48* (Serial No. 200).

Collins, L. J., Ingoldsby, B. B., & Dellman, M. M. (1984). Sexrole stereotyping in children's literature: A change from the past. *Childhood Education, 60,* 278–285.

Collins, W. A., & Russell, G. (1991). Mother–child and father–child relationships in middle childhood and adolescence: A developmental analysis. *Developmental Review, 11,* 99–136.

Condry, J., & Condry, S. (1976). Sex differences: A study of the eye of the beholder. *Child Development, 47,* 812–819.

Constantinople, A. (1973). Masculinity–femininity: An exception to a famous dictum? *Psychological Bulletin, 80,* 389–407.

Cordua, G. D., McGraw, K. O., & Drabman, R. S. (1979). Doctor or nurse: Children's perception of sex typed occupations. *Child Development, 50,* 590.

Cox, M. J., Owen, M. T., Henderson, W. K., & Margand, N. A. (1992). Prediction of infant–father and infant–mother attachment. *Developmental Psychology, 28,* 474–483.

Daniels, K. R. (1988). Artificial insemination using donor semen and the issue of secrecy: The views of donors and recipient couples. *Social Science and Medicine, 27,* 377.

Daniels, K. R., & Taylor, K. (1993). Secrecy and openness in donor insemination. *Politics and Life Sciences, 12,* 155–170.

Davidson, M. J., & Cooper, C. L. (1983). *Stress and the woman manager.* Oxford: Blackwell.

(1984). Occupational stress in female managers: A comparative study. *Journal of Management Studies, 21,* 185–205.

Davis, D. M. (1990). Portrayals of women in prime-time network television: Some demographic characteristics. *Sex Roles, 23,* 325–332.

Deaux, K. (1985). Sex and gender. *Annual Review of Psychology, 36,* 49–81.

Deaux, K., & Emswiller, T. (1974). Explanations of successful performance on sex-linked tasks: What is skill for the male is luck for the female. *Journal of Personality and Social Psychology, 29,* 80–85.

Deaux, K., & Lewis, L. L. (1983). Components of gender stereotypes. *Psychological Documents, 13,* 25.

(1984). Structure of gender stereotypes: Interrelationships among components and gender label. *Journal of Personality and Social Psychology, 46,* 991–1004.

de Lacoste, M. D., & Holloway, R. L. (1982). Sexual dimorphism in the human corpus callosum. *Science, 216,* 1431–1432.

DeLamater, J., & MacCorquodale, P. (1979). *Premarital sexuality: Attitudes, relationships, behavior.* Madison: University of Wisconsin Press.

DeLoache, J., Cassidy, D. J., & Carpenter, J. C. (1987). The three bears are all male: Mother's gender labeling of neutral picture book characters. *Sex Roles, 17,* 163–178.

De Lucia, L. A. (1963). The Toy Preference Test: A measure of sex role identification. *Child Development, 34,* 107–117.

Deutsch, H. (1933/1967). On female homosexuality. Reprinted in H. M. Ruitenbeek (Ed.), *Psychoanalysis and female sexuality* (pp. 106–129). New Haven, CT: College and University Press.

(1945). *Psychology of Women. Vol. 2: Motherhood.* New York: Grune & Stratton.

DeVries, R. (1969). Constancy of generic identity in the years three to six. *Monographs of Society in Research in Child Development, 34* (Serial No. 127).

Diamond, M. (1965). A critical evaluation of the ontogeny of human sexual behavior. *Quarterly Review of Biology, 40,* 147–175.

(1982). Sexual identity: Monozygotic twins reared in discordant sex roles and a BBC follow-up. *Archives of Sexual Behavior, 11,* 181–186.

Dittman, R. W., Kappes, M. E., & Kappes, M. H. (1992). Sexual behavior in adolescent and adult females with congenital adrenal hyperplasia. *Psychoneuroendocrinology, 17,* 1–18.

Dittman, R., Kappes, M. H., Kappes, M. E., Borger, D., Meyer-Bahlburg, H., Stegner, H., Willig, R. H., & Wallis, H. (1990). Congenital adrenal hyperplasia. II: Female salt-wasting and simple virilizing patients. Psychoneuroendocrinology, *15,* 421–434.

Dittman, R., Kappes, M. H., Kappes, M. E., Borger, D., Stegner, H., Willig, R. H., & Wallis, H. (1990). Congenital adrenal hyperplasia. I: Gender-related behavior and attitudes in female patients and sisters. *Psychoneuroendocrinology, 15,* 401–420.

Donaldson, M. (1978). *Children's minds*. New York: Norton.

Donenberg, G. R., & Hoffman, L. W. (1988). Gender differences in moral development. *Sex Roles, 18*, 701–717.

Douthitt, R. A. (1989). The division of labor within the home: Have gender roles changed? *Sex Roles, 20*, 693–704.

Downey, J., Ehrhardt, A., Morishima, A., Bell, J., & Gruen, R. (1987). Gender role development in two clinical syndromes: Turner syndrome versus constitutional short stature. *Journal of the American Academy of Child and Adolescent Psychiatry, 26*, 566–573.

Dunn, J., Bretherton, I., & Munn, P. (1987). Conversations about feeling states between mothers and their young children *Developmental Psychology, 23*, 132–139.

Dweck, C. S. (1986). Motivational processes affecting learning *American Psychologist, 41*, 1041–1048.

Dweck, C. S., Davidson, W., Nelson, S., & Enna, B. (1978). Sex differences in learned helplessness. II. The contingencies of evaluative feedback in the classroom. III. An experimental analysis. *Developmental Psychology, 14*, 268–276.

Eagly, A. H., & Johnson, B. T. (1990). Gender and leadership style: A meta-analysis. *Psychological Bulletin, 108*, 233–256.

Earls, F. (1987). Sex differences in psychiatric disorders: Origins and developmental influences. *Psychiatric Developments, 1*, 1–23.

Earls, L., & Jung, K. (1987). Temperament and home-environment characteristics as causal factors in the early development of childhood psychopathology. *Journal of the American Academy of Child Psychiatry, 26*, 491–498.

Eccles, J. S. (1987). Gender roles and women's achievement-related decisions. *Psychology of Women Quarterly, 11*, 135–172.

(1983). Expectations, values and academic behaviors. In J. T. Spence (Ed.), *Achievement and achievement motivations* (pp. 75–146). San Francisco: Freeman.

Eccles, J., Midgeley, C., & Adler, T. F. (1984). Grade-related changes in the school environment: Effects on achievement motivation. In J. Nicholls (Ed.), *Advances in motivation and achievement* (Vol. 3, pp. 283–331). Greenwich, CT: JAI Press.

Eccles, J., & Wigfield, A. (1985). Teacher expectations and student motivation. In J. B. Dusek (Ed.), *Teacher expectancies* (pp. 185–220). Hillsdale, NJ: Erlbaum.

Eccles-Parsons, J., Adler, T. F., & Kaczala, C. M. (1982). Socialization of achievement attitudes and beliefs: Parental influences. *Child Development, 53*, 310–321.

Eccles-Parsons, J., Kaczala, C. M., & Meece, J. L. (1982). Socialization of achievement attitudes and beliefs: Classroom influences. *Child Development, 53*, 322–339.

Eccles-Parsons, J., Meese, J. L., Adler, T. F., & Kaczala, C. M. (1982). Sex differences in attributions and learned helplessness. *Sex Roles*, *8*, 421–432.

Edwards, R. G., & Steptoe, P. C. (1980). *A matter of life*, London: Hutchinson.

Ehrhardt, A. A. (1975). Prenatal hormone exposure and psychosexual differentiation. In E. J. Sachar (Ed.), *Topics in psychoneuroendocrinology*, New York: Grune & Stratton.

——— (1987). A transactional perspective on the development of sex differences. In J. M. Reinisch, L. A. Rosenblum, & S. A. Sanders (Eds.), *Masculinity/feminity: Basic perspectives*, New York: Oxford University Press.

Ehrhardt, A. A., & Baker, S. W. (1974). Fetal androgens, human central nervous system differentiation and behavior sex differences. In R. C. Freeman, R. M. Richart, & R. L. Vande Wiele (Eds.), *Sex Differences in Behavior*, New York: Wiley.

Ehrhardt, A. A., Epstein, R., & Money, J. (1968). Fetal androgens and female gender identity in the early treated adrenogenital syndrome. *Johns Hopkins Medical Journal*, *122*, 160–167.

Ehrhardt, A. A., & Meyer-Bahlburg, H. F. L. (1981). Effects of prenatal sex hormones on gender-related behavior. *Science*, *211*, 1312–1318.

Ehrhardt, A. A., Meyer-Bahlburg, H. F. L., Feldman, J. F., & Ince, S. E. (1984). Sex-dimorphic behavior in childhood subsequent to prenatal exposure to exogenous progestogens and estrogens, *Archives of Sexual Behavior*, *13*(5), 457–477.

Ehrhardt, A., Meyer-Bahlburg, H., Rosen, L., Feldman, J., Veridiano, N., Zimmerman, I., & McEwen, B. (1985). Sexual orientation after prenatal exposure to exogenous estrogen. *Archives of Sexual Behavior*, *14*, 57–77.

Ehrhardt, A. A., & Money, J. (1967). Progestin-induced hermaphroditism: IQ and psychosexual identity in a study of 10 girls. *Journal of Sex Research*, *3*, 83–100.

Einwohner, J. (1989). Who becomes a surrogate: Personality characteristics. In J. Offerman-Zuckerberg (Ed.), *Gender in transition*. New York: Plenum.

Eisenberg, N. (1983). Sex-typed toy choices: What do they signify? In M. Liss (Ed.), *Social and cognitive skills: Sex roles and children's play*. New York: Academic Press.

Ekman, P. (1984). Expression and the nature of emotion. In K. Scherer & P. Ekman (Eds.), *Approaches to emotion* (pp. 329–343). Hillsdale, NJ: Erlbaum.

Elliot, J., Ochiltree, G., Richards, M., Sinclair, C., & Tasker, F. (1990). Divorce and children: A British challenge to the Wallerstein view. *Family Law*, *20*, 309–310.

Emery, R. E., & O'Leary, K. D. (1982). Children's perceptions of marital discord and behavior problems of boys and girls. *Journal of Abnormal Child Psychology, 10,* 11–24.

Englehard, G., & Monsaas, J. A. (1989). Academic performance, gender and the cooperative attitudes of third, fifth and seventh graders. *Journal of Research and Development in Education, 22,* 13–26.

Entwistle, D. R., & Baker, D. P. (1983). Gender and young children's expectations for performance in arithmetic. *Developmental Psychology, 19,* 200–209.

Erikson, E. (1968). *Identity: Youth and crisis.* New York: Horton.
    (1968/1974). Womanhood and the inner space. Reprinted in J. Strouse (Ed.), *Women and analysis* (pp. 291–319). New York: Grossman.

Etaugh, C. (1983). Introduction: The influence of environmental factors on sex differences in children's play. In M. B. Liss (Ed.), *Social and cognitive skills: Sex roles and children's play* (pp. 1–17). New York: Academic Press.

Etaugh, C., & Petroski, B. (1985). Perceptions of women: Effects of employment status and marital status. *Sex Roles, 12,* 329–339.

Evans, R. (1969). Childhood parental relationships of homosexual men. *Journal of Consulting and Clinical Psychology, 33,* 129–135.

Fabes, R. A., & Martin, C. L. (1990, June). *Gender and age stereotypes about emotionality in others.* Paper presented at the American Psychological Society, Dallas.

Fagenson, E. A. (1990). At the heart of women in management research: Theoretical and methodological approaches and their biases. *Journal of Business Ethics, 9,* 267–274.

Fagot, B. I. (1978). The influence of sex of child on parental reactions to toddler children. *Child Development, 49,* 459–465.
    (1987). Toddler's play and sex stereotyping. In D. Bergen (Ed.), *Play as a medium for learning and development* (pp. 133–135). Portsmouth, NH: Heinemann.

Fagot, B. I., & Hagan, R. (1991). Observations of parent reactions to sex-stereotyped behaviors. *Child Development, 62,* 617–628.

Fagot, B. I., & Leinbach, M. D. (1983). Play styles in early childhood: Social consequences for boys and girls. In M. B. Liss (Ed.), *Social and cognitive skills: Sex roles and children's play* (pp. 93–116). New York: Academic Press.
    (1987). Socialization of sex roles within the family. In D. B. Carter (Ed.), *Current conceptions of sex roles and sex typing: Theory and research.* New York: Praeger.
    (1989). The young child's gender schema: Environmental input, internal organization. *Child Development, 60,* 663–672.

(1993). Gender role development in young children: From discrimination to labeling. *Developmental Review*, *13*, 86–106.

Falk, P. G. (1989). Lesbian mothers: Psychosocial assumptions and family law. *American Psychologist*, *44*, 941–947.

Farmer, H. S. (1985). Model of career and achievement motivation for women and men. *Journal of Counseling Psychology*, *32*, 363–390.

Feather, N. T. (1969). Attribution of responsibility and valence of success and failure in relation to initial confidence and perceived lack of control. *Journal of Personality and Social Psychology*, *13*, 129–144.

(1988). Values, valences and course-enrollments: Testing the role of personal values within an expectancy-value framework. *Journal of Educational Psychology*, *80*, 381–391.

Fein, G. (1981). Pretend play in childhood: An integrative review. *Child Development*, *52*, 1095–1118.

Feingold, A. (1992). Gender differences in mate selection preferences: A test of the parental investment model. *Psychological Bulletin*, *112*(1), 125–139.

Ferri, E. (1976). *Growing up in a one parent family*, Slough, U.K.: NFER.

Fidell, L. S., & Marik, J. (1989). Paternity by proxy: Artificial insemination by donor sperm. In J. Offerman-Zuckerberg (Ed.), *Gender in transition: A new frontier*. New York: Plenum.

Fishman, J. (1980). Fatness, puberty and ovulation. *New England Journal of Medicine*, *303*, 42–43.

Fivush, R. (1989). Exploring sex differences in the emotional content of mother–child conversations about the past. *Sex Roles*, *20*, 675–691.

(1991). Gender and emotion in mother–child conversations about the past. *Journal of Narrative and Life History*, *1*, 325–341.

Fleming, J. E., Offord, D. R., & Boyle, M. H. (1989). Prevalence of childhood and adolescent depression in the community. *British Journal of Psychiatry*, *155*, 647–654.

Ford, M. R., & Lowery, C. R. (1986). Gender differences in moral reasoning: A comparison of the use of justice and care orientations. *Journal of Personality and Social Psychology*, *50*, 777–783.

Forehand, R., Neighbors, B., & Wierson, M. (1991). The transition to adolescence: The role of gender and stress in problem behavior and competence. *Journal of Child Psychiatry and Psychology*, *32*, 929–937.

Fowers, B. (1991). His and her marriage: A multivariate study of gender and marital satisfaction. *Sex Roles*, *24*, 209–221.

Fox, N. A., & Fein, G. (1990). *Infant day care*. Norwood, NJ: Ablex.

Fox, N. A., Kimmerly, N. L., & Schafer, W. D. (1991). Attachment to mother/attachment to father: A meta-analysis. *Child Development*, *62*, 210–225.

Frank, E. J. (1988). Business students' perceptions of women in management. *Sex Roles, 19,* 107–118.

Freud, S. (1916/1963). Introductory lectures on psychoanalysis. In J. Strachey (Ed.), *The standard edition of the complete psychological works of Sigmund Freud* (Vol. 18, pp. 15–239). London: Hogarth.

    (1931/1967). Female sexuality. Reprinted in H. M. Ruitenbeek (Ed.), *Psychoanalysis and female sexuality* (pp. 88–105). New Haven, CT: College and University Press.

Friedman, R. C. (1988). *Male homosexuality.* New Haven, CT: Yale University Press.

Frisch, R. E., & McArthur, J. W. (1974). Menstrual cycles: Fatness as a determinant of minimum weight for height necessary for their maintenance and onset. *Science, 185,* 949–951.

Garvey, C. J. (1977). *Play.* Cambridge, MA: Harvard University Press.

Gelman, R. (1979). Cognitive development. *Annual Review of Psychology, 29,* 297–332.

Gibbs, J. C., Arnold, K. D., & Burkhart, J. E. (1984). Sex differences in the expression of moral judgments. *Child Development, 55,* 1041–1043.

Gilligan, C. (1982). *In a different voice: Psychological theory and women's development.* Cambridge, MA: Harvard University Press.

Gilligan, C., & Attanucci, J. (1988). Two moral orientations: Gender differences and similarities. *Merrill-Palmer Quarterly, 34,* 223–237.

Glick, P., Zion, C., & Nelson, C. (1988). What mediates sex discrimination in hiring decisions? *Journal of Personality and Social Psychology, 55,* 178–186.

Goldberg, S., & Lewis, M. (1969). Play behavior in the year-old infant: Early sex differences. *Child Development, 40,* 21–32.

Goldberg, W. A., & Easterbrooks, M. A. (1988). Maternal employment when children are toddlers and kindergartners. In A. E. Gottfried & A. W. Gottfried (Eds.), *Maternal employment and children's development: Longitudinal research.* New York: Plenum.

Golombok, S., Bhanji, F., Rutherford, T., & Winston, R. (1990). Psychological development of children conceived by in vitro fertilization: A pilot study. *Journal of Infant and Reproductive Psychology, 8,* 37–43.

Golombok, S., & Rust, J. (1993a). The Pre-School Activities Inventory: A standardized assessment of gender role in children. *Psychological Assessment, 5,* 131–136.

    (1993b). The measurement of gender role behavior in pre-school children: A research note. *Journal of Child Psychology and Psychiatry, 34,* 805–811.

Golombok, S., Spencer, A., & Rutter, M. (1983). Children in lesbian and single parent households: Psychosexual and psychiatric appraisal. *Journal of Child Psychology and Psychiatry, 24*, 551–572.

Good, T. L., & Brophy, J. E. (1987). *Looking in classrooms* (4 ed.). New York: Harper & Row.

Goodwin, R. (1990). Sex differences among partner preferences: Are the sexes really very similar? *Sex Roles, 23*, 501–513.

Gordon, S. L. (1989). The socialization of children's emotions: Emotion culture, competence, and exposure. In C. Saarni & P. Harris (Eds.), *Children's understanding of emotion* (pp. 319–349). New York: Cambridge University Press.

Gottfried, A. E., Gottfried, A. W., & Bathurst, K. (1988). Maternal employment, family environment and children's development: Infancy through the school years. In A. E. Gottfried & A. W. Gottfried (Eds.), *Maternal employment and children's development: Longitudinal research*. New York: Plenum.

Gove, W. R. (1972). Sex roles, marital roles and mental illness. *Social Forces, 51*, 34–44.

(1979). Sex, marital status, and psychiatric treatment: A research note. *Social Forces, 58*, 89–93.

(1980). Mental illness and psychiatric treatment among women. *Psychology of Women Quarterly, 4*, 345–362.

Gove, W. R., Hughes, M., & Style, C. B. (1983). Does marriage have positive effects on the psychological well-being of the individual? *Journal of Health & Social Behavior, 24*, 122–131.

Gove, W. R., & Tudor, J. F. (1973). Adult sex roles and mental illness. *American Journal of Sociology, 78*, 812–835.

Goy, R. W., & McEwen, B. S. (1980). *Sexual differentiation in the brain*. Cambridge, MA: MIT Press.

Green, R. (1987). *The "sissy boy syndrome" and the development of homosexuality*. New Haven, CT: Yale University Press.

Green, R., Williams, K., & Goodman, M. (1982). Ninety-nine "tomboys" and "non-tomboys": Behavioral contrasts and demographic similarities. *Archives of Sexual Behavior, 11*, 247–266.

Greenfield, P. M. (1984). *Mind and media: The effects of television, video games and computers*. Cambridge, MA: Harvard University Press.

Gregory, A. (1990). Are women different and why are women thought to be different? Theoretical and methodological perspectives. *Journal of Business Ethics, 9*, 257–266.

Grossmann, K. E., Grossmann, K., Spangler, G., Suess, G., & Unzer, L. (1985). Maternal sensitivity in northern Germany. In I. Bretherton & E. Waters (Eds.), *Growing points of attachment theory and research*. Monographs of the Society for Research in Child Development, *50*, 233–256.

Gutek, B. A. (1985). *Sex roles in the workplace*. San Francisco: Jossey-Bass.

Gutek, B. A., & Cohen, A. G. (1987). Sex ratios, sex role spillover, and sex at work: A comparison of men's and women's experiences. *Human Relations, 40*, 97–115.

Gutek, B. A., & Morasch, B. (1982). Sex-ratios, sex role spillover, and sexual harassment of women at work. *Journal of Social Issues, 38*(4), 55–74.

Hackett, G., Esposito, D., & O'Halloran, M. S. (1989). The relationship of role model influences to the career salience and educational and career plans of college women. *Journal of Vocational Behavior, 35*, 164–180.

Haimes, E. (1990). Recreating the family? Policy considerations relating to the "new" reproductive technologies. In M. McNeil, I. Varcoe, & S. Yearley (Eds.), *The new reproductive technologies*. London: Macmillan.

Hall, J. A., & Halberstadt, A. G. (1980). Masculinity and femininity in children: Development of the Children's Personal Attributes Questionnaire. *Developmental Psychology, 16*(4), 270–280.

Halpern, D. (1992). *Sex differences in cognitive abilities* (2nd ed.), Hillsdale, NJ: Erlbaum.

Hamer, D., Hu, S., Magnuson, V., Hu, N., & Pattatucci, A. (1993). A linkage between DNA markers on the X chromosome and male sexual orientation. *Science, 261*, 321–327.

Hamilton, J. A., Alagna, S. W., Parry, B., Hertz, A. K., Blumenthal, S. J., & Conrad, C. (1985). An update on premenstrual depression: Evaluation and treatment. In J. H. Gold (Ed.), *The psychiatric implications of menstruation*. Washington, DC: American Psychiatric Press.

Hamilton, J. A., Parry, B. L., & Blumenthal, S. J. (1988). The menstrual cycle in context. I. Affective syndromes associated with reproductive hormonal changes. *Journal of Clinical Psychiatry, 49*, 474–480.

Hammersla, J. F., & Frease-McMahon, L. (1990). University students' priorities: Life goals vs relationships. *Sex Roles, 23*, 1–14.

Hampson, J. L., & Hampson, G. H. (1961). The ontogenesis of sexual behavior in man. In W. C. Young (Ed.), *Sex and internal secretions*, Baltimore: Williams & Wilkins.

Harmen, L. W. (1981). The life and career plans of young adult college women: A follow-up study. *Journal of Counseling Psychology, 28*, 416–427.

(1989). Longitudinal changes in women's career aspirations: Developmental or historical? *Journal of Vocational Behavior, 35*, 46–63.

Haugh, S. S., Hoffman, C. D., & Cowan, G. (1980). The eye of the very young beholder: Sex typing of infants by young children. *Child Development, 51*, 598–600.

Hawkins, J. (1985). Computers and girls: Rethinking the issues. *Sex Roles, 13*, 165–180.

Heatherington, L., Crown, J., Wagner, H., & Rigby, S. (1989). Toward an understanding of the social consequences of "feminine immodesty" about personal achievements. *Sex Roles, 20*, 371–380.

Heilman, M. E. (1980). The impact of situational factors upon personnel decisions concerning women: Varying the sex composition of the applicant pool. *Organizational Behavior and Human Performance, 26*, 386–395.

Heiman, J. R. (1975). The psychology of erotica: Women's sexual arousal. *Psychology Today, 8*, 90–94.

Heller, K. A., & Parsons, J. E. (1981). Sex differences in teachers' evaluative feedback and students' expectancies for success in mathematics. *Child Development, 52*, 1015–1019.

Henley, N. (1985). Psychology and gender. *Signs: Journal of Women in Culture and Society, 11*, 101–119.

Hennig, M., & Jardin, A. (1977). *The managerial woman.* New York: Doubleday.

Herzog, E., & Sudia, C. E. (1973). Children in fatherless families. In B. M. Campbell & H. N. Ricciuti (Eds.), *Review of child development research.* Chicago: University of Chicago Press.

Hess, R. D., & Camara, K. A. (1979). Post-divorce relationships as mediating factors in the consequences of divorce for children. *Journal of Social Issues, 35*, 79–96.

Hetherington, E. M. (1988). Parents, children and siblings six years after divorce. In R. Hinde & J. Stevenson-Hinde (Eds.), *Relationships within families.* Cambridge: Cambridge University Press.

(1989). Coping with family transitions: Winners, losers, and survivors. *Child Development, 60*, 1–14.

Hetherington, E. M., Cox, M., & Cox, R. (1982). Effects of divorce on parents and children. In M. E. Lamb (Ed.), *Nontraditional families: Parenting and child development.* Hillsdale, NJ: Erlbaum.

(1985). Long-term effects of divorce and remarriage on the adjustment of children. *Journal of the American Academy of Psychology, 24*, 518–530.

Hines, M. (1982). Prenatal gonadal hormones and sex differences in human behavior. *Psychological Bulletin, 92*(1), 56–80.

(1990). Gonadal hormones and human cognitive development. In J. Balthazart (Ed.), *Hormones, brain & behavior in vertebrates. I. Sexual differentiation, neuroanatomical aspects, neurotransmitters and neuropeptides. Comparative Physiology, 8*, 51–63.

Hines, M., & Green, R. (1990). Human hormonal and neural correlates of sex-typed behaviors. *Review of Psychiatry, 10*, 536–555.

Hite, S. (1976). *The Hite Report.* New York: Macmillan.

Hoeffer, B. (1981). Children's acquisition of sex-role behavior in lesbian-mother families. *American Journal of Orthopsychiatry, 51,* 167–184.

Hoffman, L. W. (1979). Maternal employment: 1979. *American Psychologist, 34,* 859–865.

Hoffman, L. W. (1989). Effects of maternal employment in the two-parent family. *American Psychologist, 44,* 283–292.

Hoffman, L. W., & Hoffman, M. (1973). The value of children to parents. In J. T. Fawcett (Ed.), *Psychological perspectives on population.* New York: Basic Books.

Hoffman, L. W., Thornton, A., & Marris, J. D. (1978). The value of children to parents in the United States. *Journal of Population, 1,* 91–131.

Hogrebe, M. C., Nest, S. L., & Newman, I. (1985). Are there gender differences in reading achievement? An investigation using the high school and beyond data. *Journal of Educational Psychology, 77,* 716–724.

Hopwood, N. J., Kelch, R. P., Hale, P. M., Mendes, T. M., Foster, C. M., & Beitins, I. Z. (1990). The onset of human puberty: Biological and environmental factors. In J. Bancroft & J. Reinisch (Ed.), *Adolescence and puberty.* New York: Oxford Universty Press.

Horner, M. (1972). Toward an understanding of achievement-related conflicts in women. *Journal of Social Issues, 28,* 129–156.

Horney, K. (1933/1967). The denial of the vagina. Reprinted in H. M. Ruitenbeek (Ed.), *Psychoanalysis and female sexuality* (pp. 73–87). New Haven, CT: College and University Press.

Hort, B. E., Fagot, B. I., & Leinbach, M. D. (1990). Are people's notions of maleness more stereotypically framed than their notions of femaleness? *Sex Roles, 23,* 197–212.

Howard, J., Blumstein, P., & Schwartz, P. (1987). Social or evolutionary theories? Some observations on preferences in human mate selection. *Journal of Personality and Social Psychology, 53,* 194–200.

Howes, C. (1988). Peer interaction of young children. *Monographs of the Society for Research in Child Development, 53*(217).

Humphrey, M., Humphrey, H., & Ainsworth-Smith, I. (1991). Screening couples for parenthood by donor insemination. *Social Science and Medicine, 32,* 273–278.

Hunt, M. (1974). *Sexual behavior in the 1970's.* Chicago: Playboy Press.

Huston, A. (1983). Sex typing. In E. M. Hetherington (Ed.), *Handbook of child psychology. Vol. 4: Socialization, personality and social development.* New York: Wiley.

(1985). The development of sex-typing: Themes from recent research. *Developmental Review, 5,* 1–17.

Hyde, J. S., Fennema, E., & Lamon, S. J. (1990). Gender differences in mathematics performance: A meta-analysis. *Psychological Bulletin, 107*, 139–155.

Hyde, J. S., Fennema, E., Ryan, M., Frost, L. A., & Hopp, C. (1990). Gender comparisons of mathematics attitudes and affect. *Psychology of Women Quarterly, 14*, 299–324.

Hyde, J. S., & Linn, M. C. (1988). Gender differences in verbal ability: A meta-analysis. *Psychological Bulletin, 104*, 53–69.

Imperato-McGinley, J., Peterson, R. E., Gautier, T., & Sturla, E. (1979). Androgens and the evolution of male gender identity among male pseudohermaphrodites with 5α reductase deficiency. *New England Journal of Medicine, 300*, 1233–1237.

Isabella, R., Belsky, J., & von Eye, A. (1989). Origins of infant–mother attachment: An examination of interactional synchrony during the infant's first year. *Developmental Psychology, 25*, 12–21.

Izard, C. E. (1977). *Human emotions*. New York: Plenum.

Izraeli, D. (1983). Sex effects or structural effects? An empirical test of Kanter's theory of proportions. *Social Forces, 62*, 153–165.

Jacklin, C., & Maccoby, E. (1978). Social behavior at 33 months in same-sex and mixed-sex dyads. *Child Development, 49*, 557–569.

Jennings, S. (1991). Virgin birth syndrome. *Lancet, 337*, 559–560.

Jones, D. C., Bloys, N., & Wood, M. (1990). Sex roles and friendship patterns. *Sex Roles, 23*, 133–145.

Jones, M. G., & Wheatley, J. (1990). Gender differences in teacher–student interactions in science classrooms. *Journal of Research in Science Teaching, 27*, 861–874.

Juraska, J. M. (1991). Sex differences in "cognitive" regions of the rat brain. *Psychoneuroendocrinology, 16*, 105–119.

Kandel, D. B., Davies, M., & Davies, V. H. (1985). The stressfulness of daily social roles for women: Marital, occupational and household roles. *Journal of Health and Social Behavior, 26*, 64–78.

Kanter, R. M. (1977). *Men and women of the organization*. New York: Basic Books.

Kaplan, M. (1983). A woman's view of DSM-III. *American Psychologist, 38*, 786–792.

Kaplan, M. J., Winget, C., & Free, N. (1990). Psychiatrists' beliefs about gender-appropriate behavior. *American Journal of Psychiatry, 147*, 910–912.

Kaye, H., Berl, S., Clare, J., Eleston, M., Gershwin, B., Gershwin, P., Kogan, L., Torda, C., & Wilbur, C. (1967). Homosexuality in women. *Archives of General Psychiatry, 17*, 626–634.

Kessler, R. C., & McRae, J. A. (1982). The effects of wives' employment on the mental health of married men and women. *American Sociological Review, 47*, 216–227.

Kester, P. A. (1984). Effects of prenatally administered 17-hydroxyprogesterone caproate on adolescent males. *Archives of Sexual Behavior, 13*(5), 441–455.

Kester, P. A., Green, R., Finch, S. J., & Williams, K. (1980). Prenatal "female hormone" administration and psychosexual development in human males. *Psychoneuroendocrinology, 5,* 269–285.

Kinsey, A. C., Pomeroy, W. B., & Martin, C. E. (1948). *Sexual behavior in the human male.* Philadelphia: Saunders.

(1953). *Sexual behavior in the human female.* Philadelphia: Saunders.

Kirkpatrick, M., Smith, C., & Roy, R. (1981). Lesbian mothers and their children: A comparative survey, *American Journal of Orthopsychiatry, 51,* 545–551.

Kitzinger, C. (1987). *The social construction of lesbianism.* London: Sage.

Kohlberg, L. (1966). A cognitive-developmental analysis of children's sex-role concepts and attitudes. In E. E. Maccoby (Ed.), *The development of sex differences* (pp. 82–173). Stanford, CA: Stanford University Press.

(1969). The cognitive developmental approach. In D. A. Goslin (Ed.), *Handbook of socialization theory and research.* Chicago: Rand McNally.

Kohnstamm, G. A. (1989). Temperament in childhood: Cross-cultural and sex differences. In G. A. Kohnstamm, J. E. Bates, & M. K. Rothbart (Eds.), *Temperament in Childhood.* Chichester, UK: Wiley.

Korabik, K. (1990). Androgyny and leadership style. *Journal of Business Ethics, 9,* 283–292.

Kuebli, J., & Fivush, R. (1992). Gender differences in parent–child conversations about past events. *Sex Roles, 27,* 683–698.

LaFreniere, P., Strayor, F. F., & Gauthier, R. (1984). The emergence of same sex affiliative preferences among preschool peers: A developmental/ethological perspective. *Child Development, 55,* 1958–1965.

Lamb, M. (1977). Father–infant and mother–infant interaction in the first year of life. *Child Development, 48,* 167–181.

(1986). Introduction: The emergent American father. In M. Lamb (Ed.), *The father's role: Applied perspectives.* New York: Wiley.

(Ed.) 1986. *The father's role: Applied perspectives.* New York: Wiley.

Lamb, M. E., Frodi, A. M., Hwang, C., & Frodi, M. (1982). Varying degrees of paternal involvement in infant care: Attitudinal and behavioral correlates. In M. E. Lamb (Ed.), *Nontraditional families: Parenting and child development.* Hillsdale, NJ: Erlbaum.

Lamb, M., & Oppenheim, D. (1989). Fatherhood and father–child relationships: Five years of research. In S. H. Cath, A. Gurwitt, & L. Gunsberg (Eds.), *Fathers and their families.* Hillsdale, NJ: Erlbaum.

Lamb, M. E., & Roopnarine, J. L. (1979). Peer influences on sex role development. *Child Development, 50,* 1219–1222.

Langlois, J. H., & Downs, A. C. (1980). Mothers, fathers and peers as socialization agents of sex-typed play behaviors in young children. *Child Development, 51,* 1237–1247.

Last, C. G. (1989). Anxiety disorders. In T. H. Ollendick & M. Hersen (eds.), *Handbook of child psychopathology.* New York: Plenum.

Leahy, R., & Shirk, S. (1984). The development of classificatory skills and sex-trait stereotypes in children. *Sex Roles, 10,* 281–292.

Lee, D., & Hertzberg, J. (1978). Theories of feminine personality. In I. H. Frieze, J. E. Parsons, P. B. Johnson, & D. N. Ruble (Eds.), *Women and sex roles: A social psychological perspective* (pp. 28–44). New York: Norton.

Leinbach, M. D., & Fagot, B. (1986). Acquisition of gender labeling: A test for toddlers. *Sex Roles, 15,* 655–666.

Lerman, H. (1986). From Freud to feminist personality theory: Getting here from there. *Psychology of Women Quarterly, 10,* 1–18.

LeVay, S. (1991). A difference in hypothalamic structure between heterosexual and homosexual men. *Science, 253,* 1034–1037.

Lever, J. (1976). Sex differences in the games children play. *Social Problems, 23,* 478–487.

Levy, G. D. (1989). Developmental and individual differences in preschoolers' recognition memories: The influences of gender schematization and verbal labeling of information. *Sex Roles, 21,* 305–324.

Levy, G. D., & Carter, D. B. (1989). Gender schema, gender constancy and gender role knowledge: The roles of cognitive factors in preschoolers' gender-role stereotypic attitudes. *Developmental Psychology, 25,* 444–449.

Levy, G., & Fivush, R. (1993). Scripts and gender: A new approach for examining gender role development. *Developmental Review, 13,* 126–146.

Lewin, M., & Tragos, L. M. (1987). Has the feminist movement influenced adolescent sex role attitudes? A reassessment after a quarter century. *Sex Roles, 16,* 125–135.

Lewis, C., Scully, D., & Condor, S. (1992). Sex stereotyping of infants: A re-examination. *Journal of Reproductive and Infant Psychology, 10,* 53–63.

Lewis, V. G., & Money, J. (1983). Gender identity/role. GI/R Part A. XY (androgen-insensitivity) syndrome and XX (Rokitansky) syndrome of vaginal atresia compared. In L. Dennerstein & G. Burrows (Eds.), *Handbook of psychosomatic obstetrics and gynaecology.* Amsterdam: Elsevier Biomedical Press.

Liben, L. S., & Signorella, M. L. (1980). Gender-related schemata and constructive memory in children. *Child Development, 51*, 111–118.

Lifton, P. D. (1985). Individual differences in moral development: The relation of sex, gender, and personality to morality. *Journal of Personality, 53*, 306–334.

Links, P. S., Boyle, M. H., & Offord, D. R. (1989). The prevalence of emotional disorder in children. *Journal of Nervous and Mental Diseases, 177*, 85–91.

Lipman-Blumen, J., Handley-Isaksen, A., & Leavitt, H. G. (1983). Achieving styles in men and women: A model, an instrument and some findings. In J. T. Spence (Ed.), *Achievement and achievement motives: Psychological and sociological approaches* (pp. 147–204). San Francisco: Freeman.

Lippa, R. (1991). Some psychometric characteristics of gender diagnosticity measures: Reliability, validity, consistency across domains, and relationship to the big five. *Journal of Personality and Social Psychology, 61*(6), 1000–1011.

Lippa, R., & Connelly, S. (1990). Gender diagnosticity: A new Bayesian approach to gender-related individual differences. *Journal of Personality and Social Psychology, 59*, 1051–1065.

Lopez, S. (1989). Patient variable biases in clinical judgment: A conceptual overview and some methodological considerations. *Psychological Bulletin, 106*, 184–203.

Loring, M., & Powell, B. (1988). Gender, race, and DSM-III: A study of the objectivity of psychiatric diagnostic behavior. *Journal of Health & Social Behavior, 29*, 1–22.

Lovdal, L. T. (1989). Sex role messages in television commercials: An update. *Sex Roles, 21*, 715–724.

Lummis, M., & Stevenson, H. W. (1990). Gender differences in beliefs and achievement: A cross-cultural study. *Developmental Psychology, 26*, 254–263.

Lutz, C., & White, G. W. (1986). The anthropology of emotions. *Annual Review of Anthropology, 15*, 405–436.

Lytton, H., & Romney, D. M. (1991). Parents' differential socialization of boys and girls: A meta-analysis. *Psychological Bulletin, 109*, 267–296.

Maccoby, E. E. (1988). Gender as a social category. *Developmental Psychology, 24*, 755–765.

Maccoby, E. E., & Jacklin, C. N. (1974). *The psychology of sex differences.* Stanford, CA: Stanford University Press.

(1987). Gender segregation in children. In H. W. Reese (Ed.), *Advances in child development and behavior* (Vol. 20, pp. 239–287). New York: Academic Press.

McBroom, W. H. (1987). Longitudinal changes in sex role orientations: Differences between men and women. *Sex Roles, 16*, 439–451.

McClelland, D. C. (1961). *The achieving society.* New York: Van Nostrand.

McClelland, D. C., Atkinson, J. W., Clark, R. A., & Lowell, E. L. (1953). *The achievement motive.* New York: Appleton-Century-Crofts.

McGlone, J. (1980). Sex differences in human brain asymmetry: A critical survey. *Behavioral and Brain Science, 3,* 215–263.

McGrath, E., Keita, G. P., Strickland, B. R., & Russo, N. F. (1990). *Women and depression: Risk factors and treatment issues.* Washington, DC: American Psychological Association.

McKinley, J. B., McKinley, S. M., & Brambilla, D. J. (1987). The relative contributions of endocrine changes and social circumstances to depression in mid-aged women. *Journal of Health and Social Behavior, 28,* 345–363.

Malatesta, C. Z., Culver, C., Tesman, J. R., & Shepard, B. (1989). The development of emotional expression during the first two years of life. *Monographs of the Society for Research in Child Development,* No. 219.

Malatesta, C., & Haviland, J. M. (1985). Signals, symbols and socialization: The modification of emotional expression in human development. In M. Lewis & C. Saarni (Eds.), *The socialization of emotions* (pp. 89–115). New York: Plenum.

Mandel, J., Hotvedt, M., Green, R., & Smith, L. (1986). The lesbian parent: Comparison of heterosexual and homosexual mothers and their children. *Archives of Sexual Behavior, 15,* 167–184.

Marcia, J. E. (1980). Identity in adolescence. In J. Adelson (Ed.), *Handbook of adolescent psychology* (pp. 159–187). New York: Wiley.

Marks, J. N., Goldberg, D. P., & Hillier, V. F. (1979). Determinants of the ability of general practitioners to detect psychiatric illness. *Psychological Medicine, 9,* 337–353.

Martenko, M. J., & Gardner, W. L. (1983). A methodological review of sex-related access discrimination problems. *Sex Roles, 9,* 825–839.

Martin, B., & Hoffman, J. A. (1990). Conduct disorders. In M. Lewis & S. M. Miller (Eds.), *Handbook of developmental psychopathology.* New York: Plenum.

Martin, C. L. (1989a). Children's use of gender-related information in making social judgments. *Developmental Psychology, 25,* 80–88.

(1989b, April). *Beyond knowledge based conceptions of schematic processing.* Paper presented at the Society for Research in Child Development, Kansas City.

(1993). New directions for assessing children's gender knowledge. *Developmental Review.*

Martin, C. L., & Halverson, C. (1981). A schematic processing model of sex typing and stereotyping in children. *Child Development*, 52, 1119–1134.

(1983). Gender constancy: A methodological and theoretical analysis. *Sex Roles*, 9, 775–790.

Martin, C. L., & Little, J. K. (1990). The relation of gender understanding to children's sex-typed preferences and gender stereotypes. *Child Development*, 61, 1427–1439.

Martin, C. L., Wood, C. H., & Little, J. K. (1990). The development of gender stereotype components. *Child Development*, 61, 1891–1904.

Masica, D. N., Money, J., & Ehrhardt, A. A. (1971). Fetal feminization and female gender identity in the testicular feminizing syndrome of androgen insensitivity. *Archives of Sexual Behavior*, 1, 131–142.

Masters, J. C., Ford, M. E., Arend, R., Grotevant, H. D., & Clark, L. V. (1979). Modeling and labelling as integrated determinants of children's sex-typed imitative behavior. *Child Development*, 50, 364–371.

Masters, W., & Johnson, V. (1966). *Human sexual response*. Boston: Little, Brown.

Meese, J. L., Wigfield, A., & Eccles, J. (1990). Predictors of math anxiety and its influence on young adolescents' course enrollment intentions and performance in mathematics. *Journal of Educational Psychology*, 82, 60–70.

Meyer-Bahlburg, H. (1984). Psychoendocrine research on sexual orientation: Current status and future options. *Progress in Brain Research*, 61, 375–398.

Meyer-Bahlburg, H., Feldman, J., Ehrhardt, A. A., & Cohen, P. (1984). Effects of prenatal hormone exposure versus pregnancy complications on sex-dimorphic behavior. *Archives of Sexual Behavior*, 13(5), 479–495.

Miller, P. M., Danahar, D. L., & Forbes, D. (1980). Sex-related strategies for coping with interpersonal conflicts in children aged five and seven. *Developmental Psychology*, 22, 543–548.

Miller, S. M., Boyer, B. A., & Rodoletz, M. (1990). Anxiety in children: Nature and development. In M. Lewis & S. M. Miller (Eds.), *Handbook of developmental psychopathology*. New York: Plenum.

Mischel, W. (1966). A social learning view of sex differences in behavior. In E. E. Maccoby (Ed.), *The development of sex differences*. Stanford, CA: Stanford University Press.

(1970). Sex-typing and socialization. In P. Mussen (Ed.), *Carmichael's manual of child psychology* (Vol. 2). New York: Wiley.

Money, J. (1987). Sin, sickness or status? Homosexual gender identity and psychoneuroendocrinology. *American Psychologist*, 42, 384–399.

(1988). *Gay, straight or in-between: The sexology of erotic orientation*. New York: Oxford University Press.

Money, J., & Ehrhardt, A. A. (1972). *Man and woman, Boy and Girl: The differentiation and dimorphism of gender identity from conception to maturity*. Baltimore: Johns Hopkins University Press.

Money, J., & Lewis, V. G. (1982). Homosexual/heterosexual status in boys at puberty: Idiopathic adolescent gynecomastia and congenital virilizing adrenocortism compared. *Psychoneuroendocrinology, 7*, 339–346.

(1983). Gender identity/role: GI/R Part B. A multiple sequential model of differentiation. In L. Dennerstein & G. Burrows (Eds.), *Handbook of psychosomatic obstetrics and Gynaecology*. Amsterdam: Elsevier Biomedical Press.

Money, J., & Mathews, D. (1982). Prenatal exposure to virilizing progestins: An adult follow-up study of 12 women. *Archives of Sexual Behavior, 11*, 73–83.

Money, J., & Ogurno, B. (1974). Behavior sexology: Ten cases of genetic male intersexuality with impaired prenatal and pubertal androgenization. *Archives of Sexual Behavior, 3*(3), 181–205.

Money, J., Schwartz, M., & Lewis, V. G. (1984). Adult erotosexual status and fetal hormonal masculinization and demasculinization: 46, XX congenital virilizing adrenal hyperplasia and 46, XY androgen-insensitivity syndrome compared. *Psychoneuroendocrinology, 9*, 405–414.

Money, J., & Tucker, P. (1976). *Sexual signatures: On being a man or a woman*. London: Harrap.

Moore, D. S., & Erickson, P. I. (1985). Age, gender and ethnic differences in sexual and contraceptive knowledge, attitudes, and behavior. *Family and Community Health, 8*, 38–51.

Morgan, M. (1982). Television and adolescents' sex-role stereotypes: A longitudinal study. *Journal of Personality and Social Psychology, 43*, 947–955.

Moss, H. A. (1967). Sex, age, and state as determinants of mother–infant interaction. *Merrill-Palmer Quarterly, 13*, 19–36.

Narus, L. R., & Fischer, J. L. (1982). Strong but not silent: A reexamination of expressivity in the relationships of men. *Sex Roles, 8*, 159–168.

Nelson, K. (1986). *Event knowledge: Structure and function in development*. Hillsdale, NJ: Erlbaum.

Nevell, D. D., & Schlecker, D. J. (1988). The relation of self-efficacy and assertiveness to willingness to engage in traditional/nontraditional career activities. *Psychology of Women Quarterly, 12*, 91–98.

Newcombe, M. (1985). The role of perceived relative parent personality in the development of heterosexuals, homosexuals and transvestites. *Archives of Sexual Behavior*, *14*, 147–164.

Newman, R. C., & Carney, R. E. (1981). Cross validation of sex role measures for children and parents. *Perceptual and Motor Skills*, *52*, 883–890.

Newmann, J. P. (1984). Sex differences in symptoms of depression: Clinical disorder or normal distress. *Journal of Health and Social Behavior*, *25*, 136–159.

Nieva, V., & Gutek, B. A. (1981). *Women and work: A psychological perspective*. New York: Praeger.

Noe, R. A. (1988). Women and mentoring: A review and research agenda. *Academy of Management Review*, *13*, 65–78.

Nolen-Hoeksema, S. (1987). Sex differences in unipolar depression: Evidence and theory. *Psychological Bulletin*, *101*, 259–282.

O'Connell, A. N., & Perez, S. (1982). Fear of success and causal attributions of success and failure in high school and college students. *Journal of Psychology*, *111*, 141–151.

Offord, D., Boyle, M., Szatmari, P., Rae-Grant, N., Links, P., Cadman, D., Byles, J., Crawford, J., Munroe Blum, H., Byrne, L., Thomas, H., & Woodward, C. (1987). Ontario Child Health Study: Six month prevalence of disorder and rates of service utilization. *Archives of General Psychiatry*, *44*, 832–836.

O'Leary, V. (1974). Some attitudinal barriers to occupational aspirations in women. *Psychological Bulletin*, *29*, 809–826.

O'Leary, V. E., & Johnson, J. L. (1991). Steep ladder, lonely climb. *Women in Management Review and Abstracts*, *6*, 4–9.

Paludi, M. A. (1991). Sociopsychological and structural factors related to women's vocational development. *Annals of the New York Academy of Sciences*, 157–168.

Paludi, M. A., & Strayer, L. A. (1985). What's in an author's name? Differential evaluations of performance as a function of author's name. *Sex Roles*, *12*, 353–361.

Parke, R. D. (1981). *Fathers*. Cambridge, MA: Harvard University Press.

Parke, R. D., & Sawin, D. B. (1976). The father's role in infancy: A re-evaluation. *The Family Coordinator*, *25*, 365–371.

(1980). The family in early infancy: Social interactional and attitudinal analyses. In F. Pedersen (Ed.), *The father–infant relationship: Observational studies in a family context*. New York: Praeger.

Parry, G. (1986). Paid employment, life events, social support, and mental health in working-class mothers. *Journal of Health and Social Behavior*, *27*, 193–208.

Patterson, C. J. (1992). Children of lesbian and gay parents. *Child Development*, *63*, 1025–1042.

Peplau, L. A., & Gordon, S. L. (1985). Women and men in love: Gender differences in close heterosexual relationships. In T. B. Sonderegger (Ed.), *Nebraska Symposium on Motivation: Psychology and Gender*. Lincoln: University of Nebraska Press.

Perry, D. G., & Bussey, K. (1979). The social learning theory of sex difference: Imitation is alive and well. *Journal of Personality & Social Psychology, 37*, 1699–1712.

Perry, L. C., & Sanders, D. (1992, April). *Relationships between theory of intelligence and academic performance in children: Domain differences in the influence of gender and self-esteem variables.* Poster presented at the Conference on Human Development, Atlanta, GA.

Peterson, A. C. (1988). Adolescent development. *Annual Review of Psychology, 39*, 503–607.

Pfost, K. S., & Fiore, M. (1990). Pursuit of nontraditional occupations: Fear of success or fear of not being chosen? *Sex Roles, 23*, 15–24.

Phares, V. (1992). Where's poppa? The relative lack of attention to the role of fathers in child and adolescent psychopathology. *American Psychologist, 47*(5), 656–664.

Phoenix, A., & Woollett, A. (1991). Introduction. In A. Phoenix, A. Woollett, & E. Lloyd (Eds.), *Motherhood: Meanings, practices and ideologies*. London: Sage.

Piaget, J. (1962). *Play dreams and imitation in childhood*. New York: Norton.

(1966). *The moral judgement of the child*. New York: Free Press.

(1968). *On the development of memory and identity*. Worcester, MA: Clark University Press.

Pitcher, E. G., & Shultz, L. H. (1983). *Boys and girls at play: The development of sex roles*. New York: Praeger.

Potts, M. K., Burnham, M. A., & Wells, K. B. (1991). Gender differences in depression detection: A comparison of clinical diagnosis and standardized assessment. *Psychological Assessment, 3*(4), 609–615.

Powell, B., & Jacobs, J. A. (1984). The prestige gap: Differential evaluations of male and female workers. *Work and Occupations, 11*, 283–308.

Power, T. G., & Parke, R. D. (1982). Play as a context for early learning: Lab and home analyses. In E. Sigel & L. M. Laosa (Eds.), *The family as a learning environment*. New York: Plenum.

Pratt, M. W., Golding, G., & Hunter, W. J. (1984). Does morality have a gender? Sex, sex role and moral judgment relationships across the adult life span. *Merrill-Palmer Quarterly, 30*, 321–340.

Prior, M. (1992). Childhood temperament. *Journal of Child Psychology and Psychiatry, 33*(1), 249–279.

Radin, N. (1982). Primary caregiving and role-sharing fathers. In M. E. Lamb (Ed.), *Nontraditional families: Parenting and child development*. Hillsdale, NJ: Erlbaum.

Radloff, L. S. (1975). Sex differences in depression: The effects of occupation and marital status. *Sex Roles, 1*, 249–266.

Radloff, L. S., & Rae, D. S. (1979). Susceptibility and precipitating factors in depression: Sex differences and similarities. *Journal of Abnormal Psychology, 82*, 174–181.

Raymond, C. L., & Benbow, C. P. (1989). Educational encouragement by parents: Its relationship to procodity and gender. *Gifted Child Quarterly, 33*, 144–151.

Redman, S., Webb, G. R., Hennrikus, D. J., & Gordon, J. J. (1991). The effects of gender on diagnosis of psychological disturbance. *Journal of Behavioral Medicine, 14*(5), 527–540.

Reinisch, J. (1981). Prenatal exposure to synthetic progestins increases potential for aggression in humans. *Science, 211*, 1171–1173.

Reinisch, J. M., Ziemba-Davis, M., & Sanders, S. A. (1991). Hormonal contributions to sexually dimorphic behavioral development in humans. *Psychoneuroendocrinology, 16*, 213–278.

Repetti, R. L., Matthews, K. A., & Waldron, I. (1989). Employment and women's health: Effects of paid employment on women's mental and physical health. *American Psychologist, 44*, 1394–1401.

Rheingold, H. L., & Cook, K. V. (1975). The content of boys' and girls' rooms as an index of parents' behavior, *Child Development, 46*, 459–463.

Riger, S., & Galligan, P. (1980). Women in management: An exploration of competing paradigms. *American Psychologist, 35*, 902–910.

Roberts, C. W., Green, R., Williams, K., & Goodman, M. (1987). Boyhood gender identity development: A statistical contrast of two family groups. *Developmental Psychology, 23*, 544–557.

Roberts, L. R., Sarigiani, Peterson, A. C., & Newman, J. L. (1990). Gender differences in the relationship between achievement and self-image during early adolescence. *Journal of Research in Early Adolescence, 10*, 159–175.

Roberts, T., & Nolen-Hoeksema, S. (1989). Sex differences in reactions to evaluative feedback. *Sex Roles, 21*, 725–747.

Robinson, C. C., & Morris, J. T. (1986). The gender-stereotyped nature of Christmas toys received by 36-, 48-, and 60-month old children: A comparison between requested and nonrequested toys. *Sex Roles, 15*, 21–32.

Robinson, J. (1989, April). *Sex differences in the development of empathy during late infancy: Findings from the MacArthur longitudinal twin study*. Paper presented at the Society for Research in Child Development, Seattle.

Roll, J. (1992). *Lone parent families in the European community.* London: European Family and Social Policy Unit.

Rosenberg, B. G., & Sutton-Smith, B. (1964). The measurement of masculinity and femininity in children. *Journal of Genetic Psychology, 104,* 259–264.

Ross, C. E., & Mirowsky, J. (1988). Child care and emotional adjustment to wives' employment. *Journal of Health and Social Behavior, 29,* 127–138.

Rothbart, M. K., Hanley, D., & Albert, M. (1986). Gender differences in moral reasoning. *Sex Roles, 15,* 645–653.

Rotterg, H. L., Brown, D., & Ware, W. B. (1987). Career self-efficacy expectations and perceived range of career options in community college students. *Journal of Counseling Psychology, 34,* 164–170.

Rubin, J. Z., Provenzano, F. J., & Luria, Z. (1974). The eye of the beholder: Parents' views on sex of newborns. *American Journal of Orthopsychiatry, 44,* 512–519.

Russell, G. (1986). Primary caretaking and role-sharing fathers. In M. E. Lamb (Ed.), *The father's role: Applied perspectives.* New York: Wiley.

Rutter, M. (1971). Parent–child separation: Psychological effects on the children. *Journal of Child Psychology and Psychiatry, 12,* 233–260.

(1983). Stress, coping, and development: Some issues and some questions. In N. Garmezy & M. Rutter (Eds.), *Stress, coping, and development.* New York: McGraw-Hill.

(1985). Resilience in the face of adversity. *British Journal of Psychiatry, 147,* 598–611.

(1986). The development of psychopathology in depression: Issues and perspectives. In M. Rutter, C. E. Izard, & P. B. Read (Eds.), *Depression in young people.* New York: Guilford.

Rutter, M., Tizard, J., & Whitmore, K. (1970). *Education, health, and behavior.* London: Longman.

Ryckman, D. B., & Peckham, P. (1987). Gender differences in attributions for success and failure situations across subject areas. *Journal of Educational Research, 81,* 120–125.

Safer, J., & Reiss, B. (1975). Two approaches to the study of female homosexuality: A critical and comparative review. *International Mental Health Research Newsletter, 17,* 11–13.

Saghir, M. T., & Robins, E. (1973). *Male and female homosexuality: A comprehensive investigation.* Baltimore: Williams & Wilkins.

Sagi, A. (1982). Antecedents and consequences of various degrees of paternal involvement in child rearing: The Israeli project. In M. E. Lamb (Ed.), *Nontraditional families: Parenting and child development.* Hillsdale, NJ; Erlbaum.

Sanders, S. A., Reinisch, J. M., & McWhirter, D. P. (1990). An overview. In D. P. McWhirter, S. A. Sanders, & J. M. Reinisch (Eds.), *Homosexuality/heterosexuality*. Oxford: Oxford University Press.

Sants, H. J. (1964). Genealogical bewilderment in children with substitute parents. *British Journal of Medical Psychology, 37*, 133–141.

Sayers, J. (1983). Is the personal political? Psychoanalysis and feminism revisited. *International Journal of Women's Studies, 6*, 71–85.

Schachere, K. (1990). Attachment between working mothers and their infants: The influence of family processes. *American Journal of Orthopsychiatry, 60*, 19–34.

Schank, R. C., & Abelson, R. P. (1977). *Scripts, plans, goals and understanding*. Hillsdale, NJ: Erlbaum.

Schein, V. E. (1973). The relationship between sex role stereotypes and requisite management characteristics. *Journal of Applied Psychology, 57*, 95–100.

  (1975). Relationships between sex role stereotypes and requisite management characteristics among female managers. *Journal of Applied Psychology, 57*, 89–105.

Schmidt, G., Lange, C., & Knopf, M. (1992). *Changes in adolescents' sexuality between 1970 and 1990 in West Germany*. Paper presented at the 18th Annual Meeting of the International Academy of Sex Research, Prague.

Seavey, A. A., Katz, P. A., & Zalk, S. R. (1975). Baby X: The effect of gender labels on adult responses to infants. *Sex Roles, 1*, 103–109.

Seigal, M. (1987). Are sons and daughters treated more differently by fathers than by mothers? *Developmental Review, 7*, 183–209.

Seligman, M. E. P. (1975). *Helplessness: On depression, development, and death*. San Francisco: Freeman.

Sells, L. W. (1973). High school mathematics as the critical filter in the job market. In R. T. Thomas (Ed.), *Developing opportunities for minorities in graduate education* (pp. 37–39). Berkeley: University of California Press.

Selman, R. L., Jaquette, D., & Lavin, D. (1977). Interpersonal awareness in children. *American Journal of Orthopsychiatry, 47*, 264–274.

Serbin, L. A., Marchessault, K., McAffer, V., Peters, P., & Schwartzman, A. E. (1991). *Patterns of social behavior on the playground in 9–11 year old girls and boys: Relation to teacher perceptions and to peer ratings of aggression, withdrawal and likeability*. Unpublished manuscript.

Serbin, L. A., Moller, L., Powlishta, K., & Gulko, J. (1991). *The emergence of gender segregation and behavioral compatibility in toddlers' peer preferences*. Paper presented at the meetings of the Society for Research in Child Development, Seattle.

Serbin, L. A., Powlishta, K. K., & Gulko, J. (1993). The development of sex typing in middle childhood. *Monographs of the Society of Research in Child Development, 58*(2), serial no. 232.

Serbin, L. A., & Sprafkin, C. (1986). The salience of gender and the process of sex-typing in three to seven year olds. *Child Development, 57,* 1188–1199.

Shakin, M., Shakin, D., & Sternglanz, S. H. (1985). Infant clothing: Sex labelling for strangers, *Sex Roles, 12,* 955–963.

Sheldon, A. (1990). Pickle fights: Gendered talk in preschool disputes. *Discourse Processes, 13,* 5–31.

Siegel, M., & Robinson, J. (1987). Order effects in children's gender constancy responses. *Developmental Psychology, 23,* 283–286.

Siegelman, M. (1974). Parental background of male homosexuals and heterosexuals. *Archives of Sexual Behavior, 6,* 89–96.

Signorella, M. L., Bigler, R. S., & Liben, L. (1993). Development differences in children's gender schemata about others: A meta-analytic review. *Developmental Review, 13,* 106–126.

Signorella, M. L., & Liben, L. S. (1984). Recall and reconstruction of gender-related pictures: Effects of attitude, task difficulty and age. *Child Development, 55,* 393–405.

Signorielli, N. (1989). Television and conceptions about sex roles: Maintaining conventionality and the status quo. *Sex Roles, 21,* 341–360.

Signorielli, N., & Lears, M. (1992). Children, television, and conceptions about chores: Attitudes and behaviors. *Sex Roles, 27,* 157–170.

Simmons, R. G., Burgeson, R., Carlton-Ford, S., & Blyth, D. A. (1987). The impact of cumulative change in early adolescence. *Child Development, 58,* 1220–1234.

Simpson, A. W., & Erikson, M. T. (1983). Teachers' verbal and non-verbal communication patterns as a function of teacher race, student gender and student race. *American Educational Research Journal, 20,* 183–198.

Singer, J. M., & Stake, J. E. (1986). Mathematics and self-esteem: Implications for women's career choice. *Psychology of Women Quarterly, 10,* 339–352.

Skaalvik, E. M., & Rankin, R. J. (1990). Math, verbal and general academic self-concept: The internal/external frame of reference model and gender differences in self-concept structure. *Journal of Educational Psychology, 82,* 546–554.

Slaby, R. G., & Frey, K. S. (1975). Development of gender constancy and selective attention to same sex models. *Child Development, 46,* 849–856.

Snow, M. E., Jacklin, C. N., & Maccoby, E. E. (1983). Sex-of-child differences in father–child interaction at one year of age. *Child Development, 49,* 227–232.

Snowden, R. (1990). The family and artificial reproduction. In D. R. Bromham, M. E. Dalton, & J. C. Jackson (Eds.), *Philosophical ethics in reproductive medicine.* Manchester: Manchester University Press.

South, S. J., Bonjean, C. M., Corder, J., & Markum, W. T. (1982). Sex and power in the federal bureaucracy: A comparative analysis of male and female supervisors. *Work and Occupations, 9,* 233–254.

Spence, J. T. (1984). Masculinity, femininity, and gender-related traits: A conceptual analysis and critique of current research. *Progress in Experimental Personality Research, 13,* 1–97.

(1985). Gender identity and its implications for the concepts of masculinity and femininity. In T. B. Sonderegger (Ed.), *Nebraska Symposium on Motivation: Psychology and Gender.* Lincoln: University of Nebraska Press.

(1993). Gender-related traits and gender ideology: Evidence for a multifactorial theory. *Journal of Personality and Social Psychology, 64*(4), 624–635.

Spence, J. T., & Helmreich, R. L. (1978). *Masculinity and femininity: Their psychological dimensions, correlates and antecedents.* Austin: University of Texas Press.

Spence, J. T., Helmreich, R. L., & Stapp, J. (1974). The Personal Attributes Questionnaire: A measure of sex-role stereotypes and masculinity–femininity. *JSAS Catalog of Selected Documents in Psychology, 4,* 43–44, MS 617.

(1975). Ratings of self and peers on sex role attributes and their relation to self-esteem and conceptions of masculinity and femininity. *Journal of Personality and Social Psychology, 32,* 29–39.

Spitze, G. (1988). Women's employment and family relations: A review. *Journal of Marriage and the Family, 50,* 595–618.

Sprangler, E., Gordon, M. A., & Pipkin, R. M. (1978). Token women: An empirical test of Kanter's hypothesis. *American Journal of Sociology, 84,* 160–170.

Sroufe, L. A. (1985). Attachment classification from the perspective of infant–caregiver relationships and infant temperament. *Child Development, 56,* 1614.

Stagnor, C., & Ruble, D. N. (1987). Development of gender role knowledge and gender constancy. In L. S. Liben & M. L. Signorella (Eds.), *Children's gender schemata: New directions for child development* (No. 38, pp. 5–22). San Francisco: Jossey-Bass.

Stake, J. E., & Katz, J. F. (1982). Teacher–pupil relationships in the elementary school classroom: Teacher gender and pupil gender differences. *American Educational Research Journal, 19,* 465–471.

Stasz, C., Shavelson, R. J., & Stasz, C. (1985). Teachers as role models: Are there gender differences in microcomputer-based mathematics and science achievement? *Sex Roles, 13,* 149–164.

Steil, J. M. (1983). Marriage: An unequal partnership. In B. Wolman & G. Stricker (Eds.), *The handbook of family and marital therapy.* New York: Plenum.

Steil, J. M., & Weltman, K. (1991). Marital inequality: The importance of resources, personal attributes, and social norms on career valuing and the allocation of domestic responsibilities. *Sex Roles, 24,* 161–179.

Steinberg, R., & Shapiro, S. (1982). Sex differences in personality traits of female and male master of business administration students. *Journal of Applied Psychology, 67,* 306–310.

Steinkamp, M. W., & Maehr, M. L. (1983). Affect, ability and science achievement: A quantitative synthesis of correlational research. *Review of Educational Research, 53,* 369–396.

Stern, M., & Karraker, K. H. (1989). Sex stereotyping of infants: A review of gender labeling studies. *Sex Roles, 20,* 501–522.

Stevenson, M. R., & Black, K. N. (1988). Paternal absence and sex role development: A meta-analysis, *Child Development, 59,* 793–814.

Stewart, C. R., Daniels, K. R., & Boulnois, J. D. H. (1982). The development of a psychosocial approach to artificial insemination of donor sperm. *New Zealand Medical Journal, 95,* 853–856.

Stockard, J. (1980). Sex inequities in the experience of students. In J. Stockard, P. A. Schmuck, K. Kempner, P. Williams, S. K. Edson, & M. A. Smith (Eds.), *Sex inequity in education* (pp. 49–77). New York: Academic Press.

Stockard, J., & Johnson, M. M. (1992). *Sex and gender in society.* Englewood Cliffs, NJ: Prentice Hall.

Strange, C. C., & Rea, J. S. (1983). Career choice considerations and sex role self-concept of male and female undergraduates in non-traditional majors. *Journal of Vocational Behavior, 23,* 219–226.

Straver, C. T. (1992). *Sexual development between 12 and 19.* Paper presented at the 18th Annual Meeting of the International Academy of Sex Research, Prague.

Sutton-Smith, B., & Rosenberg, B. G. (1971). Sixty years of historical change in the game preferences of American children. In R. E. Herron & B. Sutton-Smith (Eds.), *Child's Play.* New York: Wiley.

Svanum, S., Bringle, R. G., & McLaughlin, J. E. (1982). Father absence and cognitive performance in a large sample of six- to eleven-year-old children. *Child Development, 53,* 136–143.

Sweeney, P. D., Moreland, R. L., & Gruber, K. L. (1982). Gender differences in performance attributions: Students' explanations for personal success or failure. *Sex Roles, 8,* 359–372.

Tannen, D. (1990). Gender differences in topical coherence: Creating involvement in best friend's talk. *Discourse Processes, 13*, 73–90.

Tasker, F., & Golombok, S. (1992). *Adults raised as children in lesbian families*. Paper presented at the 18th Annual Meeting of the International Academy of Sex Research, Prague.

Taylor, M. C., & Hall, J. A. (1982). Psychological androgyny: A review and reformulation of theories, methods and conclusions. *Psychological Bulletin, 92*, 347–366.

Taylor, S. E., & Crocker, J. (1979). Schematic bases of social information processing. In E. T. Higgens, P. Herman, & M. P. Zanna (Eds.), *The Ontario Symposium in Personality and Social Psychology* (Vol. 1). Hillsdale, NJ: Erlbaum.

Terborg, J. R. (1977). Women in management: A research review. *Journal of Applied Psychology, 62*, 647–664.

Terman, L. M., & Miles, C. C. (1936). *Sex and personality*. New York: McGraw-Hill.

Thoma, S. J. (1986). Estimating gender differences in the comprehension and preference of moral issues. *Developmental Review, 6*, 165–180.

Thompson, C. (1943/1967). "Penis-envy" in women. Reprinted in H. M. Ruitenbeek (Ed.), *Psychoanalysis and female sexuality* (pp. 246–251). New Haven, CT: College and University Press.

Udry, J. R. (1990). Hormonal and social determinants of adolescent sexual initiation. In J. Bancroft & J. Reinisch (Eds.), *Adolescence and Puberty*. New York: Oxford University Press.

Ullman, J. B., & Fidell, L. S. (1989). Gender selection and society. In J. Offerman-Zuckerberg (Ed.), *Gender in transition: A new frontier*. New York: Plenum.

Unger, R. K. (1979). Toward a redefinition of sex and gender. *American Psychologist, 34*, 1085–1094.

Urberg, K. A. (1982). The development of the concepts of masculinity and femininity in young children. *Sex Roles, 8*, 659–668.

U.S. Department of Labor (1989). *Employment and earnings, 36*(10), Table A-22, 29.

Vance, E. B., & Wagner, N. N. (1976). Written descriptions of orgasm: A study of sex differences. *Archives of Sexual Behavior, 5*, 87–98.

Vuchinich, S., Hetherington, E. M., Vuchinich, R., & Clingempeel, W. G. (1991). Parent–child interaction and gender differences in early adolescents' adaptation to stepfamilies. *Developmental Psychology, 27*(4), 618–626.

Walker, L. J. (1984). Sex differences in the development of moral reasoning: A critical review. *Child Development, 55*, 677–691.

Walker, L. J., deVries, B., & Trevethan, S. D. (1987). Moral stages and moral orientations in real life and hypothetical dilemmas. *Child Development, 58*, 842–858.

Walkerdine, V. (1989). *Counting girls out.* London: Virago Press.

Wallerstein, J. S., & Blakeslee, S. (1989). *Second chances: Men, women and children a decade after divorce.* New York: Ticknor & Fields.

Wallerstein, J. S., Corbin, S. B., & Lewis, J. M. (1988). Children of divorce: A 10 year study. In E. M. Hetherington & J. D. Arasteh (Eds.), *Impact of divorce, single parenting and stepparenting on children.* Hillsdale, NJ: Erlbaum.

Wallerstein, J. S., & Kelly, J. B. (1980). *Surviving the breakup: How children and parents cope with divorce.* New York: Basic Books.

Wallston, B. S., & Grady, K. E. (1985). Integrating the feminist critique and the crisis in social psychology: Another look at research methods. In V. E. O'Leary, R. K. Unger, & B. S. Wallston (Eds.), *Women, gender and social psychology.* Hillsdale, NJ: Erlbaum.

Weiner, B. (1985). An attributional theory of achievement motivation and emotion. *Psychological Review, 92,* 548–573.

Weinraub, M., Jaeger, E., & Hoffman, L. W. (1988). Predicting infant outcomes in families of employed and non-employed mothers, *Early Childhood Research Quarterly, 3,* 361–378.

Weisner, T. S., & Wilson-Mitchell, J. E. (1990). Nonconventional family life-styles and sex typing in 6 year olds. *Child Development, 61,* 1915–1933.

Weissman, M. M. (1987). Advances in psychiatric epidemiology: Rates and risks for major depression. *American Journal of Public Health, 77,* 445–451.

Weissman, M. M., & Klerman, G. L. (1985). Sex differences in the epidemiology of depression. *Archives of General Psychiatry, 34,* 98–111.

Weitzman, L. J., Eifler, E. H., Hokada, E., & Ross, C. (1972). Sex-role socialization in picture books for preschool children. *American Journal of Sociology, 77,* 1125–1150.

Weitzman, N., Birns, B., & Friend, R. (1985). Traditional and nontraditional mothers' communication with their daughters and sons. *Child Development, 56,* 894–898.

Wentzel, K. R. (1988). Gender differences in math and English achievement: A longitudinal study. *Sex Roles, 18,* 691–699.

Whalen, C. K. (1989). Attention deficit and hyperactivity disorders. In T. H. Ollendick & M. Hersen (Eds.), *Handbook of Child Psychopathology.* New York: Plenum.

Whitam, F. (1977). Childhood indicators of male homosexuality. *Archives of Sexual Behavior, 6,* 89–96.

Whitely, B. E. (1983). Sex role orientation and self-esteem: A critical meta-analytic review. *Journal of Personality and Social Psychology, 44,* 765–785.

Wigfield, A., Eccles, J., Harold-Goldsmith, R., Blumenfield, P., Yoon, K. S., & Friedman-Doon, C. (1989, April). *Gender and age dif-*

ferences in children's achievement self-perceptions during elementary school. Paper presented at the meeting of the Society for Research in Child Development, Kansas City.

Williams, J. A. (1984). Women and mental illness. In J. Nicholson & H. Beloff (Eds.), *Psychology survey 5.* Leicester, UK: British Psychological Society.

Williams, J. E., & Best, D. L. (1990). *Measuring sex stereotypes: A multination study.* Newbury Park, CA: Sage.

Williams, K., Goodman, M., & Green, R. (1985). Parent–child factors in gender role socialization in girls. *Journal of the American Academy of Child Psychiatry, 26,* 720–731.

Witelson, S. F. (1989). Hand and sex differences in the isthmus and genu of the human corpus callosum, *Brain, 112,* 799–835.

Wittig, M. A. (1985). Sex-role norms and gender-related attainment values: Their role in attributions of success and failure. *Sex Roles, 12,* 1–11.

Wood, W., Rhodes, N., & Whelan, M. (1989). Sex differences in positive well-being: A consideration of emotional style and marital status. *Psychological Bulletin, 106,* 249–264.

Woollet, A. (1991). Having children: Accounts of childless women and women with reproductive problems. In A. Phoenix, A. Woollett, & E. Lloyd (Eds.), *Motherhood: Meanings, practices and ideologies.* London: Sage.

Wright, P. H. (1989). Gender differences in adults' same- and cross-gender friendships. In R. G. Adams & R. Blieszner (Eds.), *Older adult friendship* (pp. 197–221). London: Sage.

Yalom, I. D., Green, R., & Fisk, N. (1973). Prenatal exposure to female hormones. *Archives of General Psychiatry, 28,* 554–561.

Yee, D. K., & Eccles, J. S. (1988). Parent perceptions and attributions for children's math achievement. *Sex Roles, 19,* 317–333.

Zahn-Waxler, C., Cole, P., & Barrett, K. (1991). Guilt and empathy: Sex differences and implications for the development of depression. In K. Dodge & J. Garber (Eds.), *Emotion regulation and disregulation* (pp 243–272). New York: Cambridge University Press.

Zaslow, M. J. (1988). Sex differences in children's response to divorce. 1. Research methodology and postdivorce family forms. *American Journal of Orthopsychiatry, 58,* 355–378.

(1989). Sex differences in children's response to divorce. 2. Samples, variables, ages, and sources. *American Journal of Orthopsychiatry, 59,* 118–141.

Zilbergeld, B. (1978). *Male sexuality.* Boston: Little, Brown.

Zucker, K., & Green, R. (1992). Psychosexual disorders in children and adolescents. *Journal of Child Psychiatry and Psychology, 33*(1), 107–151.

Zuger, B. (1984). Early effeminate behavior in boys: Outcome and significance for homosexuality. *Journal of Nervous and Mental Disease, 172,* 90–97.

Zussman, J. U., Zussman, P. P., & Dalton, P. (1975). Postpubertal effects of prenatal administration of progesterone. *Paper presented at the meeting of the Society for Research in Child Development,* Denver.

Index